What Matters in America

Reading and Writing About Contemporary Culture

Gary Goshgarian
NORTHEASTERN UNIVERSITY
with
Kathryn Goodfellow
NORTHEASTERN UNIVERSITY

New York Boston San Francisco
London Toronto Sydney Tokyo Singapore Madrid
Mexico City Munich Paris Cape Town Hong Kong Montreal

Senior Acquisitions Editor: Lynn M. Huddon
Development Editor: Katharine Glynn
Marketing Manager: Sandra McGuire
Senior Supplements Editor: Donna Campion
Managing Editor: Valerie Zaborski
Project Coordination, Text Design, and Electronic Page Makeup: Nesbitt Graphics
Cover Design Manager: Wendy Ann Fredericks
Cover Designer: Base Art Company
Cover Photo: Jeffrey Aronson/Network Aspen
Photo Researcher: Christine A. Pullo
Senior Manufacturing Buyer: Dennis J. Para
Printer and Binder: RR Donnelley and Sons—Crawfordsville
Cover Printer: Phoenix Color Corps

For permission to use copyrighted material, grateful acknowledgment is made to the copyright holders on pp. 353–357, which are hereby made part of this copyright page.

Library of Congress Cataloging-in-Publication Data

Goshgarian, Gary.

What matters in America : reading and writing about contemporary culture / Gary Goshgarian

p. cm.

Includes bibliographical references and index.

ISBN 0-321-25029-X

1. Readers—Popular culture. 2. English language—Rhetoric—Problems, exercises, etc. 3. Report writing—Problems, exercises, etc. 4. Critical thinking—Problems, exercises, etc. 5. Popular culture—Problems, exercises, etc. I. Title.

PE1127.P6G67 2006

Please visit us at *www.ablongman.com*

ISBN 0-321-25029-X

1 2 3 4 5 6 7 8 9 10—ROC—08 07 06 05

Contents

I, FOR ONE, AM NOT WILLING TO SACRIFICE PRIVACY FOR A FALSE SENSE OF SECURITY!
HOME-LAND ACT
GEORGE BLEDSOE, FOR ONE, IS NOT WILLING TO SACRIFICE PRIVACY FOR A FALSE SENSE OF SECURITY.
PUT THAT IN HIS FILE.

OH YEAH? WELL MY THIRD WIFE'S EX-HUSBAND'S STEPMOTHER IS A CONGRESSMAN'S MISTRESS, AND HE SAYS IT'S AN INSULT TO THE SANCTITY OF MARRIAGE!!
NEWS
GAY MARRIAGE

ARE YOU SURE IT'S MINE?
IN VITRO
FROZEN EMBRYOS
CLONES
Mike Keefe

CHILDREN WHO WATCH TOO MUCH TV TEND TOWARD VIOLENCE...
WHEN TRENDS COLLIDE!
CHILDREN WHO WATCH TOO MUCH TV TEND TOWARD OBESITY...
IF I COULD CATCH YOU I'D PUNCH YOUR LIGHTS OUT!
Mike Keefe

NEWS ITEM: AMERICANS WORK MORE HOURS FOR LESS PAY THAN EVER BEFORE...
I MUST TELL YOU THAT THE POSITION YOU'VE APPLIED FOR IS A "24/7" JOB...
OOH!... I HATE THAT TERM... WHAT DOES IT PAY?...
$24,700.
PERSONNEL MGR
cagiecartoons.com

Rhetorical Contents

Comparison and Contrast: Examining Similarities and Differences

Narration: Telling a Story

Definition: Determining the Nature of Something

Persuasion and Argument: Appealing to Reason and Emotion

Illustration: Explaining with Examples and Statistics

Division and Classification: Sorting Things Out

Research and Analysis: Using Authority

Preface

Like its inspirational text, *The Contemporary Reader,* now in its eighth edition, *What Matters in America: Reading and Writing About Contemporary Culture* is designed to stimulate critical thinking skills in introductory writing students through a variety of contemporary subjects connected to popular culture, media, and society.

The book's intention is to provide a collection of well-written, thought-provoking, thematically organized readings that students can relate to—readings that stimulate classroom discussion, critical thinking, and writing. The text's study apparatus aims to elicit thoughtful response while providing students with the tools they need to approach each reading as informed, critical thinkers.

The introduction to *What Matters in America* includes strategies for critical writing. Continuing this concept throughout the book, the apparatus includes the latest and most effective rhetorical theory and practice. Preceding each reading is a short paragraph, "Connecting to the Topic," that orients the student to the subject matter. "Words in Context" provides students with the vocabulary support they may need to understand the material.

Directly following each reading are four areas of inquiry designed to help students think about the reading and the issue within a broader framework. "Considering the Issues" encourages students to think about issues raised by the reading in a thematic context. "Craft and Content" asks students to consider rhetorical and analytical issues connected to the reading itself. "Critical Thinking" and "Writing About the Issues" questions promote analytical approaches to the reading, and support thoughtful writing projects.

While visuals are interspersed throughout the text, the end of each chapter features a "Visual Connections" exercise designed to help students think about the ways images, photographs, and cartoons present ideas and concepts. Another visual element of *What Matters in America* is the editorial cartoon on the title page of each chapter followed by critical thinking questions designed to elicit thoughtful consideration of each image. Instructions on how to view editorial cartoons are included in the book's introductory material.

Each chapter closes with a "Topical Connections" section that encourages students to make broad thematic associations related to the chapter's overarching subject matter. The apparatus in this section includes group projects, research topics for further inquiry, and Web exercises.

Chapter Topics

More than 95 percent of the book's material comes from essays and articles written within the last four years. With more than 60 short essays and visuals from more than 35 periodicals, journals, and newspapers and five recently released books, the text's readings are organized into ten thematic areas, framed as questions.

1. How Does Advertising Influence Us?
2. Are There Limits to Our Right to Privacy?
3. Do the Media Promote a Culture of Fear?
4. Do Campus Speech Codes Violate Students' Rights?
5. Should Gay Marriage Be Legal?
6. Can Racial Profiling Be Justified?
7. Are Designer Humans in Our Future?
8. Can Television Violence Influence Behavior?
9. Is Fast Food Responsible for a Crisis in Public Health?
10. Why Do We Work?

These themes were chosen to reflect a wide spectrum of issues that affect all of us. Most importantly, they capture some of the conflicts and paradoxes that make our culture unique. For ours is a culture caught in conflicts; from fashion and advertising to television and privacy, we are a people who crave the modern, yet long for nostalgia. We are as much a society steeped in traditional values and identities as we are a culture that redefines itself in response to trends and new ideas.

Variety of Readings

Expository communication comes in all shapes and models. This book includes newspaper stories, editorials, political cartoons, advertisements, academic essays, magazine articles, television interviews, Internet articles from "e-zines," student essays, humor columns, and a lot more. Students will read academic articles, personal narratives, objective essays, position papers, political arguments, and research reports. Readings come from a wide variety of sources expressing many different points of view, including *Mother Jones,* the *Nation, Commentary,* the *Wall Street Journal,* the *New York Times,* the *National Review,* the *Progressive,* the *Boston Globe,* the *Atlantic, Africana, GQ, Newsweek,* and *TIME*. We have also included readings from student newspapers and campus magazines, as well as online articles from *Slate* and *Salon.*

Supplements

Instructor's Manual

The Instructor's Manual (available to qualified adopters of this text) includes suggested responses to the "Considering the Issues" and "Critical Thinking" questions in the text as well as ideas for directing class discussion and eliciting student response.

mycomplab™ 2.0

Where writing and research help is just a click away!

MyCompLab 2.0 (www.mycomplab.com) offers engaging new resources in grammar, writing, and research for composition students and instructors. This market-leading composition Web resource includes grammar diagnostics; over 3,500 grammar questions; video-, image-, and Web-based writing activities organized by different writing purposes; Exchange, an online peer review and instructor grading program; a Model Documents gallery; the highly acclaimed Avoiding Plagiarism tutorial; ResearchNavigator™ with AutoCite bibliography maker program and searchable databases of credible academic sources; and access to Longman's English Tutor Center. New for Fall 2005: Gradetracker system, in the Web site version of MyCompLab, tracks student results for all exercises and activities on the site.

Acknowledgments

Many people behind the scenes deserve gratitude for bringing this first edition of *What Matters in America* to publication. It would be impossible to thank all of them, but there are some for whose help I am particularly grateful. I would like to thank those instructors who provided their input and advice answering lengthy questionnaires on the effectiveness of the essays in the prototype chapters of the text: Virginia Brackett, Triton College; Tim Catalano, Marietta College; Ana Douglass, Truckee Meadows Community College; Tracy Duckart, Humboldt State University; Sharon Jaffe, Santa Monica College; Robert Koelling, Northwest College; Lyle W. Morgan, Pittsburgh State University; Jeff Newberry, Abraham Baldwin Agricultural College; Tony Perrello, Angelo State University; Jay Rubin, College of Alameda; Robert Schwegler, University of Rhode Island; Owen Williamson, Barton County Community College. Their helpful comments and suggestions have been incorporated into this finished volume.

A special thanks goes to Kathryn Goodfellow for her assistance in developing the content, locating articles, and writing the study apparatus. This book would not have been possible without her creativity and energy. I would also like to thank Danise Cavallaro for her help in securing permissions for the readings featured in this volume. I would also like to extend my thainks to those students who allowed us to reprint their essays in this text.

Finally, my thanks to the people of Longman Publishers, especially Lynn Huddon and Katharine Glynn, who helped conceptualize this edition as its editors, and to Joe Opiela for encouraging me to move forward on this project.

Gary Goshgarian

Introduction

Critical **Reading** and **Thinking**

What Is Critical Thinking?

Whenever you read a magazine article, newspaper editorial, or a piece of advertising and find yourself questioning its message or implications, you are exercising the basics of critical thinking. Instead of taking what you read at face value, you look beneath the surface of words and think about their meaning and significance. And subconsciously you ask the authors questions such as:

- What did you mean by that?
- Can you back up that statement?
- How do you define that term?
- How did you draw that conclusion?
- Do all the experts agree?
- Is this evidence dated?
- So what? Why does it matter?
- What is your point?
- Why do we need to know this?

You make statements such as:

- That's not true.
- You're contradicting yourself.
- I see your point, but I don't agree.
- That's not a good choice of words.
- You're jumping to conclusions.
- Good point. I never thought of that.
- That was nicely stated.
- This is an extreme view.

Whether conscious or unconscious, such responses indicate that you are thinking *critically* about what you read. You ask for definitions, weigh claims, evaluate information, look for proof, question assumptions, and make judgments. In short, you process another person's words, not just take them in.

Why Read Critically?

When you read critically, you think critically. And that means instead of blindly accepting what's written on a page, you separate yourself from the text and decide for yourself what is or is not important or logical or right. And you do so because you bring to your reading your own perspective, experience, education, and personal values, as well as your powers of comprehension and analysis. Such skills translate into every facet of your life.

Critical Reading Is a Process of Discovery

Critical reading is an active process of discovery. You discover an author's view on a subject; you begin a dialogue with the author; you discover the strengths and weaknesses of the author's thesis or argument; and you decide if you agree or disagree with the author's views. The end result is that you have a better understanding of the issue and the author. By asking the author questions and by analyzing where the author stands with respect to other experiences or views of the issue—including your own—you actively enter a dialogue or a debate. You seek out the truth on your own instead of accepting at face value what somebody else says.

Critical reading is an active and reactive process—one that sharpens your focus on a subject and your ability to absorb information and ideas. At the same time, critical reading encourages you to question accepted norms, views, and myths. You will find yourself asking tough questions—and by so doing, you develop the skills you need to be an active player in the world, and not a passive viewer.

Critical Reading Is a Lens on a Visual World

We have all heard the old saying "A picture is worth a thousand words." We constantly react to nonverbal cues in our daily lives. Symbols, images, gestures, and graphics all instantly communicate information that we must process.

To better understand how visuals work, we have interspersed throughout this text various cartoons, posters, and photographs that highlight the different ways we communicate without using words. For example, a cartoon, featured in little boxes with drawn characters, communicates a certain set of expectations before a reader even begins to examine it. We know instantly that it is a cartoon and that, as such, it is supposed to convey some form of humor. In well-known cartoons, we may even instantly recall the personalities of the characters depicted and expect certain reactions or attitudes from them.

In advertisements, cultural cues of imagery, symbolism, the use of light and dark, and the product's purpose are all used by advertisers to tap into our presumed set of expectations. Sensational photos can incite anger, sadness, fear, or joy. Take a look at the cover of a major newspaper and see how the front page photos are designed to get you to pick that paper up and read it. Look around at the ads and images that bombard you every day. When you are aware of the visual world, you are better able to understand it and react appropriately.

Critical Reading Is the Key to Good Writing

Critical reading also helps you become a better writer, because critical reading is the first step to good writing. Good readers look at another's writing the way a carpenter looks at a house: They study the fine details and how those details connect and create the whole. Likewise, they consider the particular slants and strategies of appeal. Good writers always have a clear sense of their audience—their readers' racial makeup, gender, and educational background; their political and/or religious persuasions; their values, prejudices, and assumptions about life; and so forth.

Critical reading helps you evaluate your own writing. The better you become at analyzing and reacting to another's written work, the better you will analyze and react to your own. You will ask yourself: Is my argument logical? Do my points come across clearly? Are my examples solid enough? Is this the best wording? Is my conclusion persuasive? Do I have a clear sense of my audience? What appeal strategy did I take—to logic, emotions, or ethics? In short, critical reading will help you to evaluate your own writing.

How to Read and Write Critically

To help you read critically, use these six proven basic steps:

- Keep a journal on what you read.
- Annotate what you read.
- Outline what you read.
- Summarize what you read.
- Question what you read.
- Analyze what you read.

Keep a Journal on What You Read

Unlike writing an essay or a paper, keeping a journal is a personal exploration in which you develop your own ideas without set rules. It is a process of recording impressions and exploring feelings and ideas. It is an opportunity to write without restrictions and without judgment. You don't have to worry about breaking the rules—because in a journal, anything goes.

Reserve a special notebook just for your journal—not one that you use for class notes or homework. Also, date your entries and include the titles of the articles to which you are responding. Eventually, by the end of the semester, you should have a substantial number of pages to review so you can see how your ideas and writing style have developed over time.

What do you include in your journal? Although it may serve as a means to understanding an essay you're assigned, you are not required to write only about the essay itself. Perhaps the piece reminds you of something in your personal experience. Maybe it triggered an opinion you didn't know you had. Or perhaps you wish to explore a particular phrase or idea presented by the author.

Some students may find keeping a journal difficult because it is so personal. They may feel as if they're exposing their feelings too much. Or they may feel uncomfortable thinking that someone else—a teacher or another student—may read their writing. But such apprehensions shouldn't prevent you from exploring your impressions and feelings. Just don't record anything that you wouldn't want your teacher or classmates to read; or if you do, don't show anybody your journal. You may even consider keeping two journals—one for class and one for your personal use.

Annotate What You Read

It's a good idea to underline (or highlight) key passages and to make marginal notes when reading an essay. (If you don't own the publication in which the essay appears, or choose not to mark it up, it's a good idea to make a photocopy of the piece and annotate that.) I recommend annotating on the second or third reading, once you've gotten a handle on the essay's general ideas.

There are no specific guidelines for annotation. Use whatever technique suits you best, but keep in mind that in annotating a piece of writing, you are engaging in a dialogue with the author. As in any meaningful dialogue, you may hear things you may not have known, things that may be interesting and exciting to you, things that you may agree or disagree with, or things that give you cause to ponder. The other side of the dialogue, of course, is your response. In annotating a piece of writing, that response takes the form of underlining (or highlighting) key passages and jotting down comments in the margin. Such comments can take the form of full sentences or some shorthand codes. Sometimes "Why?" or "True." or "NO!" will be enough to help you respond to a writer's position or claim. If you come across a word or reference that is unfamiliar to you, underline or circle it. Once you've located the main thesis statement or claim, highlight or underline it and jot down "Claim" or "Thesis" in the margin.

Outline What You Read

Briefly outlining an essay is a good way to see how writers structure their ideas. When you physically diagram the thesis statement, claims, and the supporting evidence, you can better assess the quality of the writing and decide how convincing it is. You may already be familiar with detailed, formal essay outlines where structure is broken down into main ideas and subsections. However, for our purposes here, I suggest a brief and concise breakdown of an essay's components. Simply jotting down a one-sentence summary of each paragraph does this.

Summarize What You Read

Summarizing is perhaps the most important technique to develop for understanding and evaluating what you read. This means boiling down the essay to its main points. In your journal or notebook, try to write a brief (about 100 words) synopsis of the reading in your own words. Note the claim or thesis of the discussion (or argument) and the chief supporting points. It is important to write these points down, rather than highlight them passively with a pen or pencil, because the act of jotting down a summary helps you absorb the argument. At times, it may be impossible to avoid using the author's own words in a summary. But if you do, remember to use quotation marks.

Question What You Read

Although we break down critical reading into discrete steps, these steps will naturally overlap in the actual process. While reading an essay you will simultaneously summarize and evaluate the writer's points in your head, perhaps adding your own ideas and arguments. If something strikes you as particularly interesting or insightful, make a mental note. Likewise, if something rubs you the wrong way, argue back. For beginning writers, a good strategy is to convert that automatic mental response into actual note taking.

In your journal, or even in the margins of the text, question and challenge the writer. Jot down any points in the essay that do not measure up to your expectations or personal views. Note anything you are skeptical about. Scratch down any questions you have about the claims, views, or evidence. If some point or conclusion seems forced or unfounded, record it and briefly explain why. The more skeptical and questioning you are, the better reader you are. Likewise, note what features of the essay impressed you—outstanding points, interesting wording, clever or amusing phrases or allusions, particular references, the general structure of the piece. Record what you learn from the reading and what aspects about the issue you would like to explore.

Of course, you may not feel qualified to pass judgment on an author's views, especially if that author is a professional writer or expert on a particular subject. Sometimes the issue discussed might be too technical, or you may not feel informed enough to make critical evaluations. Sometimes a personal narrative may focus on experiences completely alien to you. Nonetheless, you are an intelligent person with an instinct to determine if the writing impresses you or if an argument is sound, logical, and convincing. What you can do in such instances—and another good habit to get into—is think of other views on the issue. If you've read or heard of experiences different from the author's or arguments with the opposing views, jot them down.

Analyze What You Read

To analyze something means breaking it down into its components, examining those components closely and evaluating their significance, and determining how they relate as a whole. In part you already did this by briefly outlining the essay. But there is more, because analyzing what you read involves interpreting and evaluating the points of a discussion or argument as well as its presentation—that is, its language and structure.

Ultimately, analyzing an essay after establishing its main idea will help you understand what may not be evident at first. A closer examination of the author's words takes you beneath the surface and sharpens your understanding of the issue at hand.

Although there is no set procedure for analyzing a piece of prose, here are some specific questions you should raise when reading an essay, especially one that is trying to sway you to its view.

- What kind of audience is the author addressing?
- What are the author's assumptions?
- What are the author's purposes and intentions?
- How well does the author accomplish those purposes?
- How convincing is the evidence presented? Is it sufficient and specific? Relevant? Reliable and not dated? Slanted?
- How good are the sources of the evidence used? Were they based on personal experience, scientific data, or outside authorities?
- Did the author address opposing views on the issue?
- Is the author persuasive in his or her perspective?

Reading and Interpreting a Visual World

From the moment we awaken to the moment we close our eyes to sleep, we are bombarded with images competing for our attention. Some want to sell us something; others want to sway our opinion or tell a story. It is easy to allow our gut emotions to serve as our guide in a visual world, but critically approaching this world gives us an edge. When we read critically the ads and appeals around us, we are better able to make informed decisions about them.

As you review the various visual presentations throughout the text, consider the ways symbolism, brand recognition, stereotyping, and cultural expectations contribute to how such illustrations communicate their ideas. Try to think abstractly, taking into account the many different levels of consciousness that visuals use to communicate. Consider also the way shading, lighting, and subject placement in the photos all converge to make a point. "Read" them as you would any text, applying some of the points described earlier in the Introduction.

Like works of art, visuals often employ color, shape, line, texture, depth, and point of view to create their effect. Therefore, to understand how visuals work and to analyze the way visuals persuade and influence us, we must also ask questions about specific aspects of form and design. For example, some questions to ask about print images such as those in newspaper and magazine ads include:

- What in the frame catches your attention immediately?
- What is the central image? What is the background image? Foreground images? What are the surrounding images? What is significant in the placement of these images? Their relationship to one another?
- What verbal information is included? How is it made prominent? How does it relate to the other graphics or images?
- What specific details (people, objects, locale) are emphasized? Which are exaggerated or idealized?
- What is the effect of color and lighting?
- What emotional effect is created by the images—pleasure? longing? anxiety? nostalgia?
- Do the graphics and images make you want to know more about the subject or product?
- What special significance might objects in the image have?
- Is there any symbolism imbedded in the images?

Considering these questions helps us to critically survey a visual argument and enables us to formulate reasoned assessments of its message and intent.

You will notice that the title page of each unit in this book features an editorial cartoon addressing the thematic focus of the unit. Editorial cartoons have been a part of American life for over a century. They are a mainstay feature of the editorial pages in most newspapers—those pages reserved for columnists, contributing editors, and illustrators to present their views in words and pen and ink. Most editorial cartoons are political in nature, holding issues up for public scrutiny and sometimes ridicule.

The editorial cartoon presents a moment in the flow of familiar current events. Although a cartoon captures a split instant in time, it also implies what came before and, perhaps, what may happen next—either in the next moment or in some indefinite future. For the cartoon to be effective, it must make the issue clear at a glance and it must establish where it stands on the argument.

To convey less-obvious issues and figures in a glance, cartoonists resort to images that are instantly recognizable—called visual clichés—that we don't have to work at to grasp. Locales are determined by giveaway props: airports will have an airplane outside the window, the desert is identified by a cactus and cattle skull, or an overstuffed armchair and TV indicate a standard living room. Likewise, human emotions are instantly conveyed: pleasure is a huge toothy grin; fury is steam blowing out of a figure's ears; love is two figures making goo-goo eyes with floating hearts. People themselves may have exaggerated features to emphasize a point or emotion. The cartoonist is also likely to employ stock figures for their representation, images instantly recognizable from cultural stereotypes: the fat-cat tycoon, the mobster thug, the sexy female movie star. And these come to us in familiar outfits and props that give away their identities and professions. The cartoon judge has a black robe and gavel; the prisoner wears striped overalls and a ball and chain; the physician dons a smock and forehead light; the doomsayer is a scrawny long-haired guy carrying a sign saying "The end is near." These are visual clichés known by the culture at large, and we get them.

As you view the editorial cartoons in this book, consider the visual clichés the cartoonist uses. What information is important for the viewer to know? What assumptions does the cartoonist make? What issue is the cartoonist holding up for public scrutiny, and why?

Discussing What You Read

Tune in to a news talk show and you will see experts in any number of fields shouting at one another. The subject may be politics, terrorism, free speech, some social issue, or the latest tabloid courtroom case. Whatever the topic, the goal of those "talking heads" seems less like a rational exchange than a shouting match. Speakers cut each other off, shout each other down, and do whatever it takes to dominate the discussion. And if the volume level fails to do the trick, participants may resort to personal insult. Or they may ignore the question asked and simply make a statement arguing a personal view.

Obviously, a shouting match is not conducive to the exchange of ideas. Nor is the silent treatment a means of sharing opinions. Whether at a social occasion, a family holiday, or a gathering of friends, everyone has experienced a conversation or discussion brought to a halt by silence. Sometimes it may be a recent news item tossed out for discussion, or a controversial topic raised at the dinner table. Everyone freezes, and nothing is said. Such dead silence may be due to lack of information, fear of upsetting someone else with an unpopular view, or simply not wanting to bother contributing to the discourse. Whatever the cause—fear, embarrassment, lack of knowledge regarding a topic—the result is dull interaction and a discussion that goes nowhere.

It could be argued that as social creatures we all have the yearning to express ourselves freely and clearly—to contribute to open discussion and debate, to be an active participant in the group.

Ideally, the classroom is the perfect venue for students to practice communication skills—to exchange ideas and differences of opinions. With the guidance of an instructor and with the mutual support and respect of classmates, a group spirit can be established; an environment can exist where each student feels comfortable in exercising his and her discussion skills and feedback is encouraged. The result is a class that's fun, engaging, and informative—a class that enjoys a group spirit of mutual respect and attentiveness.

That's not always the case, of course. But it can be achieved, especially if each student assumes a positive sense of responsibility to the group with the goal of keeping the discussion moving forward and on track, of promoting good class interchange. Toward that end, we offer the following guidelines for discussion. And we ask that you think about your own strengths and weaknesses in this area—that you work with your instructor and classmates to make class discussions lively and engaging.

Guidelines for Class Discussion

1. Take time to process the questions your instructor or classmates have posed. Be sure you understand what is being asked before you respond.
2. If the question is unclear, ask for clarification or restate what you understood the question to be.
3. When you offer your answer, speak in an audible, clear voice.
4. Look directly at the individual who posed the question or at your classmates.

5. Work on listening carefully to answers or comments made by your classmates.
6. Take notes during the discussion so that you can refer to specific remarks. Also, jot down ideas that will help you express yourself in your own feedback.
7. Refer to comments made by other classmates in your response. Then elaborate on how your ideas agree or disagree with statements made by classmates.
8. Ask your instructor if the discussion can take place in a circle formation if that is not already the case.
9. Do not interrupt a classmate when he or she is speaking. Give the speaker a chance to finish a thought. Some people need more time than others to articulate their ideas.
10. Try to use brief codes to introduce your ideas. You may begin your response by saying, "I disagree with Tom's view that . . . because . . . ," or "I agree with what Mary just said and can offer an example . . ." or "In the piece we read by David Plotz, this idea was discussed."
11. Make sure your response addresses the topic being discussed and does not go off on a tangent.
12. Rely on the moderator of the discussion for prompting and direction. In other words, select the discussion leader. It might naturally be your instructor or another student in the class. Rely on the moderator to direct the discussion. In other words, the moderator might call on individuals to speak, ask new questions, or prompt students to explore new ideas.
13. Regard every speaker with respect—just what you would expect of others.
14. A spirited answer is acceptable, but not an aggressive, loud, or rude one.
15. If you know the topic your class will be discussing on a given day, jot down your ideas or opinions beforehand. Perhaps look up an article on the topic online before your class.

In the chapters that follow, you will discover dozens of different selections—both written and visual—that range widely across contemporary matters that we hope you will find exciting and thought-provoking. Arranged thematically into ten chapters, the writings represent widely diverse topics. Regardless of how these issues touch your own personal experience, you should understand that critical thinking, reading, writing, and viewing will open you up to a deeper understanding of society, culture, politics, and of yourself as a vital member of a broader community.

1 How Does Advertising Influence Us?

Advertising surrounds us, permeating our daily lives—on television, billboards, newspapers, magazines, the Internet, the sides of buses and trains, T-shirts, sports arenas, even license plates. Advertising is the driving force behind our consumptive economy, accounting for more than 150 billion dollars worth of commercials and print ads each year in the United States. Commercials fill 15 to 20 minutes of television airtime per hour (more for sporting events such as football games). They form the bulk of most newspapers and magazines. Advertising is everywhere we are, appealing to the root of our desires—our fantasies, hopes, wishes, and dreams—while promising us youth, beauty, social acceptance, power, sex appeal, and happiness. Through carefully selected images and words, advertising may be the most powerful manufacturer of meaning in our society. And many of us are not even aware of how it influences our lives.

Most of us are so accustomed to advertising that we barely notice its presence around us. However, if we stopped to think about how it works on our subconscious, we might be amazed at how powerful and complex a force it is. This chapter examines how advertising tempts us to buy, feeds our fantasies, and convinces us to part with our money.

The chapter closes with some sample ads for popular products and services. Use a critical eye when reviewing these advertisements, and consider some of the points about persuasion and advertising described in this chapter.

CRITICAL THINKING

1. This editorial cartoon features a great deal of visual material. What is happening in this cartoon? What does it seek to demonstrate? How effective is it in relaying its message? Explain.
2. How many scenarios exhibited in this cartoon can you relate to? Cite a few examples of how this cartoon relates to your own life experience.
3. Can you tell how the person in the cartoon feels about the issue depicted? Explain.

A Brand by Any Other Name

Douglas Rushkoff

Douglas Rushkoff is a writer and columnist who analyzes, writes, and speaks about the way people, cultures, and institutions share and influence each other's values. He is the author of many books on new media and popular culture, including *Media Virus* and *Coercion: Why We Listen to What "They" Say.* His column on cyberculture appears monthly in the *New York Times.* This essay appeared in the April 30, 2000, edition of the *London Times.*

CONNECTING TO THE TOPIC

Brand-name products target groups of consumers—Pepsi and Levi's appeal to large, diverse populations, while Fendi, Coach, or Gucci appeal to very elite ones. Brands depend on image—the image they promote, and the image consumers believe they will project by using the product. For many teens, brands can announce membership in a particular group, value systems, personality, and personal style. Today's youth are more consumer and media savvy than previous generations, forcing retailers to rethink how they brand and market goods to this group. While teens like to think that they are hip to advertising gimmicks, marketers are one step ahead of the game—a game that teens are likely to lose as they strive to "brand" themselves.

WORDS IN CONTEXT

affiliation: connection; association
psycho-physical: mind-body
phenomenon: a circumstance or fact that can be felt by the senses
utilitarian: practical
esoteric: confined to and understood by a small group only
affinity: natural attraction and liking
existential: relating to or dealing with existence
anthropology: the study of the behavior and physical, social, and cultural development of humans and human groups
predilections: preferences
angst: anxiety
compunction: sense of guilt
deconstruct: to break down and analyze

arsenal: a store of weapons of defense
opaque: impenetrable; difficult to see through and understand
sensibility: awareness and sense of feeling
coerce: to force to act or think in a certain way by use of pressure or intimidation; to compel
conflation: a mix of several things together

1 I was in one of those sports "superstores" the other day, hoping to find a pair of trainers for myself. As I faced the giant wall of shoes, each model categorized by either sports affiliation, basketball star, economic class, racial heritage or consumer niche, I noticed a young boy standing next to me, maybe 13 years old, in even greater awe of the towering selection of footwear.

2 His jaw was dropped and his eyes were glazed over—a psycho-physical response to the overwhelming sensory data in a self-contained consumer environment. It's a phenomenon known to retail architects as "Gruen Transfer," named for the gentleman who invented the shopping mall, where this mental paralysis is most commonly observed. Having finished several years of research on this exact mind state, I knew to proceed with caution. I slowly made my way to the boy's side and gently asked him, "what is going through your mind right now?"

3 He responded without hesitation, "I don't know which of these trainers is 'me.'" The boy proceeded to explain his dilemma. He thought of Nike as the most utilitarian and scientifically advanced shoe, but had heard something about third world laborers and was afraid that wearing this brand might label him as too anti-Green. He then considered a skateboard shoe, Airwalk, by an "indie" manufacturer (the trainer equivalent of a micro-brewery) but had recently learned that this company was almost as big as Nike. The truly hip brands of skate shoe were too esoteric for his current profile at school—he'd look like he was "trying." This left the "retro" brands, like Puma, Converse and Adidas, none of which he felt any real affinity for, since he wasn't even alive in the 70's when they were truly and non-ironically popular.

4 With no clear choice and, more importantly, no other way to conceive of his own identity, the boy stood there, paralyzed in the modern youth equivalent of an existential crisis. Which brand am I, anyway?

5 Believe it or not, there are dozens, perhaps hundreds of youth culture marketers who have already begun clipping out this article. They work

for hip, new advertising agencies and cultural research firms who trade in the psychology of our children and the anthropology of their culture. The object of their labors is to create precisely the state of confusion and vulnerability experienced by the young shopper at the shoe wall—and then turn this state to their advantage. It is a science, though not a pretty one.

6 Marketers spend millions developing strategies to identify children's predilections and then capitalize on their vulnerabilities. Young people are fooled for a while, but then develop defense mechanisms, such as media-savvy attitudes or ironic dispositions. Then marketers research these defenses, develop new countermeasures, and on it goes.

7 The battle in which our children are engaged seems to pass beneath our radar screens, in a language we don't understand. But we see the confusion and despair that results. How did we get in this predicament, and is there a way out? Is it your imagination, you wonder, or have things really gotten worse? Alas, things seem to have gotten worse. Ironically, this is because things had gotten so much better.

8 In olden times—back when those of us who read the newspaper grew up—media was a one-way affair. Advertisers enjoyed a captive audience, and could quite authoritatively provoke our angst and stoke our aspirations. Interactivity changed all this. The remote control gave viewers the ability to break the captive spell of television programming whenever they wished, without having to get up and go all the way up to the set. Young people proved particularly adept at "channel surfing," both because they grew up using the new tool, and because they felt little compunction to endure the tension-provoking narratives of storytellers who did not have their best interests at heart. It was as if young people knew that the stuff on television was called "programming" for a reason, and developed shortened attention spans for the purpose of keeping themselves from falling into the spell of advertisers. The remote control allowed young people to deconstruct TV.

9 The next weapon in the child's arsenal was the video game joystick. For the first time, viewers had control over the very pixels on their monitors. The television image was demystified. Then, the computer mouse and keyboard transformed the TV receiver into a portal. Today's young people grew up in a world where a screen could as easily be used for expressing oneself as consuming the media of others. Now the media was up-for-grabs, and the ethic, from hackers to camcorder owners, was "do it yourself."

10 Likewise, as computer interfaces were made more complex and opaque—think Windows—the do-it-yourself ethic of the Internet was undone. The original Internet was a place to share ideas and converse with others. Children actually had to use the keyboard! Now, the World Wide Web encourages them to click numbly through packaged content. Web sites are designed to keep young people from using the keyboard, except to enter in their parents' credit card information.

11 But young people had been changed by their exposure to new media. They constituted a new "psychographic," as advertisers like to call it, so new kinds of messaging had to be developed that appealed to their new sensibility.

12 Anthropologists—the same breed of scientists that used to scope out enemy populations before military conquests—engaged in focus groups, conducted "trend-watching" on the streets, in order to study the emotional needs and subtle behaviors of young people. They came to understand, for example, how children had abandoned narrative structures for fear of the way stories were used to coerce them. Children tended to construct narratives for themselves by collecting things instead, like cards, bottlecaps called "pogs," or keychains and plush toys. They also came to understand how young people despised advertising—especially when it did not acknowledge their media-savvy intelligence.

13 Thus, Pokemon was born—a TV show, video game, and product line where the object is to collect as many trading cards as possible. The innovation here, among many, is the marketer's conflation of TV show and advertisement into one piece of media. The show is an advertisement. The story, such as it is, concerns a boy who must collect little monsters in order to develop his own character. Likewise, the Pokemon video game engages the player in a quest for those monsters. Finally, the card game itself (for the few children who actually play it) involves collecting better monsters—not by playing, but by buying more cards. The more cards you buy, the better you can play.

14 Kids feel the tug, but in a way they can't quite identify as advertising. Their compulsion to create a story for themselves—in a world where stories are dangerous—makes them vulnerable to this sort of attack. In marketer's terms, Pokemon is "leveraged" media, with "cross-promotion" on "complementary platforms." This is ad-speak for an assault on multiple fronts.

15 Moreover, the time a child spends in the Pokemon craze amounts to a remedial lesson in how to consume. Pokemon teaches them how to want things that they can't or won't actually play with. In fact, it teaches them how to buy things they don't even want. While a child might want one particular card, he needs to purchase them in packages whose contents are not revealed. He must buy blind and repeatedly until he gets the object of his desire.

16 Meanwhile, older kids have attempted to opt out of aspiration altogether. The "15–24" demographic, considered by marketers the most difficult to wrangle into submission, have adopted a series of postures they hoped would make them impervious to marketing techniques. They take pride in their ability to recognize when they are being pandered to, and watch TV for the sole purpose of calling out when they are being manipulated.

17 But now advertisers are making commercials just for them. Soft drink advertisements satirize one another before rewarding the cynical viewer: "image is nothing," they say. The technique might best be called "wink" advertising for its ability to engender a young person's loyalty by pretending to disarm itself. "Get it?" the ad means to ask. If you're cool, you do.

18 New magazine advertisements for jeans, such as those created by Diesel, take this even one step further. The ads juxtapose imagery that actually makes no sense—ice cream billboards in North Korea, for example. The strategy is brilliant. For a media-savvy young person to feel good about himself, he needs to feel he "gets" the joke. But what does he do with an ad where there's obviously something to get that he can't figure out? He has no choice but to admit that the brand is even cooler than he is. An ad's ability to confound its audience is the new credential for a brand's authenticity.

19 Like the boy at the wall of shoes, kids today analyze each purchase they make, painstakingly aware of how much effort has gone into seducing them. As a result, they see their choices of what to watch and what to buy as exerting some influence over the world around them. After all, their buying patterns have become the center of so much attention!

20 But however media-savvy kids get, they will always lose this particular game. For they have accepted the language of brands as their cultural currency, and the stakes in their purchasing decisions as something real. For no matter how much control kids get over the media they watch, they are still utterly powerless when it comes to the manu-

facturing of brands. Even a consumer revolt merely reinforces one's role as a consumer, not an autonomous or creative being.

21 The more they interact with brands, the more they brand themselves. ◆

CONSIDERING THE ISSUES

1. When you were in junior and senior high school, did you have particular brands to which you were most loyal? Did this brand loyalty change as you got older? Why did you prefer certain brands over others? What cultural and social influences, if any, contributed to your desire for that brand?
2. How would you define your personal style and the image you wish to project? What products and/or brands contribute to that image? Explain.
3. What can a brand tell you about the person who uses it? Explain.

CRAFT AND CONTENT

4. How does Rushkoff support his argument? Evaluate his use of supporting sources. Identify some of the essay's particular strengths.
5. In paragraph 7, Rushkoff notes that things have gotten worse because they have gotten better. What does he mean by this statement? Explain.

CRITICAL THINKING

6. Look up the phrase "Gruen transfer" on the Internet. Were you aware of this angle of marketing practice? Does it change the way you think about how products are sold to you? Explain.
7. In order to stay in business, marketers have had to rethink how they sell products to the youth market. How have they changed to keep pace with the youth market? Explain.
8. In his conclusion, Rushkoff predicts that even media-savvy kids will still "lose" the game. Why will they fail? Explain.

WRITING ABOUT THE ISSUES

9. Rushkoff notes in paragraph 11 that the youth generation "constitutes a new psychographic." First, define what you think

"psychographic" means in the advertising industry. What makes this generation different from previous generations of consumers? If you are part of this generation, (ages 14–24), explain why you do or don't think you indeed represent a new "psychographic." If you are older than this group, answer the same question based on your own experience and observation of younger consumers.

10. Teens and young adults covet certain brand-name clothing because they believe it promotes a particular image. What defines brand image? Is it something created by the company, or by the people who use the product? How does advertising influence the social view we hold of ourselves and the brands we use? Write an essay on the connection between advertising, image, and cultural values of what is "in" or popular and what is not.
11. Did marketing techniques such as the one described by Rushkoff for the Pokemon trading cards and games influence your consumer habits as a child or teen? Were you aware of such techniques? Write an essay exploring the way advertising targets specific age groups. Support your essay with information from the article and your own experience. You may wish to identify particular products that use specific marketing techniques to target young consumers.

Brand Cool

Peter Belmonte

Peter Belmonte is a marketing executive. In 2004, with Peter Frost, managing director of Proficiency Group, he helped produce the "Rethink Pink" conference in London that explored how to market products to women. This essay was published in the September/October 2003 issue of *Adbusters* magazine.

CONNECTING TO THE TOPIC

The concept of "cool" is something we learn as children in grade school. For kids, cool can mean having the "right" clothing or newest toy. For teens, it could be owning popular video games, sporting particular brand names, and knowing the latest trends. Some people chase cool throughout their lives, and for many Americans it is a way of life. Having the best, most appropriate, envied, and admired stuff can mark us as "cool" and successful. But what is "cool"? How do we learn what is cool and what is not, and how does this knowledge influence our consumer habits?

WORDS IN CONTEXT

aspirational: desiring to achieve; having ambition to reach
polyethnic: many ethnicities; multicultural
faux pas: a social blunder
preempt: to take the place of; displace
nostalgia: longing for things, persons, or situations of the past

1 According to the marketing studies, our "aspirational age" is 17 years old. It's the age of Perfect Cool and everybody wants it, from 42-year-old "style fossils" to 30-something "adultescents" to eight-year-old "tartlets" who wear glitter denims and kick box to S Club Juniors. You're thinking marketing? Think sweet 17.

2 As much as the importance of being cool is discounted, it remains a timeless emotional need. Cool is a comprehensive set of life-guiding concepts, a shorthand for social survival: acceptance, popularity, fun, and success. Don't take that as a definition, though. Cool has no definition. In fact, its total undefinability is what has made "Am I cool?" the all-consuming question of our times.

3 By the 1990s, the brandmasters had begun to study teens like an anthropologist would study a foreign culture. At the same time, branding was up against its deepest challenge yet. The so-called Generation X was in active self-defense against the marketers, adopting a posture and lifestyle that resisted the very notion of cool itself. Of course, they turned out to be a market ripe for harvest. It only took the right kind of message, and Sprite nailed it with their 1995 reverse-marketing play. "Image is Nothing, Thirst is Everything," the Sprite campaign proclaimed. You remember: famous basketball players pitching the product in TV ads while bags of money representing their endorsement fees accumulated at the bottom of the screen. Anti-sell became the new sell; marketing moved from one play to the next.

4 Today's youth market is the most ethnically mingled bunch in history. Teenagers are empowered by their differences, and many pride themselves on their ability to move between peer groups and make

friends across increasingly blurry racial lines. Polyethnic plays were deployed and planted, most memorably by Gap, Hilfiger, and Benetton. Their ads are a tangle of multiculturalism: scrubbed black faces lounging with their windswept white brothers in that great country club in the sky. Is it art imitating life or life imitating art? Actually, it's what sociologists call "reflexivity" the tendency of communications to shape society. (Reports on increasing divorce rates tend to increase divorce rates; opinion polls about voter trends tend to affect the way people cast their votes.) Through reflexivity, the communications industry feeds into the streams that form cultural agendas; the media show us how we could or should be living.

5 Over the past decade, young black men in American inner cities have been the most aggressively mined by the brandmasters as a source of borrowed meaning and identity. For pioneers, think Nike and Hilfiger, both catapulted to brand superstardom in no small part by poor kids incorporating their brands into hip-hop style at the very moment when rap was being thrust into the limelight. The turning point for Tommy Hil was a single night in March 1994, when Tommy's nephew introduced the label to friends at Def Jam records and to rapper icon Snoop Doggy Dogg. Snoop swaggered onto the *Saturday Night Live* stage dressed in baggy gangsta pants, but also draped in a preppie sport jersey branded boldly with the Hilfiger logo. Hilfiger sales exploded—up $93 million the next year. As for Nike—the company is so focused on borrowing style and attitude from black urban youth that its marketers have their own word for the practice: "bro-ing."

6 But where is cool going next? What product or brand will ride high on the next wave of cool? Here's the only answer: the one that moves at the speed of reinvention.

7 A few facts to keep in mind. Number one: the whole skate/hip-hop thing is now so unbelievably commercial and mainstream that many style hoovers have completely lost interest. The post-streetwear age is looming evercloser.

8 Number two: there is a contemporary groundswell of cultural apathy towards hyped lifestyles and impossible beauty. It's not for nothing that marketing execs are studying *No Logo*. A bit of truth and authenticity? A great new play.

9 An extension of the truth construct is the re-birth of "un-cool." Getting it wrong may now be the safest, surest way of being one step ahead. Naturally, it's nothing new. As a route to instant credibility,

adopting a faux pas and making it work for you has become so obvious that everyone is doing it. What was once a means of rejecting fashion is now an attempt to preempt fashion.

10 The growing universality of un-cool/nu-cool is more than a new twist on irony. It's also a nostalgia for the carefree days before teens fell victim to their own hyper self-consciousness. Following years of logomania, fashion is experiencing a backlash against the brand. In the same way, so-called tastemakers are abandoning Wallpaper-clone bars in favor of the local pub. And yes, brandmasters are onto the game. Referencing a world previously overlooked or considered unsavory has become a new way of asserting independence and individuality. It's been good news for the revived fortunes of Camper shoes, Pringle cashmere, rainbow leg warmers and Babycham. In six months' time they'll be sporting Millets fleeces and Widdecombe bowl cuts while discussing the merits of M People and the Lighthouse Family. Then it won't be long before anti-anti-cool. The cycle goes 'round. Be ready. ◆

CONSIDERING THE ISSUES

1. Several of the essays in this section comment on the concept of "cool." What is "cool" to you? Can you define it? Is it something you can buy? Explain.
2. Marketers have determined that the ideal age to which we aspire, whether we are older or younger, is 17. How do you think marketers came up with this number? Does it ring true? From your own perspective, do you agree? What is so appealing about this age? Explain.

CRAFT AND CONTENT

3. In his first paragraph, Belmonte puts several advertising phrases or terms in quotation marks. Identify these words and what they mean. Are these coined words more effective in making his point than real ones? Explain.
4. At various points throughout his essay, Belmonte asks his readers a question. What questions does he pose to his readers, and how does he answer these questions? In your opinion, is this a good writing device? Explain.

CRITICAL THINKING

5. What challenges did advertisers face in their branding approach after 1990? Why did they need to change the way they approached branding? Explain.
6. What is the "anti-sell"? Can you think of any current commercials that employ this technique?
7. What did Snoop Doggy Dogg do for the Tommy Hilfiger brand? How did he do it? Would the brand have been as popular if he had starred in a commercial endorsing Tommy Hilfiger? Explain.

WRITING ABOUT THE ISSUES

8. Spend an evening watching different commercials on television during the prime-time viewing hours of 8:00 to 11:00 p.m. Separate the commercials into different product categories (automobiles, electronics, cell phone/Internet service, food, popular stores, etc.). Describe how these products or services are marketed to you as a viewer. Do they speak directly to you? Let you in on a joke? Admit that they know that you know that they are advertising? Tell a story? Try to determine if there are any trends in advertising thematically by product or service, or overall. Can you make any parallels between what you viewed and Belmonte's observations in his essay? Explain.
9. Belmonte notes that logos are becoming so overblown that they may become passé. "Uncool" may become the new cool. Write an essay in which you expand on this idea and foretell what the branding landscape might look like in ten years based on your personal knowledge of trends.

On Sale at Old Navy: Cool Clothes for Identical Zombies!

Damien Cave

Damien Cave is a writer and Phillips Foundation Fellow. This article first appeared in the November 22, 2000, issue of the e-zine *Salon*.

CONNECTING TO THE TOPIC

Mass-market retail stores like Old Navy, Gap, Pottery Barn, and Ikea have enjoyed enormous popularity in recent years. Part of their appeal is that they market the concept of "cool." We believe that they represent a "with it" lifestyle that we literally buy into. But are these stores just marketing conformity under the guise of "cool"? Are they crushing our individuality? Are we moving rapidly to the day where we will all dress the same, have the same furniture, and want the same things? If the things we own and the clothes we wear help create our identity, are chain stores just helping us join the cult of conformity?

WORDS IN CONTEXT

pugnacious: scornful or hostile; disapproving and critical
homogenous: of the same or similar nature or kind
urbanite: a city dweller
equate: to consider, treat, or depict as equal or equivalent
Pavlovianly: referring to Russian scientist Ivan Petrovich Pavlov, known for discovering the conditioned response. In one experiment, by ringing a bell when feeding dogs, he eventually was able to get the dogs to salivate just by hearing the bell, even when no food was present. His experiment proved that animals could be conditioned to expect a consequence on the results of previous experience.
commodify: to turn into or treat as a product that can be sold; make commercial
pessimistic: tending to stress the negative or unfavorable viewpoint
duality: state of having two sides
insidious: sinister; intended to entrap by stealth; having a harmful allure

1 Thomas Frank walks by the candy-cane-adorned displays of Old Navy, passing the sign exclaiming "priced so low, you can't say no," and into the chain's San Francisco flagship store. The all-devouring Christmas rush hasn't started yet, but it's clear from the frown on Frank's face that he's not being seduced by the cheap but stylish clothes, the swirling neon and the bass-heavy hip-hop pounding in his ears.

2 "Oh God, this is disgusting," Frank says. This reaction isn't surprising. The bespectacled Midwesterner is a pioneering social critic—one of the first writers to document how, starting in the '60s, American businesses have co-opted cool anti-corporate culture and used it to

seduce the masses. His arguments in the *Baffler*, a pugnacious review Frank founded in 1988, and in 1997's "The Conquest of Cool" read like sermons, angry wake-up calls for consumers who hungrily ingest hipper-than-thou ("Think Different") marketing campaigns without ever questioning their intent.

3 Old Navy and other cheap but tasteful retailers provide perfect fodder for Frank's critique. Their low prices and hip-but-wholesome branding strategy are supposed to present a healthy alternative to the conspicuous consumption of a Calvin Klein. But critics like Frank and Naomi Klein, author of "No Logo," argue that the formula is really nothing more than the wolf of materialism wrapped in cheaper sheep's clothing.

4 Consumers are being scammed, says Klein, arguing that stores like Old Navy and Ikea are duping millions, inspiring mass conformity while pretending to deliver high culture to the masses. "It's this whole idea of creating a carnival for the most homogenous fashions and furniture," says Klein. "It's mass cloning that's being masked in a carnival of diversity. You don't notice that you're conforming because everything is so colorful."

5 Klein and Frank say that few consumers recognize just how conformist their consumption habits have become. And certainly, it's hard to argue that Ikea's and Old Navy's items haven't become icons of urbanite and suburbanite imagination. Watch MTV, or rent "Fight Club," to see Ikea's candy-colored décor, then truck down to your local Old Navy flagship store. When you arrive, what you'll find is that hordes of people have beaten you there. At virtually every opening of Old Navy's and Ikea's stores—in the New York, Chicago and San Francisco areas, for example—tens of thousands of people appeared in the first few days. Even now, long after the stores first opened, lines remain long.

6 What's wrong with these people? Nothing, say defenders of the companies. The popularity of brands like Ikea and Old Navy, they argue, derives from the retailers' ability to offer good stuff cheap. "They provide remarkable value," says Joel Reichart, a professor at the Fordham School of Business who has written case studies on Ikea. "They're truly satisfying people's needs."

7 Despite his irritation with the way companies like Old Navy market themselves, Frank acknowledges that businesses have always sought to offer cheap, relatively high-quality merchandise and concedes that there is some value in their attempts. He even admits that consumerism is good for the economy.

8 But he and other critics argue that in the end we're only being conned into thinking that our needs are being satisfied. What's really happening, they argue, is that clever marketers are turning us into automatons who equate being cool with buying cheap stuff that everyone else has. Under the stores' guise of delivering good taste to the general public, any chance we have at experiencing or creating authenticity is being undermined. Ultimately, our brave new shopping world is one in which we are spending more time in the checkout line than reading books, watching movies or otherwise challenging ourselves with real culture.

9 "Shopping is a way of putting together your identity," laments "Nobrow" author John Seabrook. And the "homogenized taste" of today's Old Navy and Ikea shoppers proves, he says, that Americans either are consciously choosing to look and live alike or are determined not to notice that that is what they're doing.

10 According to Christine Rosen, a professor in the Haas School of Business at UC-Berkeley, people who fill their closets, homes and lives with Old Navy and Ikea—or Pottery Barn or a host of other slick stores—are simply new examples of the trend toward conformity that started when the first "brands" appeared in the 1910s and '20s. "We're Pavlovianly trained to respond to this," she says.

11 And we're also just too damn lazy. That's the theory floated by Packard Jennings, an anti-consumerism activist who says that stores like Old Navy are designed to numb the brain and remove all semblance of creativity from the purchasing process. "Ikea pre-arranges sets of furniture in its stores, thereby lessening individual thought," he says. Once people are in the store, they can't resist. "Entire households are purchased at Ikea," he says.

12 Indeed, Janice Simonsen, an Ikea spokeswoman, confirmed that a large part of the chain's demographic consists of "people who come in and say, 'I need everything.'" Meanwhile, those who don't want everything usually end up with more than they need, says Fordham's Reichart. "The way they design their stores"—with an up escalator to the showroom and no exit until the checkout—"you end up going through the entire store," he says.

13 Old Navy plays by the same sneaky rules. When Frank and I entered the San Francisco store, clerks offered us giant mesh bags. Ostensibly, this is just good service, but since the bags are capable of holding at least half a dozen pairs of jeans and a few shirts, it's obvious that they're also meant to encourage overconsumption.

14 Frank called the bags "gross" but not out of line with other state-of-the-art retailing practices. But according to Klein, the sacks, in conjunction with Old Navy's penchant for displaying T-shirts in mock-1950s supermarket coolers, prove that the company is aiming to do something more. The idea behind this "theater for the brand" architecture is to commodify the products, to make them "as easy to buy as a gallon of milk," Klein says. "The idea is to create a Mecca where people make pilgrimages to their brand," Klein says. "You experience the identity of the brand and not the product."

15 Disney, which opened its first store in 1987, was the first to employ this strategy. And since then others have appeared. Niketown, the Body Shop, the Discovery Store—they all aim to sell products by selling a destination.

16 Old Navy and Ikea, however, are far more popular than those predecessors—and, if you believe the more pessimistic of their critics, more dangerous. Not only are the two chains remaking many closets and homes into one designer showcase, says Klein, but they are also lulling consumers to sleep and encouraging them to overlook some important issues.

17 Such as quality. People think they're getting "authenticity on the cheap," says David Lewis, author of "The Soul of the New Consumer." But the truth may be that they're simply purchasing the perception of quality and authenticity. "Because [Ikea and Old Navy] create these self-enclosed lifestyles," Klein explains, "you overlook the fact that the products are pretty crappy and fall apart." Adds Jennings, "Things may be cheaper, but you keep going back to replace the faulty merchandise."

18 Then there is the trap of materialism. Survey after survey suggests that people who place a high value on material goods are less happy than those who do not, says Eric Rindfleisch, a marketing professor at the University of Arizona. The focus on bargains, incremental purchases and commodification plays to a uniquely American blind spot.

19 "We operate with a duality," explains Rindfleisch, who has conducted studies linking materialism with depression. "Americans know that money doesn't buy happiness, but most people somehow believe that increments in pay or goods will improve our lives. It's a human weakness—particularly in America."

20 The most insidious danger may be more abstract. The anti-consumerism critics argue that by elevating shopping to cultural status,

we are losing our grip on real culture. We live in a time where college kids think nothing of decorating their rooms with Absolut vodka ads and fail to realize that they're essentially turning their rooms into billboards. Meanwhile, museum stores keep getting larger, Starbucks sells branded CDs to go with your coffee and because Ikea and other stores now look like movie theaters or theme parks, we don't just shop, "we make a day of it," as Klein puts it.

21 This only helps steer us away from other endeavors. When people spend so much time buying, thinking and talking about products, they don't have time for anything else, for real conversations about politics or culture or for real interaction with people.

22 Ultimately, the popularity of Old Navy, Ikea and their ilk proves that we're stuck in what Harvard professor Juliet Schor calls "the cycle of work and spend." Breaking that cycle may not be easy, but if one believes critics like Frank, it's essential if we are to control our own culture, instead of allowing it to be defined by corporations.

23 The cycle may not be possible to break. Frank, for one, is extremely pessimistic about our chances for turning back the tide of conformity and co-opted cool. Maybe that's one reason why he wanted to get out of Old Navy as fast as he could.

24 But I'm not so sure. When "Ikea boy," Edward Norton's character in "Fight Club," watched his apartment and his Swedish furniture explode in a blaze of glory, I wasn't the only one in the theater who cheered. ◆

CONSIDERING THE ISSUES

1. Cave notes several businesses in his essay that he calls "mass-market" sellers of "cool." What stores does he specifically identify? Do you shop at any of these stores? If so, why do you shop there? Because they are "cool"? Affordable? Hip? Popular? Explain.
2. In paragraph 20, Cave observes that "college kids think nothing of decorating their rooms with Absolut vodka ads and fail to realize that they're essentially turning their rooms into billboards." What decorating choices have you made to your personal space? In what ways has your decorating style been influenced by outside forms of advertising? Explain.

CRAFT AND CONTENT

3. Cave quotes many different people in his essay. Identify all of his sources and group them as either "inside advertising/marketing," or "outside critics/academics." Whom does he rely upon more? How do the quotes he uses from both groups support his argument?
4. Can you tell what position Cave supports on the issue of mass consumption and on the stores he describes in his essay? Identify a few specific statements he makes in his essay that reveal his point of view.
5. How does Cave's title connect to his subject matter? What images does it create? How does it influence the reader's interpretation of his argument? Explain.

CRITICAL THINKING

6. In paragraph 2, Cave notes that American businesses have "co-opted cool anti-corporate culture." What does he mean? What is "anti-corporate" culture and why is it "cool"? What started it and how are businesses using it to their advantage? In what ways is this ironic? Explain.
7. What techniques do mass-market stores employ to squeeze the maximum profit from consumers who enter them? Were you aware of these techniques? Have you fallen victim to them yourself? Explain.

WRITING ABOUT THE ISSUES

8. In paragraph 9, author John Seabrook comments, "Shopping is a way of putting together your identity." Consider the ways your shopping habits put together your identity. Are you influenced by some of the techniques described in this essay? Consider in your response not just what you buy, but where you shop, why you shop, and with whom. How do your shopping companions influence your choices? How does advertising appeal to your desire to buy particular things as part of your own personal identity? Explain.
9. Several critics in this essay fear that mass-marketing chains aim to make shopping the primary characteristic of American culture. "By elevating shopping to cultural status, we are losing our

grip on real culture. When people spend so much time buying, thinking, and talking about products, they don't have time for anything else, for real conversations about politics or culture or for real interaction with people." Write a response to this assertion expressing your own point of view.

With These Words I Can Sell You Anything

William Lutz

William Lutz teaches English at Rutgers University and is the author of several books, including *Beyond Nineteen Eighty-Four* (1984) and *Doublespeak Defined* (1999). The following essay is an excerpt from Lutz's book *Doublespeak*.

CONNECTING TO THE TOPIC

Words such as "help" and "virtually" and phrases such as "new and improved" and "acts fast" seem like innocuous weaponry in the arsenal of advertising. But not to William Lutz, who analyzes how such words are used in ads—how they misrepresent, mislead, and deceive consumers. In this essay, he alerts us to the special power of "weasel words"—those familiar and sneaky little critters that "appear to say one thing when in fact they say the opposite, or nothing at all." The real danger, Lutz argues, is how such language debases reality and the values of the consumer.

1 One problem advertisers have when they try to convince you that the product they are pushing is really different from other, similar products is that their claims are subject to some laws. Not a lot of laws, but there are some designed to prevent fraudulent or untruthful claims in advertising. Generally speaking, advertisers have to be careful in what they say in their ads, in the claims they make for the products they advertise. Parity claims are safe because they are legal and supported by a number of court decisions. But beyond parity claims there are weasel words.

2 Advertisers use weasel words to appear to be making a claim for a product when in fact they are making no claim at all. Weasel words get their name from the way weasels eat the eggs they find in the nests of other animals. A weasel will make a small hole in the egg, suck out the insides, then place the egg back in the nest. Only when the egg is examined closely is it found to be hollow. That's the way it is with weasel words in advertising.

"Help"—The Number One Weasel Word

3 The biggest weasel word used in advertising doublespeak is "help." Now "help" only means to aid or assist, nothing more. It does not mean to conquer, stop, eliminate, end, solve, heal, cure, or anything else. But once the ad says "help," it can say just about anything after that because "help" qualifies everything coming after it. The trick is that the claim that comes after the weasel word is usually so strong and so dramatic that you forget the word "help" and concentrate only on the dramatic claim. You read into the ad a message that the ad does not contain. More importantly, the advertiser is not responsible for the claim that you read into the ad, even though the advertiser wrote the ad so you would read that claim into it.

4 The next time you see an ad for a cold medicine that promises that it "helps relieve cold symptoms fast," don't rush out to buy it. Ask yourself what this claim is really saying. Remember, "helps" means only that the medicine will aid or assist. What will it aid or assist in doing? Why, "relieve" your cold "symptoms." "Relieve" only means to ease, alleviate, or mitigate, not to stop, end, or cure. Nor does the claim say how much relieving this medicine will do. Nowhere does this ad claim it will cure anything. In fact, the ad doesn't even claim it will do anything at all. The ad only claims that it will aid in relieving (not curing) your cold symptoms, which are probably a runny nose, watery eyes, and a headache. In other words, this medicine probably contains a standard decongestant and some aspirin. By the way, what does "fast" mean? Ten minutes, one hour, one day? What is fast to one person can be very slow to another. Fast is another weasel word.

5 Look at ads in magazines and newspapers, listen to ads on radio and television, and you'll find the word "help" in ads for all kinds of products. How often do you read or hear such phrases as "helps stop . . . ," "helps overcome . . . ," "helps eliminate . . . ," "helps you feel . . . ," or

"helps you look . . ."? If you start looking for this weasel word in advertising, you'll be amazed at how often it occurs. Analyze the claims in the ads using "help," and you will discover that these ads are really saying nothing.

Virtually Spotless

6 One of the most powerful weasel words is "virtually," a word so innocent that most people don't pay any attention to it when it is used in an advertising claim. But watch out. "Virtually" is used in advertising claims that appear to make specific, definite promises when there is no promise. After all, what does "virtually" mean? It means "in essence of effect, although not in fact." Look at that definition again. "Virtually" means not in fact. It does not mean "almost" or "just about the same as," or anything else.

7 The next time you see the ad that says that this dishwasher detergent "leaves dishes virtually spotless," just remember how advertisers twist the meaning of the weasel word "virtually." You can have lots of spots on your dishes after using this detergent and the ad claim will still be true, because what this claim really means is that this detergent does not in fact leave your dishes spotless. Whenever you see or hear an ad claim that uses the word "virtually," just translate that claim into its real meaning. So the television set that is "virtually trouble free" becomes the television set that is not in fact trouble free, the "virtually foolproof operation" of any appliance becomes an operation that is in fact not foolproof, and the product that "virtually never needs service" becomes the product that is not in fact service free.

New and Improved

8 If "new" is the most frequently used word on a product package, "improved" is the second most frequent. In fact, the two words are almost always used together. It seems just about everything sold these days is "new and improved." The next time you're in the supermarket, try counting the number of times you see these words on products.

9 Just what do these words mean? The use of the word "new" is restricted by regulations, so an advertiser can't just use the word on a product or in an ad without meeting certain requirements. For example,

a product is considered new for about six months during a national advertising campaign. If the product is being advertised only in a limited test market area, the word can be used longer, and in some instances has been used for as long as two years.

10 What makes a product "new"? Some products have been around for a long time, yet every once in a while you discover that they are being advertised as "new." Well, an advertiser can call a product new if there has been "a material functional change" in the product. What is "a material functional change," you ask? Good question. In fact it's such a good question it's being asked all the time. It's up to the manufacturer to prove that the product has undergone such a change. And if the manufacturer isn't challenged on the claim, then there's no one to stop it. Moreover, the change does not have to be an improvement in the product. One manufacturer added an artificial lemon scent to a cleaning product and called it "new and improved," even though the product did not clean any better than without the lemon scent. The manufacturer defended the use of the word "new" on the grounds that the artificial scent changed the chemical formula of the product and therefore constituted "a material functional change."

11 Which brings up the word "improved." When used in advertising, "improved" does not mean "made better." It only means "changed" or "different from before." So, if the detergent maker puts a plastic pour spout on the box of detergent, the product has been "improved," and away we go with a whole new advertising campaign. Or, if the cereal maker adds more fruit or a different kind of fruit to the cereal, there's an improved product. Now you know why manufacturers are constantly making little changes in their products. Whole new advertising campaigns, designed to convince you that the product has been changed for the better, are based on small changes in superficial aspects of a product. The next time you see an ad for an "improved" product, ask yourself what was wrong with the old one. Ask yourself just how "improved" the product is. Finally, you might check to see whether the "improved" version costs more than the unimproved one.

12 "New" is just too useful and powerful a word in advertising for advertisers to pass it up easily. So they use weasel words that say "new" without really saying it. One of their favorites is "introducing," as in, "Introducing improved Tide," or "Introducing the stain remover." The first is simply saying, here's our improved soap; the second, here's our

ADVERTISING DOUBLESPEAK QUICK QUIZ

Test your awareness of advertising doublespeak. The following is a list of statements from some recent ads. Your job is to figure out what each of these ads really says.

DOMINO'S PIZZA: "Because nobody delivers better."
SINUTAB: "It can stop the pain."
TUMS: "The stronger acid neutralizer."
LISTERMINT: "Making your mouth a cleaner place."
CASCADE: "For virtually spotless dishes"
NUPRIN: "Little. Yellow. Different. Better."
ANACIN: "Better relief."
ADVIL: "Advanced medicine for pain."
ALEVE COLD AND SINUS: "12 hours of relief."
PONDS COLD CREAM: "Ponds cleans like no soap can."
MILLER LITE BEER: "Tastes great. Less filling."
PHILIPS MILK OF MAGNESIA: "Nobody treats you better than MOM."
BAYER: "The wonder drug that works wonders."
KNORR: "Where taste is everything."
ANUSOL: "Anusol is the word to remember for relief."
DIMETAPP: "It relieves kids as well as colds."
LIQUID DRANO: "The liquid strong enough to be called Drano."
JOHNSON & JOHNSON BABY POWDER: "Like magic for your skin."
PURITAN: "Make it your oil for life."
PAM: "Pam, because how you cook is as important as what you cook."
TYLENOL GEL-CAPS: "It's not a capsule. It's better."
ALKA-SELTZER PLUS: "Breaks up your worst cold symptoms."

new advertising campaign for our detergent. Another favorite is "now," as in, "Now there's Sinex," which simply means that Sinex is available. Then there are phrases like "Today's Chevrolet," "Presenting Dristan," and "A fresh way to start the day." The list is really endless because advertisers are always finding new ways to say "new" without really saying it.

Acts Fast

13 "Acts" and "works" are two popular weasel words in advertising because they bring action to the product and to the advertising claim. When you see the ad for the cough syrup that "Acts on the cough control center," ask yourself what this cough syrup is claiming to do. Well, it's just claiming to "act," to do something, to perform an action. What is it that the cough syrup does? The ad doesn't say. It only claims to perform an action or do something on your "cough control center." By the way, what and where is your "cough control center"? I don't remember learning about that part of the body in human biology class.

14 Ads that use such phrases as "acts fast," "acts against," "acts to prevent," and the like are saying essentially nothing, because "act" is a word empty of any specific meaning. The ads are always careful not to specify exactly what "act" the product performs. Just because a brand of aspirin claims to "act fast" for headache relief doesn't mean this aspirin is any better than any other aspirin. What is the "act" that this aspirin performs? You're never told. Maybe it just dissolves quickly. Since aspirin is a parity product, all aspirin is the same and therefore functions the same.

Works Like Anything Else

15 If you don't find the word "acts" in an ad, you will probably find the weasel word "works." In fact, the two words are almost interchangeable in advertising. Watch out for ads that say a product "works against," "works like," "works for," or "works longer." As with "acts," "works" is the same meaningless verb used to make you think that this product really does something, and maybe even something special or unique. But "works," like "acts," is basically a word empty of any specific meaning.

Like Magic

16 Whenever advertisers want you to stop thinking about the product and to start thinking about something bigger, better, or more attractive than the product, they use that very popular weasel word, "like." The word "like" is the advertiser's equivalent of a magician's use of misdirection. "Like" gets you to ignore the product and concentrate on the claim the advertiser is making about it. "For skin like peaches and cream" claims

the ad for a skin cream. What is this ad really claiming? It doesn't say this cream will give you peaches-and-cream skin. There is no verb in this claim, so it doesn't even mention using the product. How is skin ever like "peaches and cream"? The ad is making absolutely no promise or claim whatsoever for this skin cream. If you think this cream will give you soft, smooth, youthful-looking skin, you are the one who has read that meaning into the ad.

17 The wine that claims "It's like taking a trip to France" wants you to think about a romantic evening in Paris as you walk along the boulevard after a wonderful meal in an intimate little bistro. Of course, you don't really believe that a wine can take you to France, but the goal of the ad is to get you to think pleasant, romantic thoughts about France and not about how the wine tastes or how expensive it may be. That little word "like" has taken you away from crushed grapes into a world of your own imaginative making. Who knows, maybe the next time you buy wine, you'll think those pleasant thoughts when you see this brand of wine, and you'll buy it. Or, maybe you weren't even thinking about buying wine at all, but now you just might pick up a bottle the next time you're shopping. Ah, the power of "like" in advertising.

The World of Advertising

18 A study some years ago found the following words to be among the most popular used in U.S. television advertisements: "new," "improved," "better," "extra," "fresh," "clean," "beautiful," "free," "good," "great," and "light." At the same time, the following words were found to be among the most frequent on British television: "new," "good-better-best," "free," "fresh," "delicious," "full," "sure," "clean," "wonderful," and "special." While these words may occur most frequently in ads, and while ads may be filled with weasel words, you have to watch out for all the words used in advertising, not just the words mentioned here.

19 Every word in an ad is there for a reason; no word is wasted. Your job is to figure out exactly what each word is doing in an ad—what each word really means, not what the advertiser wants you to think it means. Remember, the ad is trying to get you to buy a product, so it will put the product in the best possible light, using any device, trick, or means legally allowed. Your only defense against advertising (besides taking up permanent residence on the moon) is to develop and use a strong critical reading, listening, and looking ability. Always ask yourself

what the ad is really saying. When you see ads on television, don't be misled by the pictures, the visual images. What does the ad say about the product? What does the ad not say? What information is missing from the ad? Only by becoming an active, critical consumer of the doublespeak of advertising will you ever be able to cut through the doublespeak and discover what the ad is really saying. ◆

CONSIDERING THE ISSUES

1. Consider the phrases used in advertising such as "new and improved" and "cleans like a dream." Do you think about such advertising phrases? How much do such phrases influence you as a consumer? Explain.
2. Do you think that most people fail to comprehend how advertising works on them? When you read or watch ads, do you see through the gimmicks and weasel words?

CRAFT AND CONTENT

3. What do you think of Lutz's writing style? Is it humorous? Informal? Academic? What strategies does he use to involve the reader in the piece?
4. The author uses "you" throughout the article. Do you find the use of the second person stylistically satisfying? Do you think it is appropriate for the article?
5. Review Lutz's "Doublespeak Quick Quiz." Choose five items and analyze them using dictionary meanings to explain what the ads are really saying.

CRITICAL THINKING

6. How did "weasel words" get their name? Does it sound like an appropriate label? Why, according to Lutz, do advertisers use them?
7. According to the author, how can consumers protect themselves against weasel words?

WRITING ABOUT THE ISSUES

8. As Lutz suggests, look at some ads in a magazine or newspaper (or television and radio commercials). Then make a list of all uses of "help" you find over a 24-hour period. Examine the ads to determine exactly what is said and what the unwary consumer thinks is being said. Write up your report.
9. Invent a product and have some fun writing an ad for it. Use as many weasel words as you can to make your product shine.
10. Lutz characterizes the language used in ads as "weasel words," that is, language that pretends to do one thing while really doing another. Explore your campus for examples of "weasel words." Look not only at ads, but at material such as university brochures and pamphlets that are sent to prospective students, and/or any political contests taking place (e.g., students running for the student government or candidates for office speaking at your campus). Write down all examples of weasel words and explain why they are empty words.

SAMPLE ADS AND STUDY QUESTIONS

The following section features five recently published magazine advertisements. Diverse in content and style, some ads use words to promote the product, while others depend on emotion, name recognition, visual appeal, or association. They present a variety of sales pitches and marketing techniques.

Following each ad is a list of questions to help you analyze how the ads work their appeal to promote their products. When studying them, consider how they target our social perception and basic desires for happiness, beauty, and success. Approach each as a consumer, an artist, a social scientist, and a critic with an eye for detail.

CRITICAL THINKING

1. How does this photograph capture your attention? Can you tell at a glance what this ad is selling? How long does it take to figure out what the product is? Is this a positive or negative aspect of the ad?
2. What visual conventions does this ad employ? What symbolism does it use? How much does this ad rely on symbol recognition? What are the implications of this symbolism toward the product? If you didn't know what the symbolism was in this ad, would it fail to effectively sell the product? Explain.
3. Consider the text at the bottom of the ad. What does it say about the product? About the person who buys the product?
4. Rate this advertisement on a scale of 1 to 10 in terms of appeal, with 10 being a perfect score. What score would you give it, and why does it deserve such a ranking?

Honda

honda.com 1-800-33-Honda EX model shown. ©2003 American Honda Motor Co., Inc.
*NHTSA NCAP frontal crash test: October 2000; side crash test: November 2000.

YOUR RIGHT BRAIN AND YOUR LEFT BRAIN WILL FINALLY BE OF THE SAME MIND. A car that can quench your emotional side and satiate your rational side. The stylish and 5-star-crash-test-rated* Civic Coupe.

HONDA

Vans

where the beach >>>>>>>>> meets the street >>>>>>>>>
where the beach >>>>>>>>> meets the street >>>>>>>>>

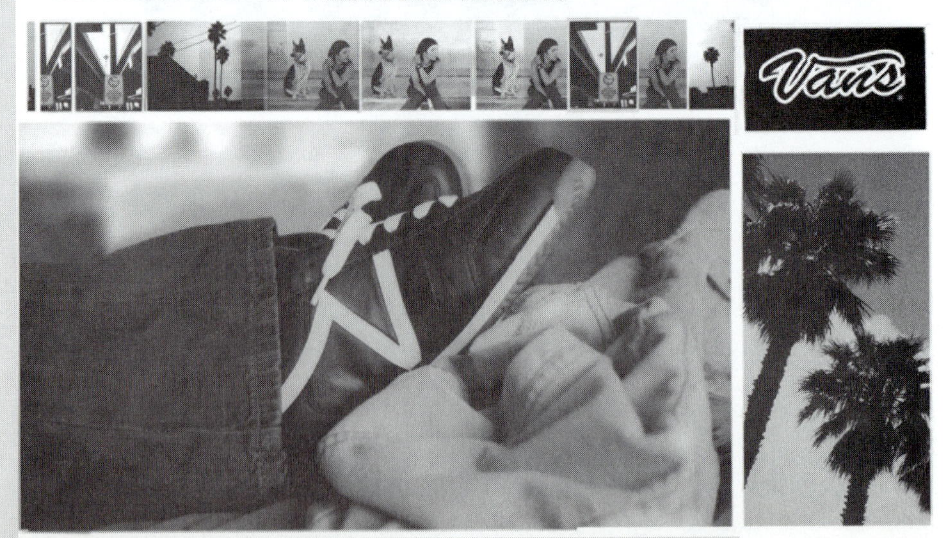

CRITICAL THINKING

1. Analyze the different images featured in the ad. What do they depict? How do the different photos contribute to the tone the ad wishes to set?
2. Do you know who the woman is in the ad? What sort of person do you imagine her to be? What is she wearing? Why is her clothing important in promoting the product—sneakers? How does her location promote the product's image?
3. Why is there a dog included in an ad for sneakers? Would the ad be different if the woman was alone? With a man? Explain.
4. Who would you say is the target audience for this ad, and why? Consider age, gender, lifestyle, etc., in your response.
5. Consider the different angles at which photographs included in this ad were taken. How would its impact be different if it were shot from above? What if the woman in the photo was looking away from the camera? Explain.

BP

Though we do have some options. As we continue to invest in alternative energy sources like solar, the immediate need for oil and gas still remains. Over the next 10 years, we're investing $15 billion in the Gulf of Mexico to find and produce new energy supplies. Today, nearly 70% of the oil we use to make fuels in the U.S. comes from North America.

It's a start.

CRITICAL THINKING

1. At first glance, whom do you look at first in the ad? Why?
2. Who are the people in the ad? What do they do? Why do you think BP mentions their profession in the ad? Explain.
3. What is the woman in the ad doing? Why do you think she is there? Would the ad be any different if it were just the man featured in the ad? Explain.
4. What do you think is happening in this ad? What situation does it aim to convey? Where are the subjects located?
5. After reading this ad, have you learned something that you did not know about foreign and domestic energy sources? Did it serve to educate you? Do you think that is the purpose of the ad?

The Michael J. Fox Foundation for Parkinson's Research

Maybe I was supposed to get Parkinson's.

Maybe the last 20 years were just a warm-up for this moment. After all, my career has given me a certain stature (even for a short guy). And people seem to pay attention when I speak. So listen to this: Of all the brain disorders, Parkinson's is the one that scientists truly believe may be closest to a cure. Yet it remains severely underfunded. In fact, with enough funding, they feel they can crack it within 10 years. And if they can cure Parkinson's, then similar diseases like Alzheimer's, Huntington's, and ALS (Lou Gehrig's Disease) may not be far behind. You can help make that happen. Go to my Web site. Or call to make a donation. You have the power to wipe out this disease. To affect millions of lives. Okay, okay. I'll get off my soapbox now.

CRITICAL THINKING

1. Do you find this ad particularly compelling? Why or why not? What kind of an impact does the spokesman's statement have on his audience? Explain.
2. What is the man standing on? Why?
3. Who is the man in the advertisement? What is his connection to the "product"? How is he dressed and posed? Do these photographic elements make the ad more effective? If so, why?
4. How does the text featured at the bottom of the ad work to complement the overall ad, including the quote at the top? What tense and voice does it use? To whom is it addressed?

iPod

CRITICAL THINKING

1. If you did not know what an iPod was, could you determine anything about it from this ad? Explain.
2. How important is brand/name recognition to the success of this ad? Who would know what this brand was, and what it was selling?
3. Who is the target audience for this brand? How does this ad appeal to that audience?
4. How does this ad use graphics to catch your eye? If you were leafing through a magazine and saw this ad, would you stop and look at it? Why or why not?

VISUAL CONNECTIONS

Follow the Flock

CONNECTING TO THE TOPIC

Adbusters magazine is a nonprofit, reader-supported, 120,000-circulation journal that provides critical commentary on consumer culture and corporate marketing agendas. Articles and issues from the magazine have been featured on MTV and PBS, the *Wall Street Journal, Wired,* and in hundreds of other newspapers, magazines, and television and radio shows around the world. They are "dedicated to examining the relationship between human beings and their physical and mental environment" and striving to create a "world in which the economy and ecology resonate in balance." This ad, a spoof on the Tommy Hilfiger brand, appeared both in their magazine and on their Web site, at www.adbusters.org.

CONSIDERING THE ISSUES

1. What expectations do we have of brand names and brand name products? Do we expect them to be better quality? To promote an image? To convey status? To be admired by others? Explain.
2. What brands do you use and why?

CRITICAL THINKING

3. What message is *Adbusters* trying to convey with this ad? Explain.
4. Locate a few real Tommy Hilfiger ads from popular magazines and compare it to this one. What similarities exist? How does the spoof ad play on conventional images and messages used in the real ones? Explain.

TOPICAL CONNECTIONS

GROUP PROJECTS

1. Working in a group, develop a slogan and advertising campaign for one of the following products: sneakers, soda, a candy bar, or jeans. How would you apply the principles of advertising language to market your product? After completing your marketing plan, "sell" your product to the class. If time permits, explain the reasoning behind your selling technique.
2. With your group, think of some advertising campaigns that created controversy (Camel cigarettes, Calvin Klein, Carl's Jr., etc.) What made them controversial? What was the impact on sales?

WEB PROJECTS

3. Access the Web sites for several popular soft drinks, such as www.pepsi.com, www.coke.com, www.drpepper.com, etc. How do the Web sites promote the product? Who is the target audience, and how do the sites reflect this audience? What techniques do they use to sell? Write an essay on the differences between online and paper advertising for soft drinks. Will the Web be the next great advertising venue? Will paper ads become obsolete? What considerations are unique to each? Is advertising on the Web a passing fad, or the wave of the future? Consider the information on advertising provided in this chapter when developing your response.
4. *Adbusters* addresses the unethical ways advertisers manipulate consumers to "need" products. However, if we consider ads long enough we can determine for ourselves the ways we may be manipulated. Write a paper in which you consider the techniques of advertising. Support your evaluation with examples of advertising campaigns with which you are familiar. Make an argument for the effectiveness or exploitative nature of such campaigns. You may draw support from the articles by authors such as Rushkoff, Belmonte, Cave, and Lutz, as well as from your personal experience as a consumer.

FOR FURTHER INQUIRY

5. You are an advertising executive. Select one of the products featured in the sample ads section and write a new advertising campaign for it. Do you use "weasel words" or tap into popular consciousness? Do you use sex appeal or power to promote your product? How do you create a need or desire for the product? Defend your campaign to your supervisors by explaining what motivates your creative decisions.
6. Write an essay evaluating advertising techniques in the twentieth and twenty-first centuries. Have ads changed over the last 50 years or so? What accounts for similarities or differences? Has advertising become more or less ethical? Creative? Focused? Be sure to explain your position and support it with examples from real advertisements.

2 Are There Limits to Our Right to Privacy?

"Do what you want—it's a free country!" is an expression that we often hear and would like to believe. Most Americans take personal freedom for granted and are startled when our rights seem to be threatened. Over the last decade, personal privacy rights have become a subject of concern and controversy. The aftermath of 9/11, the advent of the Internet, and improved technology have raised new questions connected to personal privacy. Should we have national identification cards as a measure to thwart terrorism? Do Internet companies have the right to track our movements online? Do surveillance cameras in stores, parking lots, and public spaces deter criminal activity? Does an employer have the right to ask us for a urine sample? Can the government require that we reveal our race?

Most Americans assume that their right to privacy is protected by the Fourth Amendment of the Constitution, which ensures "the right of the people to be secure in their persons, houses, papers, and effects, against unreasonable searches and seizures." But does the Fourth Amendment actually protect our right to privacy in the way that we think? How do we define an "unreasonable" search? And does the Fourth Amendment protect us from things such as Internet cookies or public surveillance cameras? Police, if they believe there is probable cause, may enter our homes or even tap our phones. Airport security guards may search our bags and our persons. Is privacy something we must sacrifice in order to live in a safer society? This chapter takes a closer look at some of the privacy issues Americans face today.

CRITICAL THINKING

1. What is happening in this cartoon? What happened first, and what could happen next? Explain.
2. Why do you think the cartoonist chose to depict an elderly couple for this cartoon? Explain.
3. What do you need to know about the political climate in order to understand the point of this cartoon? Explain.

Privacy Is Overrated

David Plotz

David Plotz is a writer and deputy editor for Slate.com. His articles have appeared in many publications, including *Harper's Magazine*, the *New York Times Magazine*, *Rolling Stone,* and the *New Republic.* He is a recipient of the National Press Club's Sandy Hume Award for Political Journalism. This essay first appeared in *GQ* magazine in 2003.

CONNECTING TO THE TOPIC

What privacy rights do we surrender in the name of safety, convenience, and even health? Is this sacrifice a fair exchange? For example, did you know that every time you log on to the Internet, information engines can put "cookies" on your computer to track your movements? When you visit their site again, these cookies are able to remember who you are as well as your preferences. Cookies may also gather information about you as a consumer. Is our privacy the price we pay for the convenience of the Internet? And are the rights that we give up a small price to pay when we consider the benefits we get in exchange?

WORDS IN CONTEXT

cookies: a collection of information stored on an Internet user's computer that identifies visitors of particular Web sites
paranoia: extreme, irrational distrust of others
pundits: critics
Orwellian: relating to the works of author George Orwell, especially the satirical novel *1984*, which depicts a futuristic totalitarian state
Big Brother: referring to a character in George Orwell's novel *1984*, an omnipresent figure representing an authoritarian government's total control over individual lives. The figure symbolizes a political or social situation in which one's actions are closely monitored by an authoritarian figure or group.
crusade: a campaign or concerted movement for a cause
hypocrisy: falseness
nostalgia: a longing for things, persons, or situations of the past
entrepreneurship: the act of organizing, operating, and assuming the risk for a business venture
titanic: enormous

stigmatized: marked as disgraceful
egocentric: holding the view that oneself is the center, object, and norm of all experience
fallacy: incorrect reasoning or beliefs
monolithic: massive
encryption: to render undecipherable by use of a secret code to prevent unauthorized parties from viewing particular information

1 Let's start by invading my privacy. I own a three-bedroom house on Cortland Place in Washington D.C. I am married to Hanna Rosin. We have a two-year-old child. I drive a 2001 Volkswagen Passat.

2 I have no criminal record. I have never been party to a lawsuit. I have no tax liens against me. I have never declared bankruptcy (unlike 2 of the 11 other David Plotzes in the United States). I have no ties to organized crime, though I do hold stock options in Microsoft.

3 The James Mintz group, a leading corporate investigation firm headquartered in New York City, learned all this about me in a few hours with a computer, an Internet connection and a single phone call—without even bending the law.

4 If you spent a bit more time, you would discover my Social Security number and how much I paid for the house. You would find out that I bank at Bank of America. You could have my listed home telephone number in two mouse clicks and my unlisted cell phone number if you paid the right data broker.

5 Corporations, meanwhile, are recording my every move. I don't watch what I eat, but Safeway does, thanks to my club card. Telecoms can pinpoint where I am when I make my cell phone calls. Clothing stores analyze my purchases in detail, recording everything from the expansion of my waist (up to 35 from 32) to my recent infatuation with three-button suits.

6 The credit reporting agencies know every time I have made a late payment to my Citibank MasterCard (number 6577 . . . I'm not that stupid) and every time I have applied for credit. This is all going on my permanent record.

7 Surveillance cameras are watching me in malls and sometimes on public streets. Even my own computer is spying on me. A scan of my hard drive turns up 141 cookies, deposited by companies that track me around the Web. I recently surfed a porn site (just because a high school

friend runs it, I swear). The cookies may know about it. My employer probably does too. After all, my employment contract permits my boss to track all my on-the-job Web surfing, and read all my work e-mail too.

8 If my company isn't watching, perhaps the FBI is: Its Carnivore program rafts through vast rivers of e-mail flow in search of criminal activity.

9 They—a *they* that includes the feds, a thousand corporations, a million telemarketers, my employer, my enemies and maybe even my friends—know all this about me, and more. And unless you are a technophobe hermit who pays for everything in cash, they know all this about you too.

10 To which I say, "Hallelujah!"

11 I'm in the minority. Privacy paranoia has become a national obsession. Pundits, politicians and privacy activists have been shouting about the latest government intrusion on privacy. The Defense Department's office of Total Information Awareness plans to collect massive quantities of information about all Americans—everything from what you buy to where you travel—in gigantic databases, and then sift through the information for clues about terrorism. Total Information Awareness has been denounced as Orwellian, and there are efforts to stop the program.

12 You could fill a library with privacy-alarmism books (*The End of Privacy*; *Privacy: How to Protect What's Left of It*). Congress and the state legislatures are awash in proposals to protect privacy. Horror stories fuel the fire of anxiety. The sailor the Navy tried to book out after he used the word *gay* in a supposedly confidential AOL profile. The stalker who bought his target's address from a Web information broker, tracked her down, and murdered her. The sale of Social Security numbers by LexisNexis.

13 You can more or less distill the essence of the privacy-rights movement to this idea: Big Brother and Big Business observe us too often, without our consent. The most intimate details of our lives are being sold and used secretly to make judgments about us, and we have no control over it.

14 It sounds appalling. But in fact, the privacy crusade is built on a foundation of hypocrisy, paranoia, economic know-nothingism and bogus nostalgia.

15 The first flaw of privacy: People care a great deal about their own, but not at all about anyone else's. We figure, why should anyone get to review my real-estate records or get to read my divorce proceedings? My life is my own business.

16 But I bet you want to know if your baby-sitter has ever been convicted of child abuse, if your business partner has a history of bankruptcy, if your boyfriend is still married. When your husband flees the

state to duck child support payments, wouldn't you use his Social Security number, driving records, real estate filings and whatever else you could get your hands on to track him down?

17 You don't want the Total Information Awareness office to know what you bought at the hardware store or where you take vacations. But if your neighbor is stockpiling fertilizer and likes to holiday in Iraq, don't you want the government to notice? If government had been using even basic data-mining techniques before September 11, at least 11 of the hijackers might have been stopped, according to a report by the Markel Foundation. Wouldn't that be worth letting the feds know you bought an Xbox last month?

18 Hysteria is growing that companies are shadowing us constantly. They are. But here, too, privacy is a silly value, both because "protecting" it is enormously costly and because it's not really being violated.

19 Ignorant companies are bankrupt companies. A recent study found that restricting marketing data would raise catalog clothing prices up to 11 percent, costing shoppers $1 billion per year. By buying address lists and consumer profiles, Victoria's Secret knows to send a catalog to my house, and International Male knows not to bother. Their marketing costs plummet. We get less junk mail, lower prices, and catalogs for clothing we might buy.

20 Your father probably shopped with a clothier who knew he wore a 44 long suit and preferred a faint pinstripe. Such friendships are extinct, murdered by megastores and armchair shopping. But today, when I log on to Amazon.com, I am pitched another book about privacy, because Amazon has learned that I am the kind of guy who buys books on privacy. They are saving me time (which is money) by delivering what I like.

21 Information sharing is also an engine of entrepreneurship. Thanks to cheap mailing lists, upstarts can challenge titanic businesses, lowering prices and bringing clever products to market.

22 Losing privacy has made it much cheaper to use a credit card or buy a house. Credit card and mortgage companies collect and share information about who pays, who doesn't, etc. Because they have an idea who will default, they offer significantly lower rates to people with good records and make credit much more available to poorer customers.

23 It's true that identity theft has become easier. On the other hand, credit card fraud—a much more common crime—is harder. Companies often catch a thief before a customer even notices her card is missing. (Their observant computers notice that her buying habits have suddenly changed.)

24 Similarly, surveillance cameras reduce shoplifting and stop ATM robberies, while cameras in police cars reduce incidents of police brutality. Lack of privacy actually tends to fight crime, not cause it.

25 There is one notable exception to the argument for transparency, however. If medical records are unsealed, especially to employers, people may avoid treatment, fearing they will be stigmatized or fired for their health problems.

26 Philosophically, many people don't like the idea that a soulless corporation records that they buy sexy underwear, subscribe to *Penthouse* and collect heavy metal CDs. Friends were freaked out to receive ads for infant formula soon after they gave birth. How did the company know? Is the hospital selling your baby already?

27 But this worry is an example of the egocentric fallacy: the belief that because people know something about you, they care. One wonderful, terrible thing about modern capitalism is that companies don't care. You are not a person. You are a wallet.

28 Privacy advocates like to say, "It didn't used to be this way." They hark back to a time—it generally sounds like 19th-century rural America—when stores didn't record your every purchase and doctors didn't report your ailments to a monolithic insurance company. You could abandon a bad life in one state, reinvent yourself 50 miles away, and no one needed to know. Nothing went down on your permanent record, because there was no permanent record.

29 This nostalgia imagines a past that never existed. Small town America never guarded anyone's privacy. In small towns, as anyone who lives in one can attest, people can be nosy and punish nonconformity viciously.

30 The right to privacy is not mentioned in the Constitution, and was not even conceived until 1890. Censuses in the 18th and 19th centuries demanded answers to intrusive questions, such as compelling Americans to reveal any history of insanity in the family.

31 Nostalgists fail to recognize that technology is creating a golden age from what they actually care about: real privacy. This is nothing that Amazon.com cares about. Nothing that Total Information Awareness can track down. Nothing that needs to be protected by encryption.

32 The opposite of privacy is not invasion of privacy: it is openness. Real privacy is what allows us to share hopes, dreams, fantasies, fears, and makes us feel we can safely expose all our faults and quirks and still be loved. Privacy is the space between us and our dearest—where everything is known and does not matter.

33 There has never been a better time for real privacy. The Internet allows people who have peculiar interests, social awkwardness or debilitating health problems to create communities that never could have existed before. Online, they can find other folks who want to re-enact the Battle of Bull Run or sunbathe nude or whatever your bag is, baby.

34 By surrendering some privacy—that is, by revealing our humanity with all its peculiarity in chat rooms or on e-mail or in newsgroups—we gain a much greater privacy: an intimacy with others, a sense of belonging. To be less private sometimes is to have more privacy. To be less private is to be more ourselves. ◆

CONSIDERING THE ISSUES

1. How much do you value your privacy? Do you ever think about this right? Plotz notes that while we tend to value our own privacy, we do not value the privacy of others. What do you feel others have a right to know about you? What do you think you have a right to know about other people? Explain.
2. Do you think we have more or less privacy than we did 50 years ago? Discuss with an older adult their perception of privacy in America now and 50 years ago. What factors, such as where we live and the lifestyle we lead, contribute to the level of privacy we have? Explain.

CRAFT AND CONTENT

3. Why does Plotz begin his essay by revealing his personal information? How does it help support the points he outlines in his essay? As a reader, how did you react to his divulging of so much personal information? Explain.
4. Identify specific areas where Plotz uses humor in his essay. Does his use of humor help him connect with his audience, or does it trivialize a serious subject? Explain.

CRITICAL THINKING

5. According to Plotz, why is our concern over privacy rights an "egocentric fallacy"? Do you agree with his argument? Why or why not?
6. What level of privacy do the "nostalgists" believe we enjoyed in the past? Why does Plotz say this memory is incorrect? Explain.

WRITING ABOUT THE ISSUES

7. At the end of his essay, Plotz states, "the opposite of privacy is not invasion of privacy: It is openness." Develop your own definition of privacy. How does it compare to Plotz's viewpoint?
8. Plotz begins his article by revealing information that is easily accessible about him through the Internet. Conduct an Internet search of yourself or a parent and see how much information you can locate. You may try online phone books, a Google search, and other information systems such as www.whowhere.com. After conducting your search, write your own narrative about what someone could find about you and how you feel about the availability of personal information online.

The Case for a National ID Card

Margaret Carlson

Margaret Carlson has been writing the column "Public Eye" for *TIME* magazine since 1994. In addition to writing for *TIME*, she serves as a panelist on CNN's political programs *Inside Politics* and *The Capital Gang*. Her articles have appeared in many publications, including the *New Republic*, *Esquire*, and *Washington Weekly*. This column was first published in the January 14, 2002, issue of *TIME*.

CONNECTING TO THE TOPIC

Most Americans are used to carrying identification cards: a Social Security card, a library card, a driver's license, a student college ID. Other cards we carry include credit cards, bank cards, even cards to allow us to take out DVDs and video games. After the terrorist attacks of September 11, discussion over whether we should carry "national identification cards" dramatically increased, with even Larry Ellison, chief of the information mega-giant Oracle, offering to provide the software for such cards. What would a national ID card be used for? Would it make us safer? More open to governmental scrutiny? Is this the next card we can expect to be carrying in our wallets?

WORDS IN CONTEXT

Nazis: the National Socialist German Workers' Party, founded in Germany in 1919 and gaining notoriety in 1933 under the direction of Adolf Hitler.
trove: a collection of valuable items discovered or found; a treasure trove
pertinent: relevant to the matter
noncommittal: refusing to commit to a particular opinion or idea
civil libertarian: someone who advocates for the protection of individual rights guaranteed by law
anonymity: the state of being unknown or having one's identity unacknowledged

1 After Michigan representative John Dingell was asked to drop his pants at Washington's National Airport, some people felt safer. Others, like me, decided that we'd lost our collective minds. A near strip search of a 75-year-old Congressman whose artificial hip has set off a metal detector—while a suspected al-Qaeda operative like Richard Reid slips onto a Paris-to-Miami flight with a bomb in his shoe—doesn't make us safer. It's making us ridiculous for entrusting our security to an unskilled police force that must make split-second decisions on the basis of incomplete data.

2 Incidents like this—and airport waits longer than the flight itself—have pushed me into the camp of the national ID card. Yes, a tamperproof ID smacks of Big Brother and Nazis intoning "Your papers, please," but the federal government already holds a trove of data on each of us. And it's less likely to mess up or misuse it than the credit-card companies or the Internet fraudsters, who have just as much data if not more.

3 The idea of a national ID card leaped into the headlines just after Sept. 11. Oracle chairman Larry Ellison offered to donate the pertinent software. Ellison went to see Attorney General John Ashcroft, who was noncommittal despite his obvious enthusiasm for expanding government powers into other areas that trouble civil libertarians.

4 Enter Richard Durbin. In concert with the American Association of Motor Vehicle Administrators (yes, the dreaded DMVs have their own trade group), the Illinois Senator proposed legislation that would create a uniform standard for the country's 200 million state-administered driver's licenses. Durbin noticed that the driver's license has become "the most widely used personal ID in the country. If you can produce one, we assume you're legitimate," he says. At present, nearly anyone can get a

license; 13 of the 19 hijackers did. Having those licenses "gave the terrorists cover to mingle in American society without being detected."

5 Since we're using the driver's license as a de facto national ID, Durbin argues, let's make it more reliable. As it stands, the chief requirement is that one knows how to drive. This is fine if the only intent is to ensure that someone behind the wheel has mastered turn signals, but it shouldn't be sufficient to get someone into a federal building, the Olympics or an airplane. All a terrorist needs to do is shop around for a lax state (Florida still doesn't require proof of permanent residency) or resort to a forger with a glue gun and laminator.

6 A high-tech, hard-to-forge driver's license could become a national E-ZPass, a way for a law-abiding citizen to move faster through the roadblocks of post-9/11 life. It's no digitalized Supercard, but the states would have uniform standards, using bar codes and biometrics (a unique characteristic, like a palm print) and could cross-check and get information from other law-enforcement agencies. Polls show 70% of Americans support an even more stringent ID. But Japanese-American members of Congress and Transportation Secretary Norman Mineta are keenly sensitive to anything that might single out one nationality. Yet an ID card offers prospects of less profiling. By accurately identifying those who are in the U.S. legally and not on a terrorist watch list, the card would reduce the temptation to go after random members of specific groups.

7 It is not ideal to leave a national problem to the states, but because of the general squeamishness about federal "papers" in the Congress, Durbin's proposal—congressional oversight of state DMVs—may be the best way to go. And if the government doesn't act, corporations will. Delta and American Airlines already provide separate lines for premium passengers; Heathrow Airport in London has an iris scan for people who have registered their eyeballs. An airline-industry association is at work on a Trusted Traveler card. Do we really want frequent-flyer status to be the basis for security decisions, or more plastic cards joining the too many we already have?

8 This ID would require one virtual strip search instead of many real ones. Durbin says the card would remove the anonymity of a Mohamed Atta but not the privacy of others. With a card, Dingell could have confirmed his identity (though he made a point of not pulling rank). With the presumption that he wasn't a terrorist, a once-over with

a wand—with his pants on—would have lent credence to his claim that he possessed an artificial hip, not a gun. The Durbin card would at least let us travel with our clothes on. ◆

CONSIDERING THE ISSUES

1. When were you last asked to produce identification? What were the circumstances? Were you asked by a person, or did you need identification of some form to access a building or pick up an item? What form of identification did you produce?
2. What personal information are you willing to give out? For example, if a cashier asks you to provide a zip code or telephone number when making a purchase, do you give out this information? What about online? Do you consider your privacy when responding to requests for personal information? Explain.

CRAFT AND CONTENT

3. What is the position of the author on the issue of national ID cards? Identify specific areas of her essay in which she reveals her position.
4. Carlson notes that national ID cards "smack of Big Brother and the Nazis." Why does she use this reference? Who is "Big Brother"? How does the concept of Big Brother connect to the idea of a national ID card and set the tone of her essay? Explain.

CRITICAL THINKING

5. Carlson presents congressman John Dingell's experience at Washington's National Airport as an example of a security blunder. Evaluate this example. Does it demonstrate her point? Did the security guards act appropriately? Would a national ID card have prevented this situation in the first place? Explain.
6. In paragraph 6, Carlson states that "Japanese-American members of Congress and Transportation Secretary Norman Mineta are keenly sensitive to anything that might single out one nationality." Why are Japanese-American members of Congress particularly cautious of a national ID system? Why would they be more concerned than other groups?

WRITING ABOUT THE ISSUES

7. Do you think that a national identification card is a good idea? Why or why not? Do you think it would deter terrorism? Make U.S. citizens safer? Explain your point of view.
8. In paragraph 6, Carlson notes that polls indicate that 70% of Americans support more stringent ID. Considering that this article was published only four months after September 11, conduct your own poll to see if Americans still feel this way. Ask at least 40 to 50 people if they support a national identification card. Based on your results, write a short essay analyzing the data. Incorporate any opinions expressed by the people you poll if appropriate.

National ID Cards: 5 Reasons Why They Should Be Rejected

ACLU

The American Civil Liberties Union (ACLU) was founded in 1920. Since its beginning, the nonprofit, nonpartisan ACLU has grown from a small group of civil liberties activists to an organization of nearly 400,000 members with offices in almost every state. The ACLU's mission is to fight civil liberties violations wherever and whenever they occur. It is also active in national and state government arenas and is dedicated to upholding the Bill of Rights.

CONNECTING TO THE TOPIC

The preceding essay presented the idea that national ID cards might not be a bad idea in the post-9/11 world. The next piece explains why the ACLU believes national ID cards would be a colossal failure. Not only would such cards *not* solve the very problems that inspire them, but they would ultimately cause more harm than good.

WORDS IN CONTEXT

superficial: only on the surface; insubstantial
thwarted: prevented

naïve: simple; lacking in experience or understanding
prohibition: a policy or law that forbids something
visceral: instinctive
aversion: intense dislike or disgust
totalitarian: referring to a government or political body that exercises total control over the individual lives of citizens within a state, usually with the suppression of all dissenting viewpoints
sentries: guards or officials with authority
stigma: a mark of disgrace

1 The terrorist attacks of September 11 have revived proposals for a national identity card system as a way to verify the identity of airline passengers and prevent terrorists from entering the country. For example, the Chairman and CEO of Oracle Corp., Larry Ellison, recently called for the creation of a national ID system and offered to provide the software for it without charge.

2 The newest calls for a national ID are only the latest in a long series of proposals that have cropped up repeatedly over the past decade, usually in the context of immigration policy, but also in connection with gun control or health care reform. But the creation of a national ID card remains a misplaced, superficial "quick fix." It offers only a false sense of security and will not enhance our security—but will pose serious threats to our civil liberties and civil rights. A national ID will not keep us safe or free.

Reason #1: A National ID Card System Would Not Solve the Problem That Is Inspiring It

3 A national ID card system will not prevent terrorism. It would not have thwarted the September 11 hijackers, for example, many of whom reportedly had identification documents on them, and were in the country legally.

4 Terrorists and criminals will continue to be able to obtain—by legal and illegal means—the documents needed to get a government ID, such as birth certificates. Yes, these new documents will have data like digital fingerprints on them, but that won't prove real identity—just that the carrier has obtained what could easily be a fraudulent document.

5 And their creation would not justify the cost to American taxpayers, which according to the Social Security Administration would be at least $4 billion. It is an impractical and ineffective proposal—a simplistic and naïve attempt to use gee-whiz technology to solve complex social and economic problems.

Reason #2: An ID Card System Will Lead to a Slippery Slope of Surveillance and Monitoring of Citizens

6 A national ID card system would not protect us from terrorism, but it would create a system of internal passports that would significantly diminish the freedom and privacy of law-abiding citizens. Once put in place, it is exceedingly unlikely that such a system would be restricted to its original purpose. The original Social Security Act contained strict prohibitions against use of Social Security cards for unrelated purposes, but those strictures have been routinely ignored and steadily abandoned over the past 50 years. A national ID system would threaten the privacy that Americans have always enjoyed and gradually increase the control that government and business wields over everyday citizens.

Reason #3: A National ID Card System Would Require Creation of a Database of All Americans

7 What happens when an ID card is stolen? What proof is used to decide who gets a card? A national ID would require a governmental database of every person in the U.S. containing continually updated identifying information. It would likely contain many errors, any one of which could render someone unemployable and possibly much worse until they get their "file" straightened out. And once that database was created, its use would almost certainly expand. Law enforcement and other government agencies would soon ask to link into it, while employers, landlords, credit agencies, mortgage brokers, direct mailers, private investigators, civil litigants, and a long list of other parties would begin seeking access, further eroding the privacy that Americans have always expected in their personal lives.

Reason #4: ID Cards Would Function as "Internal Passports" That Monitor Citizens' Movements

8 Americans have long had a visceral aversion to building a society in which the authorities could act like totalitarian sentries and demand "your papers please!" And that everyday intrusiveness would be conjoined with the full power of modern computer and database technology. When a police officer or security guard scans your ID card with his pocket bar-code reader, for example, will a permanent record be created of that check, including the time and your location? How long before office buildings, doctors' offices, gas stations, highway tolls, subways and buses incorporate the ID card into their security or payment systems for greater efficiency? The end result could be a nation where citizens' movements inside their own country are monitored and recorded through these "internal passports."

Reason #5: ID Cards Would Foster New Forms of Discrimination and Harassment

9 Rather than eliminating discrimination, as some have claimed, a national identity card would foster new forms of discrimination and harassment of anyone perceived as looking or sounding "foreign." That is what happened after Congress passed the Employer Sanctions provision of the Immigration Reform and Control Act of 1985: widespread discrimination against foreign-looking American workers, especially Asians and Hispanics. A 1990 General Accounting Office study found almost 20 percent of employers engaged in such practices. A national ID card would have the same effect on a massive scale, as Latinos, Asians, Caribbeans and other minorities became subject to ceaseless status and identity checks from police, banks, merchants and others. Failure to carry a national ID card would likely come to be viewed as a reason for search, detention or arrest of minorities. The stigma and humiliation of constantly having to prove that they are Americans or legal immigrants would weigh heavily on such groups. ◆

CONSIDERING THE ISSUES

1. When asked to provide proof of identity, do you consider it an invasion of your privacy or simply a reality of modern life? Explain.
2. Many of us take the idea of privacy for granted. Think about the number of times in a given day when your actions may be tracked by others (for example, if you use a student ID card to gain access to the cafeteria or if you purchase something with a credit card). How often is your privacy at risk? Does it matter? Why or why not?

CRAFT AND CONTENT

3. The ACLU lists five reasons why national ID cards are a bad idea. Evaluate the relevancy and logic of the reasons they cite. Are they valid points? Off track? Can you think of any additional reasons that they might have left out? Alternatively, if you do not think their reasons hold merit, explain why.
4. What is a "slippery slope"? Why would national ID cards create a "slippery slope of surveillance"? Explain.

CRITICAL THINKING

5. Why does the ACLU believe that national ID cards would be a "superficial quick fix" that poses a serious threat to our civil liberties? What liberties do they fear will be sacrificed? Do you agree with their position? Why or why not?
6. Both this article by the ACLU and Carlson's essay before it mention the idea of totalitarian governments. In your opinion, would a national ID policy contribute to such a government or legal system? How would a national ID card be different from a driver's license or a Social Security card? A passport? Explain.

WRITING ABOUT THE ISSUES

7. This article by the ACLU lists five arguments for why a national ID system would threaten our civil liberties. Assuming the position of Oracle chairman Larry Ellison who encouraged a na-

tional ID system, draft a list of five arguments for why a national ID system is a good policy for Americans to adopt.

8. Write an essay exploring the ways a national ID system could be abused. How could it contribute to a society similar to that of George Orwell's totalitarian state depicted in his novel *1984*? To review this short novel, look it up at www.online-literature.com.

SAMPLE AD AND STUDY QUESTIONS

One concern many Americans have regarding their privacy is identity theft. As more Web sites and retail establishments store information online, it is possible for hackers to access personal information. In 2005, many banks and credit companies reissued thousands of cards after their security systems were breached, exposing an unprecedented number of people to the possibility of identity theft. How do we protect ourselves from identity theft without unnecessarily complicating our lives? Or is this just another example why we must be more vigilant than ever in safeguarding our privacy?

CRITICAL THINKING

1. Consider the faces of the people in this ad. What sort of conclusions might a viewer draw from their expressions? Would the ad be as effective if the images were reversed? Why or why not?
2. Can you tell what this ad is trying to accomplish without reading the fine print at the bottom of the ad? Explain.
3. What does this ad imply about your privacy?
4. What is your gut reaction to this ad? How does it play with our fears and insecurities? Are these fears founded? Why or why not?

Identity Theft

I Spy

Wendy Kaminer

Lawyer and social critic Wendy Kaminer is a senior correspondent for the *American Prospect* and a contributing editor at the *Atlantic Monthly*. Her latest book is *Sleeping with Extra-Terrestrials: The Rise of Irrationalism and Perils of Piety*. Other books she has written include *It's All the Rage: Crime and Culture*, *I'm Dysfunctional, You're Dysfunctional*, and *A Fearful Freedom: Women's Flight from Equality*. Her articles have appeared in many publications, including the *New York Times*, the *Wall Street Journal*, the *Nation*, and *Newsweek*. This essay appeared in the August 18, 2000, issue of the *American Prospect*.

CONNECTING TO THE TOPIC

While reality television programs are fodder for critics, there is no denying their popularity. Far from a passing fad, reality television programs are more numerous than ever before. Several programs have emerged as constant hits, including *Survivor*, *The Bachelor, American Idol,* and *Extreme Makeover*. In a culture that claims to covet its privacy and fears the invasion of our privacy rights, we certainly like to take a peek at the lives of others—from *Cops*, to Court TV, to the newest reality television gimmick. Are we simply a society of contradictions? Do we say one thing but do another? Why are we so nervous about protecting our own privacy, if we are so willing to sacrifice the privacy of others as a form of entertainment?

WORDS IN CONTEXT

exalts: praises; glorifies
rife: full of
paradoxical: seemingly contradictory
convergence: intersection of two or more things; a meeting point
cede: to give away; to release
incessantly: constantly; without interruption
encroachment: a gradual taking away
ubiquitous: ever-present
cognitive dissonance: in psychology, a term describing a condition of conflict that results from a disparity between one's beliefs and one's actions

forums: venues that promote the open exchange of ideas and opinions
voyeur: someone who likes to view sensational or forbidden activities, usually while hidden
stoicism: impassivity or lack of emotion
discretion: the practice of being discreet
equated: identified as equal
repression: the act of repressing someone or something; holding back
pathologized: described in terms of disease
wrested: taken away by force
resilient: enduring; able to recover quickly
paparazzi: photographers who pursue famous people
presciently: with foresight; predicatively
usurps: takes over, usually illegally

1 American culture thrives on contradictions. It exalts individualism yet is rife with the conformity so essential to consumerism. It preaches self-reliance and personal accountability (especially for poor people) while enriching pop psychologists who provide excuses for sins of the middle class. It nurtures feminism and encourages face-lifts.

2 So we shouldn't be entirely surprised by the paradoxical convergence of reality TV shows with a growing concern about privacy, although the intensity of these opposing trends is particularly dramatic. Democratic and Republican pollsters attest to a "groundswell" of concern about privacy, which politicians rush to address. George W. Bush declares himself a "privacy rights person." Congress considers hundreds of privacy protection bills.

3 Still, people cede their privacy voluntarily every day for the promise of security. They willingly turn over photo IDs to airline clerks, in the vain hope of preventing terrorism (as if terrorists haven't figured out how to fake IDs). They give government the power to wiretap. They support a war on drugs that has eviscerated the Fourth Amendment and the privacy rights it was intended to protect. They welcome surveillance cameras in elevators, in parking garages, or at ATMs. They feel entitled to spy on others: New computer programs allow people to monitor their spouses' e-mail or online reading habits. Cameras in day care centers allow parents to keep children and day care workers under constant watch. Armed with video cameras, people

tape their children incessantly; the middle class is apt to raise a generation of performers.

4 While media stories on privacy abound, media encroachments on privacy astound. Over 20 million people tune in to watch *Survivor* and *Big Brother*, a show that confines 10 strangers to a house for 100 days and subjects them to constant and ubiquitous surveillance. Reporters poll experts to find out what this phenomenon says about our psyche. If you don't watch reality TV, you can always read about it—while you worry about your anonymity if you're reading online. The press loves the story of reality TV but covers the privacy debate as well, mirroring our cognitive dissonance.

5 We're attracted to and revolted by surveillance. It's puzzling, to be sure, but nothing new. Talk shows have long provided forums for the exhibitionists among us and entertainment for the voyeurs. Popular therapies have demonized silence and stoicism, promoting the belief that healthy people talk about themselves—sometimes incessantly and often in public. Secrets are "toxic." Discretion about your private life is likely to be equated with repression. In the age of the memoir, privacy is pathologized. Still, people who voluntarily surrender their privacy may not want it wrested from them, and American culture harbors a resilient strain of respect for the tough individualist who keeps his troubles to himself. Over a century ago, when Louis Brandeis and Samuel Warren published a famous law review article conceptualizing a legal right to privacy, they were appealing to a traditional American value: "the right to be let alone."

6 With the digital revolution making privacy seem as obsolete as a rotary phone, it's worth remembering that this landmark nineteenth-century treatise on privacy was inspired by new technology, mainly photography, which gave birth to the paparazzi. Brandeis and Warren were concerned with the "unauthorized circulation of portraits of private persons" in the press and with the rise of gossip. No longer an idle pastime, gossip was becoming "a trade," they warned, presciently describing the dangers it posed to civil society: Gossip appeals to our baser instincts, the "weak side of human nature" that takes pleasure in the "misfortunes and frailties" of others. It is dignified by print and "crowds space available" for discussion of public issues. "It usurps the place of interest in brains capable of other things."

7 Brandeis and Warren were intent on creating a remedy for involuntary, "unwarranted" invasions of privacy. (They realized that privacy rights should not always protect public figures engaged in matters of public interest, recognizing as well the difficulties of distinguishing between public and private concerns.) They saw privacy as essential to human dignity and lived at a time when exhibitionism was not respectable, much less a sign of mental health. It would have been hard for them to imagine that dignity would one day seem a small price to pay for a moment of fame. "The general object in view is to protect the privacy of private life," Brandeis and Warren wrote. What happens when private life virtually ceases, when, like trees falling in the forest, people want someone watching to make sure they exist?

8 Some applaud the "openness" (or shamelessness) of the new exhibitionism, in the belief that it will bring us all together. But community, as well as individualism, is at risk. The more public space expands, the more it threatens public life. Would you enter willingly into relationships with people from whom nothing could be hidden? Secrecy is essential to social relations. ◆

CONSIDERING THE ISSUES

1. Do you watch reality TV programs? If so, which ones? What inspires you to watch these programs? Do you consider reality television programs an invasion of privacy for the contestants on these programs? What about programs such as *Cops* or courtroom television shows? Explain.
2. If you could be a contestant on a reality television program, which one would you go on, and why? Would privacy be an issue in your decision to participate in a reality television program? Why or why not?

CRAFT AND CONTENT

3. Kaminer begins her essay by stating, "American culture thrives on contradictions." What example of contradictions does she identify? Can you think of others?
4. Consider Kaminer's title for her essay. Why does she choose this title? What does it mean in the context of her essay? Explain.

CRITICAL THINKING

5. In what ways is gossip an invasion of privacy? Do you consider gossip to violate privacy rights? Explain.
6. Why is America's obsession with reality television an ironic contrast to our desire to protect our privacy rights? Do you think that the two issues are connected? Why or why not?

WRITING ABOUT THE ISSUES

7. Write about a time in which you felt that your privacy rights were violated. Describe the circumstances and how you dealt with the situation. How did you feel? Explain.
8. Develop your own reality television program. Include the show's premise, its object and goal, why people would want to watch it, and who would be a typical contestant. In your description of your program, describe in what ways it would—or would not—infringe on individual privacy.

When Cameras Are Too Candid

Jane Black

Jane Black is a technology reporter covering privacy issues for *Business Week Online.*

CONNECTING TO THE TOPIC

Surveillance cameras monitor us in department stores and at ATMs. They are present in elevators and offices, parking lots, sporting arenas, and police cars. In Great Britain, more than three million cameras have become fixtures in public spaces. All this monitoring can seem creepy and invasive, but when a camera captures child abuse or abduction on film, such surveillance can prove a useful law enforcement tool. Is surveillance a price we should pay for a safer society? Is it a fair trade-off for an invasion of our personal privacy? Or is this a case where the ends do not justify the means?

WORDS IN CONTEXT

pummel: to relentlessly beat with fists
condemnation: severe reproach
heinous: horrible
politicized: made a political issue
forfeited: surrendered, given up

1 It was Friday the 13th, and Madelyn Gorman Toogood was having a bad day. But when she left Kohl's department store in Mishwaka, Indiana, her troubles had barely even begun. Toogood crossed the parking lot with her four-year-old daughter, Martha, and helped the child into a white Toyota SUV. Then, after checking to see who might be watching, the 25-year-old mother began to pummel Martha.

2 For 30 seconds, she pulled her daughter's hair and punched her in the head and face. The entire incident was caught on a surveillance tape—which was then played virtually nonstop on the 24-hour cable-news channels.

3 Even before the video hit the air, Toogood hit the road with Martha, getting as far as New Jersey before a warrant was issued for her arrest. On Sept. 21, Toogood returned to South Bend, Indiana, to face both condemnation and charges of child battery—and a possible three years in jail. Martha is in foster care.

4 Coming as it does amid a nationwide debate over the merits of security vs. the right to privacy, the Toogood case illustrates how complicated the issue really is—and how difficult it will be to preserve Americans' cherished freedoms while meeting the heightened challenge of keeping them safe.

5 Everyone agrees, of course, that in young Martha's case video surveillance worked for the greater good. Even the normally vocal privacy advocates can't find anything to complain about in the way events unfolded. After all, Toogood's privacy wasn't invaded: Her SUV was parked on Kohl's property, which the store clearly had the right to monitor. More important, the surveillance exposed a heinous act. Even if she avoids jail and is reunited with her daughter, being exposed may have had some effect on Toogood.

6 "I'm mortified. It was the worst moment of my life," the shamed mother said on CBS's *Early Show* on Sept. 22—just one of many stops on her post-arrest media tour. She has said that she and her husband will take parenting classes. The case is a victory for child-welfare advocates, who hope that the media circus surrounding the incident will make other short-tempered parents think twice before raising their hands to their children.

7 At first glance, it would seem that the Toogood case is also a significant victory for Bush Administration officials and others who believe that more surveillance will help reduce crime and prevent terrorism. America both shuddered and cheered when Toogood was exposed, making little Martha the poster child for increased surveillance. So why not take it a step further and simply install cameras everywhere—and, for good measure, tell everyone they're being watched?

8 Unfortunately, it's not that simple, and the value of video surveillance is debatable. For one thing, a pile of evidence shows that these cameras do little to deter crime. Britain has had 3 million of them in place since the mid-1980s. By some estimates, a Londoner is caught on film as many as 300 times per day. And yet, the results of a 1999 study commissioned by the British government and conducted by the Scottish Center for Criminology suggests that these cameras had little or no effect on crime.

9 Surveillance experts have come to similar conclusions in the U.S. In the mid-1990s, the Oakland California police department promoted using surveillance cameras in public places. Sparing no expense, the department bought sophisticated devices capable of reading the fine print on a flyer from hundreds of yards away or recognizing a license plate or a face at a distance of more than a mile.

10 Yet in a 1997 report to Oakland's city council, Chief of Police Joseph Samuels Jr. wrote that though his department had hoped to be ". . . among the pioneers in the field of taped video camera surveillance" it ultimately found that ". . . there is no conclusive way to establish that the presence of video surveillance cameras resulted in the prevention or reduction of crime."

11 "The problem with taking a cold look at the claims made on behalf of surveillance cameras is that intuitively many people feel that cameras should be effective fighting crime," Johnny Barnes, executive director of the American Civil Liberties Union of the District of Columbia,

told a House of Representatives panel in March. "But feel-good is not the same thing as do-good."

12 Granted, even if surveillance doesn't deter crime, it can help uncover such behavior as Toogood's—though it would be hard to pinpoint just how often that happens. The question is whether catching the occasional drug dealer or slap-happy mom justifies the cost and intrusion of putting cameras everywhere—and recording millions of acts of everyday citizens that are no big deal.

13 In the wake of September 11, Washington's judgment has been that it is justified. Yet Chris Hoofnagle, legislative counsel at the Washington D.C.-based advocacy group the Electronic Privacy Information Center, says cameras are being used not only to track terrorists but to catch jaywalkers.

14 Federal Appeals Court Judge J. Braxton Craven Jr. once wrote: "The right to be let alone is the only non-political protection of that vast array of human activities which, considered separately, may seem trivial but together make up what most individuals think of as freedom." Americans are coming dangerously close to seeing this right politicized—and perhaps forfeited.

15 As the Toogood case demonstrates, sometimes such surveillance can be valuable. The evidence suggests, however, that most of the time it isn't. And it can be dangerous when used to intimidate and chill free speech, as it was in the 1960s when the FBI monitored citizens engaged in civil disobedience.

16 What the surveillance camera at Kohl's really showed is that balancing privacy and security is even harder to achieve than most of us imagined. ◆

CONSIDERING THE ISSUES

1. Most people are aware that surveillance cameras help loss prevention officers catch shoplifters at department stores. In England, over three million cameras are used to help law enforcement offices keep the peace. Would knowing you could be caught on film influence your behavior? How would you feel if you lived in a society that could track you on film up to 300 times a day in different places? Would you care? Why or why not?

2. Do you think cameras in public places are a good law enforcement tool? If you ran a municipal law enforcement operation, where would you put surveillance cameras, and why? Or would you choose to not use cameras at all? Explain.

CRAFT AND CONTENT

3. In paragraph 12, Black wonders whether "catching the occasional drug dealer or slap-happy mom justifies the cost and intrusion of putting cameras everywhere." Answer her question with your own opinion on this issue.
4. Black incorporates many quotes into her essay. How do these quotes support her argument? Would her essay be stronger if she had merely paraphrased them? Why or why not?

CRITICAL THINKING

5. Black recounts the highly publicized case of Madelyn Toogood, who was caught on film hitting her daughter in a Kohl's department store parking lot. How does this case support the argument that surveillance cameras should be used? Would this case be different if the camera had caught Toogood in a public area such as a park or beach rather than a privately owned parking lot?
6. In paragraph 14, Black states, "Americans are coming dangerously close to seeing this right politicized—and perhaps forfeited." What does she mean? How can our privacy rights become "politicized"?
7. What is the author's opinion of cameras in public spaces? Can you tell? Explain.

WRITING ABOUT THE ISSUES

8. Write a short essay in which you express your own opinion on whether surveillance cameras should be used in public spaces. Following Black's format, cite a real or create a hypothetical situation in which cameras could be used or abused, and build your essay around this example.
9. Write an essay describing what you feel personal freedom is. How does personal freedom connect to privacy rights? Do you feel your personal freedom has been violated by public and private surveillance practices? Explain.

VISUAL CONNECTIONS

Caught on Camera

CONNECTING TO THE TOPIC

As the previous essay by Jane Black describes, surveillance cameras have become familiar fixtures in our lives. From department stores to airports to tollbooths, cameras are everywhere. Are these cameras invading our privacy? Is it permissible for private property owners to use them, but not public law enforcement? Should we be alerted that we could be watched on camera before entering a building? Or are cameras just another way to keep us safer in a society troubled by crime and terrorism?

CONSIDERING THE ISSUES

1. When you are watched on camera, do you feel your privacy is invaded, or do you accept cameras as a fact of modern life? Do law-abiding citizens need to worry about surveillance cameras at all?
2. Does knowing that surveillance cameras are on a particular site make you feel safer? Why or why not?

CRITICAL THINKING

3. What assumptions do we make about the people who are watching surveillance screens? For example, who do you think the man in this photo is? What is he doing? How will he use the information he views? Explain.
4. What is happening in this photo? How could a caption explaining what is happening change our opinion of the photograph? Does it matter exactly what is being monitored? A hospital? A department store? An awards ceremony or movie theater? An apartment building? Explain.

TOPICAL CONNECTIONS

GROUP PROJECT

1. In the first essay in this section, David Plotz states that the infringements on our privacy are a small price to pay for the protections we enjoy for this sacrifice. As a group, compile a list of ways that you must sacrifice your privacy. You may include airport security checks, locker searches, and even having to produce identification to pay with a check. Is this forfeiture of privacy rights worth it? Are some more invasive than others? Discuss your list and assess the costs and benefits of privacy loss. After group discussion, share your opinions with the rest of the class.

WEB PROJECT

2. This chapter addresses many issues connected to our concept of privacy. Many of us are unclear about what our privacy rights actually are. Visit the Privacy Rights Clearinghouse Web site at www. privacyrights.org for fact sheets on privacy and your privacy rights. What assumptions do you make about your privacy? Write an essay in which you explore privacy rights in American society.

FOR FURTHER INQUIRY

3. While some authors in this section imply that we are subjected to more invasions of privacy than ever before, others infer that we are more anonymous now than we were a century ago. What are your impressions of this issue? Interview fellow students, parents, grandparents, and older relatives and ask them for their viewpoints on privacy. Assess whether we have more or less privacy today. Then address how Americans feel about privacy.
4. Watch the movie *The Net*, starring Sandra Bullock, or *The Truman Show*, with Jim Carrey. Write a short review of either film addressing specifically how the movie illuminates privacy issues in modern life.

3 Do the Media Promote a Culture of Fear?

We live in a media-driven world. We are constantly under the influence of media, in newspapers, magazines, television and radio programs, music, the Internet, and advertising. The mass media compete for our eyes and ears, to ensure that we are exposed to the advertising that forms their backbone. Newspapers, television programs, magazines, and most radio programs are supported by the marketing industry. The goal is getting us to pay attention. And in today's world, we seem to pay attention to scary stories.

It is human nature to pay attention to that which is distressing—whether it is a car wreck on the freeway, or a mass murder in a restaurant in the Midwest, or a child abduction a few states away. And while such incidents are indeed distressing, we also pay attention to other "horror" stories—from moldy basements making people sick, high mercury levels in tuna fish, and exploding cigarette lighters, to dangerous trans fats in our doughnuts.

Knowing how to critically analyze different media, to use and maximize their many benefits, and to defend against their sneaky manipulations. A media literate person can sift through the hype. The articles in this chapter examine the ways the media grab our attention and prey on our deepest fears and natural tendency to hear about what a dreadful world we live in. Do the media have a responsibility to the public to balance hype with fact? Or is it our responsibility to decipher fact from fiction? Can we find a reasonable middle ground?

CRITICAL THINKING

1. What is the effect of the boy's single word in such a large bubble? If the word was larger, or the bubble smaller, would the effect be the same? Explain.
2. Is there more than one possible interpretation of this cartoon? What do you think the cartoonist is trying to say here? Can you think of other interpretations in addition to your first one? Explain.
3. How does this cartoon connect to the larger theme of "media hype"? Explain.

Extreme Reality: How Media Coverage Exaggerates Risks and Dangers

John Stossel

John Stossel is coanchor of ABC's *20/20* and the recipient of 19 Emmy awards for reporting. He is the author of *Give Me a Break: How I Exposed Hucksters, Cheats, and Scam Artists and Became the Scourge of the Liberal Media* (2004). The article that follows was part of a *20/20* segment airing on July 12, 2002.

CONNECTING TO THE TOPIC

News programs such as *20/20*, *Dateline*, *60 Minutes*, and *48 Hours*, and newsmagazines such as *Time* and *Newsweek*, tend to rely on sensational stories in order to grab viewers' eyeballs and keep them for the hour. Sometimes the information they provide can be quite helpful and illuminating. And sometimes they twist an obscure incident into a national epidemic. The trick for the audience, of course, is to figure out which is which.

WORDS IN CONTEXT

amid: surrounded by; in the middle of
circular logic: a fallacy in reasoning in which the premise is used to prove the conclusion, and the conclusion used to prove the premise—e.g., *steroids are dangerous because they ruin your health*
conglomerate: a corporation made up of a number of different companies that operate in diversified fields
infinitesimally: immeasurably or incalculably minute
mundane: relating to or concerned with the commonplace and the ordinary.
ramp up: to increase, usually in violence
rivet: to engross or hold (as in one's attention)

1 If you watch television news regularly, you can't help but think that the world is a very scary place.

2 You'll be hammered with a whole host of frightening stories about crime, terror threats, strange new diseases, or scary old ones. It's the

media's job to inform us of these dangers, but does the amount of coverage reflect the risk we really face?

3 Remember 2001's coverage of shark attacks? It seemed everywhere you looked someone in the press was talking about the "Summer of the Shark." You may have believed that shark attacks were on the rise. That's what some television stations reported. But it wasn't true.

4 In 2002, shark attacks off American beaches were hardly different from previous years. Most of the reports mentioned that, but that important truth got lost amid the blare and blur of frightening headlines and images. While the media were busy scaring us out of the water, scientists said there was no increase in the number of sharks off our beaches and stressed that sharks were so unlikely to kill you that you're about 25 times more likely to be killed by lightning.

5 If television isn't frightening you, then news magazines are ready to step in and fill that void. *Newsweek*, for example, claimed Americans were being "driven to destruction" by road rage. In their report, they quoted a study saying we were "increasingly being shot, stabbed, beaten and run over." Then television echoed with its own flurry of road-rage reports. On *20/20*, ABC NEWS introduced a story by telling viewers that they're surrounded by "strangers in their cars, ready to snap." We called road rage a frightening trend and a growing American danger.

6 The hype surrounding the reporting blew the real dangers out of proportion. Bob Lichter, president of the Center for Media and Public Affairs, which studies media coverage, has concluded that the media often distort or exaggerate threats. He said, "If road rage is something that's increasing . . . we should see more fatalities on the road. There should be more reports of reckless driving. But these things are going down instead of up."

7 A justification for the media hype surrounding road rage was a study sponsored by the American Automobile Association (AAA) that chronicled reports of aggressive driving. According to a *Time* magazine story, which based its information on the AAA report, road rage was up 51 percent in the first half of the 1990s.

8 Stefanie Faul, a spokeswoman for the AAA, said the consumer group based its analysis mostly on the number of road rage and aggressive driving incidents reported in the press. It was a strange sort of circular logic that fueled the spiraling coverage of road rage. The AAA

study looked at police reports as well, but was largely based on media accounts.

9 Lichter said people have been yelling at each other in their cars for years. Journalists just found a term for it. A few years back, Lichter noted, a person might come and complain that somebody yelled at them from his car. Today, people go home and say they're victims of "road rage."

10 AAA's Faul said that the idea of violent death by strangers is a very common topic in news reports. "You know that if you get people excited about an issue . . . that's what makes it appealing as a topic." She also added that small organizations like hers can't take on huge media conglomerates. Still, she admits that she didn't make an effort to correct the mischaracterization she saw in the press.

11 And before there was road rage, there were carjackings. The media told us that carjackings were making a comeback on Americans streets in the '90s. Greg McCrary, of the Threat Assessment Group, which works to point out that life's real dangers are far less dramatic than what the media may lead you to believe, said the chance of being killed in a carjacking is infinitesimally small.

12 McCrary said the mundane things pose greater risks on the road—things like drunken driving and failing to fasten our seat belts. Like Faul, McCrary said these sorts of things just aren't attention-grabbing. "It doesn't sell on TV. Sex and violence sells," he said.

13 Lichter agrees with McCrary's assessment. His organization noted that press coverage of murders increased by 700 percent in the 1990s, but the murder rate had fallen by half during the decade. Lichter said, "It's easier to point a camera at a blood-stained wall where a victim has just been taken away, than it is to dig into a book of dull, dry statistics."

14 According to Lichter, when there's not a major news story that has some dramatic element to it, newspapers and television stations will ramp up their coverage of things like shark attacks and carjackings to keep us buying papers and tuning in. Lichter said, "Journalists unconsciously train themselves to look for the story that really rivets your attention. And that story is, 'Wow, here's a disaster, oh my God.'"

15 A few years ago, for example, there were as many shark attacks, but it wasn't a summer of the shark. Perhaps because the media were busy covering the election. Back in 1995 there were 46 shark attacks, but the spotlight was on O.J. Simpson's murder trial. In 1998, the Monica Lewinsky story kept the shark attacks in the shadows.

16 Lichter said that reporters may have the best of intentions when they pursue a story, but often they stir up problems that really aren't there. This, Lichter said, poses a real danger to the public. Lichter said, "Bad journalism is worse than no journalism, because it leaves people thinking they know something that is, in fact, wrong." ◆

CONSIDERING THE ISSUES

1. In his article, Stossel notes several media-hyped issues: shark attacks, road rage, and carjackings. Coverage of these issues contributes to our perception that it is a very dangerous world out there. What fears do you have regarding the society in which we live? For example, are you afraid that you could be a victim of road rage? Murder? Make a list of the things that worry you about today's society. Include even small things that may not seem dangerous but concern you nonetheless.
2. Have you ever changed your behavior based on a news report? For example, did you avoid swimming because of shark attacks, or avoid driving in a certain area for fear of road rage or carjackings? Or stop eating a particular food because it might cause cancer or another disease? Explain.

CRAFT AND CONTENT

3. What was the "circular logic" of the media hype surrounding road rage (paragraph 7)? What was faulty with this logic, and how did it mislead the public's perception of road rage?
4. Review Stossel's last paragraph in which he quotes Bob Lichter: "[The media] stir up problems that really aren't there . . . this . . . poses a real danger to the public." Can this paragraph be viewed as making some of the same media errors Stossel challenges in his essay? Explain.

CRITICAL THINKING

5. John Stossel is a media journalist. Does the fact that he is reporting on a problem in his own industry make his comments seem more credible? Why or why not?

6. Greg McCrary, of the Threat Assessment Group, observes, "Sex and violence sells." Why do we find these things more interesting than more mundane things? What is it about sex and violence that holds such appeal?

WRITING ABOUT THE ISSUES

7. In the closing paragraph, Bob Lichter states, "Bad journalism is worse than no journalism, because it leaves people thinking they know something that is, in fact, wrong." Write a response to this statement from the viewpoint of a television journalist. You may agree or disagree with his comment. (Remember that Stossel seems to agree and he is a television journalist himself.)
8. Stossel notes that the summer of 2002 was "the summer of the shark." Review the last year and try to identify the sensationalized stories that marked certain seasons. For example, some people may think that the winter of 2004 was marked by stories about Lacey Peterson and the Atkins diet ("Carb Wars"). Visit Web sites such as www.cnn.com and www.msnbc.com/top10.asp for current hot news topics. After compiling your list, try to determine which topics were likely hyped up for the consumer audience.

Who's Taking the Kids?

Jonathan Alter

Jonathan Alter is a senior editor for *Newsweek* and author of its "Between the Lines" column, which examines politics, media, and society at large. He is also a correspondent for NBC News. His articles have appeared in many publications including the *New Republic*, *Esquire*, and *Rolling Stone*. This article appeared in the July 29, 2002, issue of *Newsweek*.

CONNECTING TO THE TOPIC

With all the media hype, you'd think we can no longer send a 13-year-old to pick up a quart of milk or that children are not safe riding their bikes around the block. Is it dangerous for children to play in their front yards? Are we creating a culture in which a stranger cannot stop and ask for directions anymore? How much of our fear is common sense caution and how much is fueled by media hype preying on our insecurities? In our attempt to keep children safe, are we making them even more fearful than we are?

WORDS IN CONTEXT

boffo: slang for extremely successful; great
fugitive: one who has run away or fled, usually hiding from legal authority
bureaucrat: an official who is rigidly devoted to the details of administrative procedure
predator: one that victimizes, plunders, or destroys, especially for one's own gain

1 When I was tempted last week to leave my 8-year-old daughter in the car for literally 90 seconds while I picked up laundry, I quickly came to my senses. Sure, in the 1960s my parents would leave us alone in the car for what seemed like 90 minutes, but times change and it's the summer of "Child Abductions." Visions of that Avila creep charged with killing 5-year-old Samantha Runnion flooded my brain, so I took my daughter inside the dry cleaner with me, though she wasn't wearing any shoes.

2 Even so, I can't help thinking that many people—including well-meaning officials of the U.S. government—are overreacting to all of these stories, and the effect will be to continue changing our children's lives for the worse. The media, of course, are leading the way. Let's be honest: covering child kidnappings is inexpensive and gets boffo ratings.

3 Bush, taking a leaf from Clinton (who mastered the art of responding like a fireman to any public concern), held a White House conference on missing and runaway children on Sept. 24, 2002. That's fine, but the press attention is not likely to be on the half million teens who run away from home each year. And it will be hard to get people talking about the more than 200,000 "family abductions," despite the fact that such custody battles are often terribly cruel, with the children forced to live like fugitives and told the other parent doesn't love them.

4 Instead, the focus will likely be on what scares but doesn't truly threaten parents like me, parents who vote—namely, "non-family

abductions." How worried should we be? The Web site touted by Bush, missingkids.com, is confusing on the numbers. To make us feel better, the site notes that of the 58,200 kids abducted by non-family members in 1999, only 115 were taken by strangers in ways ultimately dangerous to the child.

5 So who grabbed the other 58,085? Dad's drug dealer? Mom's pimp? The site doesn't explain, beyond noting that "abductions in this category involved forcibly moving or detaining the children for a relatively short period of time, usually in connection with another crime."

6 And of course you have to go elsewhere to locate FBI statistics (far more easily accessible through a Google search than through the pathetic FBI search engine) to find that the number of missing persons last year was the lowest since 1992. Juvenile abductions are down 5 percent since 2000.

7 Obviously, those 115 stranger abductions a year are 115 too many, especially since 40 percent of these kids end up dead and many times that number are molested. But the truth is, in a country of nearly 300 million people, the odds of your child being abducted and killed by a stranger are exceedingly small.

8 I don't mean to minimize people's fears or to suggest that all of the government's advice to parents on how to protect their children is wrong. We need the advice but we do pay a price, just as we do in protecting ourselves against terrorism.

9 For instance, the Justice Department's missingkids.com Web site suggests that younger children should be trained to say: "I always take a friend with me when I go places or play outside." Always? How about if mom is fixing dinner and she wants you to go in the backyard to work off a little energy? Is that now evidence of bad parenting?

10 Even teens are advised to "always take a friend when walking or riding your bike to and from school." What world are these bureaucrats living in? In the real world, that's impossible, unless your classmate happens to live right next door. Is the Justice Department suggesting that even though the number of stranger abductions is small and shrinking, we can no longer send our 13-year-old to the corner to pick up a quart of milk? Not reasonable. Not rational.

11 Clearly, the emphasis in recent years on child safety has been a tremendous life saver. For children under age 14, the death rate from unintended injuries is down 46 percent since 1980. Car seats have saved thousands of lives, and bike helmets have contributed to a 60 percent decline in bicycle-related injuries. But youth bike-riding itself is also down, the result of other childhood interests like video games,

but also from a sense of "stranger danger." The childhood many of us remember—riding around on our bikes unsupervised; going downtown on the bus alone—is fading into the American past. In the name of safety, kids are losing a sense of independence that is fun for them and important to their development.

12 We don't need a White House Conference on Striking the Right Balance. But it's something to think about the next time breathless coverage of a child abduction tempts us to coop up the kids in the house—safe from predators but also from healthy adventures, alive but at a distance from life. ◆

CONSIDERING THE ISSUES

1. When you were a child, what things did your parents allow you to do that might be considered risky today? For example, were you left unattended in a car while your mother ran into the supermarket? Were you allowed to ride your bike alone? Did you take walks in the woods with your friends without an adult? Would you let your own children do the things you were allowed to do? Why or why not?
2. What is the purpose of news reporting? Why do you watch the news, and what do you hope to get from the experience? Do you expect information? Advice? Guidance? Explain.

CRAFT AND CONTENT

3. What is Alter's argument in this essay? What is he trying to express? What is his motivation for writing this piece? Summarize his points in one paragraph.
4. Alter begins his essay with an example from his own experience. How does his example demonstrate the point he is trying to make in his essay? Do you think he could have left his child in the car? Does his story help readers understand his point of view? Explain.

CRITICAL THINKING

5. In paragraph 3, Alter notes that media attention on child abductions focuses on non-family kidnappings but doesn't address the 200,000 children taken by parents or relatives. Is the media doing a disservice to the public by not balancing the issue or giving it equal time? Explain.

6. Alter observes that "in the name of safety, kids are losing a sense of independence that is fun for them and important to their development." Are parents' fears, fueled by media hype, ruining childhood? Or stifling normal developmental experiences? What do you think?

WRITING ABOUT THE ISSUES

7. In the summer of 2003, when child abductions seemed to make weekly headlines, kidnapping was actually down 5% from 2000. Does this information surprise you? Should this information have been included in the commentary? Does it demonstrate a disconnect between reality and media hype? Write a short essay on what responsibility, if any, the media have in providing statistical information when reporting headline stories.
8. Alter observes that the media provide a necessary service. "We need the advice but we do pay a price . . . ." What price do we pay? Is this price too much in your opinion? Explain.
9. The Justice Department makes several recommendations to parents about how to keep children safe on the Web site www.missingkids.com, including playing with a buddy when outside and bike riding with other children to destinations such as school. Alter feels that these recommendations are largely unrealistic for parents and could even harm kids. Write a short essay providing your own recommendations on keeping children safe in the area in which you live. Explain the reasoning behind each recommendation.

The Female Fear Factor

Myrna Blyth

Myrna Blyth served as the editor for the magazine *Ladies' Home Journal* from 1981 to 2002. Before joining *Ladies' Home Journal*, Blyth was the executive editor of the women's magazine *Family Circle*. This article is excerpted from her 2004 exposé book, *Spin Sisters: How the Women of the Media Sell Unhappiness and Liberalism to the Women of America*.

CONNECTING TO THE TOPIC

American women today are the most prosperous, healthy, well-educated, and advantaged ever. Yet many feel unhappy—overwhelmed, unsafe, stressed, and even victimized. From morning shows to women's magazines, journalists influence how women see the world. As a member of the female journalistic elite, Myrna Blyth knew firsthand just how to twist a story to sell magazines. This twisting of information, or *spin* as it is known in the industry, promotes sensationalized stories in order to get women to watch a program, read an article, or listen to a news broadcast. Do the media feed on women's natural insecurities? If so, is such manipulation unethical, or simply part of media culture? And, to take a page out of the media hype playbook, could spin be creating a culture of fear?

WORDS IN CONTEXT

solemnly: earnestly, with grave seriousness
wont: likely
chaser: something closely following another thing, from the informal reference to a drink, such as beer or water, taken after hard liquor
incensed: extremely angry; infuriated
Alar: the trade name for daminozide, a chemical plant growth regulator, formerly used to increase the storage life of fruit
asbestos: a chemical-resistant, fibrous mineral form of impure magnesium silicate, used for fireproofing, electrical insulation, building materials, brake linings, and chemical filters
Alzheimer's: a degenerative brain disease marked by memory loss and dementia
mitigate: to moderate (a quality or condition) in force or intensity; alleviate
tuberculosis: an infectious disease usually of the lungs
diluted: made thinner or less concentrated by adding a liquid such as water

1 When Diane Sawyer looks me in the eye and tells me "sleeping on a conventional mattress is like sleeping on kerosene," she gets my attention— and that's the point. It was a March 30, 2000, *Good Morning America* segment. I stopped making the bed, grabbed my coffee, and sat glued to the set watching a fairly typical and typically scary network report on the dangers of non-flame-resistant mattresses.

2 Watching, with a pro's eye—hey, maybe this is a story for my magazine, too—I noted that the report had everything a woman needs . . . to start the day wrong. It had:

1. **Fear**—"This is a mattress study called 'The Big Burn' conducted by the California Bureau of Home Furnishings back in 1991." (Meaning nine whole years had passed before the show, but who's counting?) "It was a test to see how long it would take for a fire to consume a mattress like the one you just spent the night on. Firefighters . . . say they are well aware of the risk," solemnly intoned reporter Greg Hunter.
2. **A threat that endangers children**—"Stacey Hernandez's son, Damon, set a polyurethane foam mattress on fire in California back in 1993 . . . " (Seven years before the show.) "Third-degree burns over half his body."
3. **A distraught mother**—"If I had known that that was so unsafe I would rather we had slept on the floor."

3 The story also featured a bit of a debate and a doubter or two, but any and all criticisms of the story's basic premise were passed over faster than a size 14 at a fashion shoot. "The Consumer Product Safety Commission and the mattress industry insist that the greater fire hazard is what's on the mattress, [namely] the bedclothes. Not the polyurethane on the inside." Great. Now, what are the odds of finding a comforting little fire-resistant tag still on those sheets I've slept on through at least three presidents?

4 Then, as television is wont to do, we were given a chaser of reassurance after the scare session: "The federal government has required mattresses to be cigarette resistant since 1973," which I had already guessed is the cause of most bedroom fires.

5 Still, I sat there watching a terribly disfigured child, a weeping mom, and an incensed Diane. "This is really stunning," she said.

6 But what should be done about it? If I wanted to get a flame-retardant mattress right away, like before tonight when I might once again be "sleeping on kerosene," where do I find one?

7 "Only in some state prisons," Greg tells me.

8 Now, that's very helpful. Let me run right out and rob a bank.

9 That short *Good Morning America* piece was pretty standard fare, and a good illustration of the way editors and television producers construct human interest stories and consumer reports that are the bread

and butter of media aimed at women. Next time you watch *48 Hours* or *Dateline NBC*, look at the way the story is told. They all tend to have the same format: High volume on the emotions, low volume on everything else (facts, balance, debate, assessment of risks, advice you can really use).

10 But even knowing how the media overdoes stories, my basic reaction to the *GMA* piece was probably just what yours would have been. How very sad about that child. And even though I know that most safety officials are neither uncaring nor unwise, I was left with the uneasy feeling that we are often in danger, even in our own beds.

11 And that's what *GMA*, *20/20*, *Today*, *Dateline*, *Lifetime*, and other network series—all of them want you to feel. Afraid. Worried that the next victim might be you or your child. When it comes to selling fear, television and women's magazines live by one rule—there's no such thing as overkill, no pun intended.

12 For years, we have been warned and warned again about so many terrible things—benzene in our bottled water, Alar on our apples. We may not have Alar to be afraid of anymore but never fear, there's always asbestos in our school buildings, secondhand smoke in our environment, the hole in the ozone layer, the ozone in the ozone layer, high-tension power lines, cell phones that cause brain cancer, and lead paint peeling off our walls. That old lead paint fear was recycled in a recent *Redbook* article that claimed that living in any house built before 1978—which means 40 percent of all homes in America—could be a serious danger to your children. So now I know my kids spent their entire childhood in danger, not just when they came home after curfew.

13 We have also been warned by the Center for Science in the Public Interest, a.k.a. the food police, that popcorn, margarine, red meat, Chinese, Italian, French, and Mexican food along with McDonald's French fries contribute to heart disease. Still ordering fettuccine Alfredo? Heart attack on a plate, sister! Aluminum and zinc may contribute to Alzheimer's. And almost everything else including alcohol, birth control pills, bottled water, silicone breast implants, exhaust fumes, chlorine, caffeine, dairy products, diet soda, hot dogs, fluoridation, grilled meat, hair dyes, hydrogen peroxide, incense, jewelry, kissing, laxatives, low-fiber diets, magnetic fields, marijuana, olive oil, orange juice, peanut butter, playground equipment, salt, "sick" buildings, sun beds, sunlight, sunscreen, talc, testosterone, tight bras, toast, tooth fillings, vinyl toys, and wallpaper may cause cancer.

14 More than twenty years ago, political scientist Aaron Wildavsky looked around America and wrote, "How extraordinary! The richest, longest-lived, best-protected, most resourceful civilization with the highest degree of insight into its own technology is on its way to becoming the most frightened." We have arrived.

15 And the media is largely to blame, even media reporters fess up to that. As David Shaw wrote in the *Los Angeles Times*, "The media, after all, pays the most attention to those substances, issues and situations that most frighten their readers and viewers. Thus, almost every day, we read and see and hear about a new purported threat to our health and safety."

16 Says TV commentator Jeff Greenfield, "It's a basic rule of journalism—to get the human angle. But with a complicated technical story . . . the concerns, the worries, the fears of people . . . will always carry more weight than the disputes and the cautions of the experts." In other

words, let's not clutter up a perfectly good horror story with any mitigating facts.

17 Human drama, human emotions are what work. And pictures—dramatic pictures of a sobbing mother, an injured child, a disfigured teenager. Such pictures and the stories that go with them are easy for women to empathize with and understand. And that's the name of the game—attracting women. So why should we be surprised that so many of these pieces are for and about women. For example, on *20/20* there was a segment, in the early summer of 2001, introduced by Barbara Walters telling us:

> How do you like to be pampered? For millions . . . especially women, especially as summer approaches, the answer is a visit to a nail salon. Maybe you're headed there tomorrow. Well, we have to warn you, you may come home with more than beautiful fingers and toes, because there is something ugly going on at some nail salons. Customers who don't know how to protect themselves are really getting nailed.

18 "Getting Nailed" was about a California nail salon where a group of women were infected by tuberculosis-related bacteria that were found in the drain of the foot basin, which had not been carefully cleaned. The rest of the piece took us along as undercover inspectors raided other salons in various states. Many, owned by immigrants, were found to be violating local health codes, reusing emery boards and swabbing counters down with diluted disinfectant. Only one salon was shown to have seriously injured any clients, but the legs of the women who had become infected did, I grant you, look quite gruesome.

19 At the end of the piece, Barbara Walters shared that "I wanted to have a pedicure this week," but she said she didn't. Why not? Did the *20/20* piece make her as fearful as it was supposed to make us? Not really. Barbara told us, "Once and again I've been too busy." She didn't say she would be sure to do a safety check the next time she hits Frederic Fekkai's exclusive salon as she advised her loyal viewers to do.

20 Still, e-mails flew around my office and across the Internet—the world's biggest party line—as women warned their sister sandal wearers of the newly discovered dangers of the pedicure. This was real news we can use from one of television's most respected women journalists warning us that pampering can be hazardous to your health.

21 And we do depend on media to tell us what's important in the world, good news and bad. Whether it's *Dateline NBC* or Peter Jennings or *Ladies' Home Journal*, the media is our information source, and we want the truth. And there's the rub. Although we might like to think so, journalists and editors don't just transmit the facts, ma'am. They select and shape it and make facts, fit into emotional stories that tug at our heartstrings or send a chill up our spines. I've done it myself. That's because news is most effective when it tells a story that confirms our deep-seated beliefs and stokes our deep-seated fears. As psychology professor Paul Slovic of the University of Oregon says, "We trust people who tell us we're in danger more than people who tell us we're not in danger." And when we hear someone is harmed, we want a simple explanation for her pain. A very simple explanation. Editors and producers know that.

22 Look, I'm not telling you that all these "fear factor" pieces you read in magazines and see on the networks are untrue. Those women on *20/20* did get a nasty infection from their pedicures. Through the years I published many articles about wrongs against women and families, and stories about health that were fair and honest. I believed I was giving good sensible information. But there is always the temptation to play gotcha! To simplify and dramatize in order to hold the attention of the reader or viewer. And I can't deny that those of us in media, like a little girl who keeps crying long after her stubbed toe has stopped hurting, tend to exaggerate and do a lot of it for effect.

23 That's why even though women and men are safer and healthier than we have ever been, we are also more afraid of what we eat, drink, touch, and breathe. Eleanor Singer and Phyllis Endreny, two social scientists, did a study of risk coverage by the media and concluded, "A direct comparison between hazards as topics of news stories and as causes of death show essentially no relationship between the two." So we're really okay, but we are being told not to feel okay. That's because the media, in order to attract readers and viewers, "often overplays risks of dubious legitimacy. Scientific studies show that many of the alleged hazards the media trumpet are either misstated, overstated, nonexistent or there just is not enough scientific evidence yet to yield reliable guidance on the true risk for the average American." Which, I admit, is a kind of shabby way to get readers or ratings. ◆

CONSIDERING THE ISSUES

1. Blyth's introduction describes a television program segment that drew her to sit and watch. What types of news story "hooks" are likely to get your attention? Have you stayed up later than you intended or watched a news program because the "hook" statement before the show or news segment grabbed your interest? Explain.
2. What makes you buy a particular magazine? Is it the content? The advertisements? The stories? The layout? Do the headlines on the magazine influence you to buy it? Do you ever think about how the headlines might be manipulating you? Explain.

CRAFT AND CONTENT

3. In paragraphs 3 through 5, Blyth notes three things that Diane Sawyer's story used to hold a woman riveted to the television set. Analyze these elements and explain why they work to capture the intended audience. Would they work on you to grab and hold your attention? Why or why not?
4. Like John Stossel at the beginning of this chapter, Myrna Blyth is an "insider" to the journalism industry. Drawing from your experience with the format of most stories in popular magazines, in what ways does Blyth's article resemble the story format typical in many women's magazines? Does this format make her argument more accessible to her readers? (If you are unfamiliar with this format, take a look at some articles from the magazines she cites in your library or at a newsstand, and then review the article again.)

CRITICAL THINKING

5. In paragraph 15, Blyth quotes *Los Angeles Times* reporter David Shaw, "The media, after all, pays the most attention to those substances, issues, and situations that most frighten their readers and viewers. Thus, almost every day, we read and see and hear about a new purported threat to our health and safety." Respond to Shaw's statement with your own opinion. Is this practice

acceptable? Does it allow the reader to determine what information is important, and what is not? Explain.

6. Blyth reveals how women's magazines target women's fears in order to sell magazines. What techniques are used to hook men's eyeballs on magazines? How do men and women's magazines differ? Can the same principles be applied to popular men's magazines such as *Details*, *Maxim*, *GQ*, and *Esquire*? Explain.

WRITING ABOUT THE ISSUES

7. Blyth notes that "When it comes to selling fear, television and women's magazines live by one rule—there's no such thing as overkill, no pun intended." Visit your local library and scan the headlines on some popular women's magazines. Write down any headlines that seem to fit Blyth's assertion. How does the magazine twist the story to grab the viewer's attention? Is this technique ethical? Is it simply the way magazines market their material? Explain.
8. Create your own magazine cover for a women's magazine presenting stories in a factual and unsensationalized way. Select a real magazine and create an alternative cover for it after reading the articles and analyzing them with a critical eye.

Heads Above the Hype

Peter Phillips

Peter Phillips is an associate professor of sociology at Sonoma State University in California and director of Project Censored, a media research organization. He is the lead editor of the "Censored Stories" series, most recently, *Censored 2004: The Top 25 Censored Stories.* Phillips frequently speaks on media censorship and various sociopolitical issues on radio and television talk shows, including *Talk of the Nation*, *Public Interest*, and *Democracy Now!* This article was published in the October 2001 issue of *Briarpatch* magazine.

CONNECTING TO THE TOPIC

Are the media "programming" us to believe certain things about the American way of life—namely that we live in a cold, heartless, violent, corrupt, self-centered nation? Media activist Peter Phillips examines the programming we face every day, and wonders how we can overcome it in order to keep touch with reality. How do we slog through the hype and get to the truth?

WORDS IN CONTEXT

electorate: a body of qualified voters
prurient: exceedingly interested in matters of sex, vice, and scandal
opulence: great wealth and affluence
gluttony: excess in eating or drinking, self-indulgence
innately: inborn
acquisition: act of acquiring
invariably: unlikely to change; constantly
amplify: to exaggerate
essence: the essential nature or indispensable properties that characterize or identify something
alienate: to cause to become withdrawn or isolated; to dissociate emotionally

1 Are Americans becoming heartless?

2 Are we less sensitive to others?

3 Is our society really becoming corrupt and degraded?

4 As we follow American corporate media today we could only answer "yes" to each of these questions. Washington sex scandals, celebrity exposes, gruesome murders, schoolyard attacks, gangs, crime, corruption and conspicuous consumption fill the airwaves and newspapers. Media representatives say they need to protect their bottom-line, and that these types of news and fictionalized stories increase ratings. Corporate media seem to have abdicated their First Amendment responsibility of keeping the public informed. The traditional journalist values of supporting democracy by maintaining an educated electorate now take second place to profits and ratings.

5 When questioned about the appropriateness of sensationalized news coverage and heartless human episodes, corporate media responds

by saying, "we are just giving the public what it wants." Media shift the responsibility for sensationalized coverage to a prurient citizenry's market demands for more blood, gore, and opulence.

6 Is the public really screaming for more body dissections, crime coverage, and gossip news? Are ordinary people to blame for this daily parade of heartless gluttony? Somehow I firmly believe that as a society we are just as innately compassionate and sensitive as ever. I ask my freshmen classes each semester what the most important values are in their lives. After a brief discussion, wealth and material acquisitions are invariably dismissed and core personal values of love, friendship and trustfulness emerge to the forefront.

7 As a former director of a family service center in Dixon, California, I remember the dozens of phone calls offering help when our local newspaper covered the plight of a homeless family. The willingness to care, love, build friendships and respond to the needs of others is very much alive in American society. Regretfully, we have been led to believe otherwise. Because of the enormous coverage of stories on people such as Gary Condit, Monica Lewinski, and Columbine, we tend to believe that we are all somehow less then we were—that we live in a "Survivor" society. We watch with increasing numbness the killings and scandals. Through limited daily personal interactions we amplify the very essence of our numbness through media fed gossip with our friends and associates. We blame human nature and believe the worst about ourselves. The spiral turns inward, twisting the soul of society into an alienated artificiality. We hide in gated communities, consuming media-supplied episodes of fear, disgust, and lovelessness.

8 How can we resist? Individual isolation or rejection of all media is not a societal answer. (I gave my TV away years ago, but I remain a media activist.) Responsibility for media content lies with the media themselves. We need to collectively ask corporate media to return to covering the important issues of our day and away from sensationalized hype. If they fail to listen, our task is to re-diversify media by creating media options in our daily lives. By using the technologies available to us today, we can connect with independent news and entertainment services all over the world and share our stories. In recent years a global Internet news system has emerged, involving over 65 independent news centers in a dozen countries, with another 30 planning to

come online in the next few months. They can be seen on the Internet at www.indymedia.org. There is now Indymedia radio and special files for printing newspapers for local distribution. Indymedia and similar groups show us that we can rebuild media from the bottom up. We can share our success stories, maintain an informed electorate, and reconnect to our communities' heartfelt values.

9 Independent media comes from the people and is emerging around us. Local cable TV, independent radio and micro-transmitted radio, alternative newsmagazines and newspapers are everywhere. We can add to and expand these vital sources of news and entertainment and, in the process, reconnect with our society and ourselves. We can tell the stories of struggling and overcoming together—stories that strengthen and unite our hearts. ◆

CONSIDERING THE ISSUES

1. Do you think that we live in a more cold and violent world today than we did when you were a child or when your parents were children? Explain.
2. Phillips states that the media depict a shallow, cold, violent, and heartless world. His own experience, however, negates this view. How does your real-life experience compare to the media's image of society and culture? Explain.

CRAFT AND CONTENT

3. Evaluate Phillips' use of language—especially adjectives—in this essay. What adjectives does he use to describe the media and the world they depict? How does his use of language influence the reader?
4. In paragraph 5 Phillips writes, "When questioned about the appropriateness of sensationalized news coverage and heartless human episodes, corporate media respond by saying, 'we are just giving the public what it wants.'" Is this statement a valid argument? If the media are just giving the viewing public what it wants—as demonstrated by sales and ratings—is there anything wrong with sensationalizing stories? What do you think?

CRITICAL THINKING

5. What solutions does Phillips offer to address the problem of media hype? Do you think his ideas are realistic? Why or why not?
6. Phillips leads into his article by posing three questions to his readers. How would you answer these questions, based on your experience of the world? How do you think a news journalist would answer them?

WRITING ABOUT THE ISSUES

7. Watch at least two television media-journal programs such as *20/20*, *Dateline*, or *60 Minutes*. Summarize the stories featured in an evening's program. Do the segments featured on the programs match the "cold world" image Phillips says is being promoted by the media? Based on your analysis of the programs, respond to Phillips' concerns in a short essay.
8. Phillips refers to the First Amendment in paragraph 4, "Corporate media seem to have abdicated their First Amendment responsibility of keeping the public informed." Review the First Amendment. Write a short essay exploring the responsibilities of the media to the public as described in the First Amendment.

Calling All Angels

Train

The band Train formed in 1994 when Pat Monahan met Rob Hotchkiss (who left the band in 2003) in Los Angeles. They moved to San Francisco, where Charlie Colin (bass) and Jimmy Stafford (guitar) soon joined them. Scott Underwood (drummer) came on board shortly thereafter. Their first big hit, "Drops of Jupiter (Tell Me)," dominated the charts from March of 2001 to April 2002. "Meet Virginia" enjoyed similar success. Train's third album, *My Private Nation*, was released in June 2003 and featured the song reprinted on the following page, "Calling All Angels."

1 I need a sign to let me know you're here
All of these lines are being crossed over the atmosphere
I need to know that things are gonna look up
Cause I feel us drowning in a sea spilled from a cup
5 When there is no place safe and no safe place to put my head
When you can feel the world shake from the words that I said

And I'm calling all angels
And I'm calling all you angels

And I won't give up if you don't give up
10 I won't give up if you don't give up
I won't give up if you don't give up
I won't give up if you don't give up

I need a sign to let me know you're here
Cause my TV set just keeps it all from being clear
15 I want a reason for the way things have to be
I need a hand to help build up some kind of hope inside of me

And I'm calling all angels
And I'm calling all you angels

When children have to play inside so they don't disappear
20 While private eyes solve marriage lies cause we don't talk for years
And football teams are kissing queens and losing sight of having dreams
In a world where all we want is only what we want until it's ours

And I'm calling all angels
And I'm calling all you angels ◆

CRITICAL THINKING

1. In what ways does Train's song reflect current public perspectives about American society? Explain.
2. Does Train's song reinforce our fears that we live in a dangerous world? Does it have any power to influence our perception of the world?
3. What references does Train's song make to hot issues in the media today? Explain.

The Violence Reporting Project: A New Approach to Covering Crime

Jane Ellen Stevens

Jane Ellen Stevens has been a journalist and science writer for 25 years. She is currently a science and technology video journalist for *New York Times* television and has been writing about violence issues for several years. She is the author of *Reporting on Violence: A Handbook for Journalists.* This article appeared in the *Nieman Reports* published by the Nieman Foundation for Journalism at Harvard University.

CONNECTING TO THE TOPIC

In 1995, Jane Ellen Stevens embarked on a collaborative venture, the Violence Reporting Project, with Lori Dorfman, director of the Berkeley Media Studies Group, a public health research organization, and Esther Thorson, a statistician and associate dean at the University of Missouri School of Journalism. The project focuses on ways to educate journalists about the need to incorporate a public health perspective in their reporting about violence. Do the media have a responsibility to its public? If so, what are those responsibilities? Is it more important to sell headlines? Is there a middle ground?

WORDS IN CONTEXT

epidemic: widely prevalent; affecting many individuals
discipline: a branch of knowledge or teaching
interaction: the process in which two or more things act upon each other
emergence: the act or process of coming forth
epidemiology: the branch of medicine that deals with the study of the causes, distribution, and control of disease in populations
nuclear family: a family unit consisting of a mother and father and their children
communicable: transmittable between persons or species; contagious
reverberate: to have a prolonged or continuing effect
perpetrator: one who commits or is responsible for an action, especially a crime
incarcerate: state of being jailed or locked up; confinement
psychological: relating to or arising from the mind or emotions

1 In 1977, a group of physicians in the U.S. Public Health Service met to draw up a list of steps to prevent premature deaths in the United States—those that occur before age 65. To their surprise, among the top five at that time were violent injuries, homicide and suicide. More than two decades later, these are still among the top 10, and the highest rates of violent death and injury occur among children and adolescents.

2 Out of this meeting emerged a new medical and scientific specialty that studies violence as an epidemic. Specialists in this new discipline put violence in the same category and apply the same tools as those that are being used to reduce and control other epidemics, such as lung cancer and heart disease. They study the interaction among the victim, the agent of injury or death, and the environment; define risk factors; and develop methods to prevent injury or death.

3 Few would deny that violence in the United States is epidemic. In 1984, U.S. Surgeon General C. Everett Koop declared that violence was as much a public health issue for today's physicians as smallpox was for the medical community in previous generations. Even with the recent decrease in homicide, the United States still ranks first among industrialized nations in its rate of violent deaths.

4 I began reporting on violence epidemiology in 1993. Among the stories I wrote was one that dispelled some myths of violence. When my editors expressed surprise at what the data showed—that most women who are murdered die at the hands of someone they know, that most male homicide victims are killed by strangers, that children are at greater risk of death caused by abusive family members than from disease, that teenagers are at greater risk of crime than the elderly—an alarm went off in my mind. If news organizations were reporting crime on a regular basis, why were these facts a surprise to journalists?

5 I discovered that the answer lies in the way journalists report crime. We do so only from a law enforcement and criminal justice standpoint. With the emergence of violence epidemiology, it became clear to me that there is a third and essential part of the violence story that we are missing, not because the information isn't available, but because most reporters don't know it exists.

6 The U.S. Centers for Disease Control and Prevention initiated a program on violence prevention in 1983, and since then hundreds of states and city public health departments have established offices of violence prevention. For more than 15 years, epidemiologists have been

identifying violence risk factors. Among those they now track regularly are the availability of firearms and alcohol, racial discrimination, unemployment, violence in the media, lack of education, abuse as a child, witnessing violent acts in the home or neighborhood, isolation of the nuclear family, and belief in male dominance over females.

7 But, so far, the journalism community has not taken full advantage of this knowledge.

8 Traditionally, news organizations report many fewer violent incidents than occur in their communities. The violent incidents are thus treated, and regarded by readers, as isolated, random events instead of predictable and preventable problems.

9 But few violent incidents are isolated or random. Each violent incident that occurs in a community has more of the characteristics of a deadly communicable disease than of an isolated event involving the individual participants. Furthermore, each incident reverberates through the families of perpetrator and victim with long-term economic consequences (loss of job, loss of home, loss of income, medical bills, attorney bills) and psychological consequences (sense of loss, fear, alienation, hopelessness, repeated violence). The incident also affects the community with economic consequences (cost of medical treatment, rehabilitation, incarceration, trial, welfare, reduction in property values, business flight) and long-term psychological consequences (feelings of fear for personal safety, mistrust of members of community).

10 From reading or viewing reports of violence and crime, the public is learning little about the public health approach to preventing violence. That is because, in reporting violence and crime, news organizations, generally speaking, do not regularly inform readers or viewers about the status of the different types of violence in their communities. Nor do they provide readers or viewers with information about the economic and psychological consequences of the different types of violence in their communities. Readers and viewers are rarely given enough information to put reported violent incidents into context to know what violence is "usual" and able to be prevented, and what is unusual and thus unlikely to be preventable. Information about the methods being developed by the public health community (or not being developed, as the case may be) to prevent violence, is rarely reported. This means that readers and viewers don't find out about whether their

local communities are implementing these preventive approaches and, if they are, whether these approaches are successful.

11 Most news organizations' coverage of violence emphasizes unusual violent incidents, such as a kidnapping, rape and murder of a middle-aged woman by a stranger; violent incidents in which many people are killed by one person, such as the school murders in Oregon and Alabama; and more common violent incidents in which famous people are involved, such as the O.J. Simpson spousal murder case and the Pamela Lee spousal abuse case. The media give much less attention and space to common violent incidents, those that involve people who are not famous, or those in which only one person is killed or injured by an acquaintance or relative.

12 News organizations occasionally do excellent features or projects on violence issues, often as the result of a follow-up to a story to which much attention and space has been given. But months, sometimes years, go by without an investigative report or in-depth feature story about the status of a particular type of violence.

13 In March 1998, there were at least 67 murders, 175 rapes and 4,042 aggravated assaults in Los Angeles County (Los Angeles County Sheriff's Department and Los Angeles Police Department reports only). During that same time, *The Los Angeles Times* reported on 24 murders, three rapes and 39 aggravated assaults. In San Francisco, over a three-month period in 1997, there were 19 murders, 955 aggravated assaults and 55 rapes. *The Examiner* covered eight homicides, seven aggravated assaults, and none (0) of the rapes. Our analysis of newspapers' content compared with actual crime statistics found comparable disparities in Philadelphia, San Jose and Sacramento.

14 Most journalists respond to the presentation of such findings by saying: "That's what we do. We report the unusual." But that's only a part of what journalists do when we report on other topics. Newspapers regularly report in-depth the status of sports, business, political campaigns, weather and local entertainment. By not reporting on the status of violence, we are missing the most important story about the bulk of "ordinary" violent incidents that are actually doing the greatest harm to a community. And by not including a public health approach in our violence reporting, we don't offer readers and viewers enough of the kind of information they need to work toward preventing violent incidents that are causing them and their community the greatest harm.

15 Clearly, no news organizations can cover each individual act of violence. However, a newspaper can report on violent incidents in a way that doesn't get rid of the traditional "good crime stories," often the unusual, but transforms "the usual" into "good stories" that give readers and viewers enough information to reduce violence in their communities.

16 With an expanded approach to reporting violence, a news organization provides readers and viewers with more information on the context and consequences of crime. It covers violence from an investigative standpoint, strengthening its role as a community watchdog. It reports violent incidents, but does not wait for them to occur to report to readers on that particular type of violence. In this way, readers and viewers obtain knowledge of the ongoing status of violence in their communities, the toll taken on families and the community, and the success or failure of measures taken to prevent it. Through its Web site's morbidity and mortality section, a news organization can serve as a community's repository of information about statistics that are vital for them to know as well as the interpreter of changes in those statistics. Readers will be able to access enough information to know when it is appropriate to take personal action and when and how they can influence their communities and governing bodies to prevent violence. ◆

CONSIDERING THE ISSUES

1. Take a look at the front page of one or two major newspapers in your area. What headlines are featured? If you were from another country and had to make an assessment of the city or even the country based on these headlines, what would you think? Explain.
2. Visit the Centers for Disease Control and Prevention Web site's listing of the top ten "Actual Causes of Death in the U.S." at www.cdc.gov/nccdphp/publications/pdf/methods.pdf. Does the information listed on their fact sheet surprise you? What cause is likely to appeal to the public's appetite for news, and what is unlikely to sell newspapers or magazines? Explain.

CRAFT AND CONTENT

3. In paragraph 3, Stevens states, "Few would deny that violence in the United States is epidemic." What assumptions does Stevens make about her audience? How does this statement imply collective agreement? Explain.
4. Stevens compares violent crime to disease. Identify areas in her essay that make this analogy. How does she use this comparison to clarify her point? Is it an effective way to present her argument? Explain.

CRITICAL THINKING

5. While writing a story in 1993 on victims of violent crime, Stevens discovered some interesting facts not reflected in media coverage. How did this story change her perspective on media coverage of violent crime? Explain.
6. Stevens notes that "the media give much less attention and space to common violent incidents, those that involve people who are not famous, or those in which only one person is killed or injured by an acquaintance or relative." What accounts for this phenomenon? If the media were to report more often on "regular people" would it be as successful? Do readers want to read about "common" violence? Explain.

WRITING ABOUT THE ISSUES

7. You are an editor of a major metropolitan newspaper. Write a business plan for your reporters on what types of stories to report on and why. Will you assume a responsible position to aid public health, or favor hype stories to sell papers? Or will you try to strike a balance between the two? Explain the rationale for your plan in one or two paragraphs.
8. How can the Internet help balance news media's desire to entertain through hype and the public's need for factual information? Drawing from some points Stevens makes in her article, develop your own list of recommendations to improve media outreach to the public.

VISUAL CONNECTIONS

It's a Scary World

Pulitzer Prize winner Jim Borgman's comic strip "Zits" describes the teen-angst-ridden life of 15-year-old Jeremy and his family and friends. Since its debut in July 1997, the syndicated strip appears in 875 newspapers around the world and is translated into at least seven languages, including German, Chinese, Spanish, and Finnish.

CONSIDERING THE ISSUES

1. Can you recall a time when you knew your parents were frightened? How did you react? Explain.
2. Usually, children end up in their parents' room after having a nightmare. Is it significant that the parents turn to their teenage son for "protection" from their "nightmare"? Explain.

CRITICAL THINKING

3. What is this cartoon about? What cultural theme does it employ? What does the audience need to understand in order to "get" the comic's twist?
4. Who is the audience for this cartoon? How does it tap into popular fears? Explain.

TOPICAL CONNECTIONS

GROUP PROJECTS

1. Using a major metropolitan newspaper, make a list of the headlines in each section. Using this list, conduct a poll on which stories grab attention or seem the most interesting. Ask the participants of your survey to rank the headlines from most to least interesting. Then, ask them to explain why they picked the top three headlines they ranked as most compelling. Based on the information you gather, what conclusions can you make about the media and the public's appetite for information?
2. Question 1 asked you to make a list of all the headlines included in a major metropolitan newspaper. Working with such a list, analyze the language used in each headline. Are the headlines straightforward and factual, or do they put some "spin" on language in order to hook the reader? How does the headline connect to the actual content of the story? As a group, rewrite the headlines in your own words to better reflect the content of the story it modifies.

WEB PROJECT

3. The evening news broadcast that is a staple in many American homes is more than simply a recounting of the day's events. Most programs carefully consider what they will present in order to catch—and hold—viewers' eyeballs. Visit the PBS Web site "Inside the Local News" examining how media pick and present stories to the public at www.pbs.org/wnet/insidelocalnews. Examine the entire site, but carefully read the sections on "Behind the Story" and "The Ratings Game." Based on research gathered on this site, design your own news broadcast based on current events and explain in detail the reasons behind your design and story selection.

FOR FURTHER INQUIRY

4. While a critical eye may be able to cut through media hype that helps "sell" a story, media bias may be harder to decipher. Read the article on bias featured on the Rhetorica Network's Web site at http://rhetorica.net/bias.htm. Apply the questions Rhetorica lists in its six "Critical Questions for Detecting Media Bias" to a television, newspaper, or magazine journal article. Choose a "hot" issue that has gotten a great deal of press coverage in recent weeks. How does the article stand up to the test? What media bias can you detect, if any?

4 Do Campus Speech Codes Violate Students' Rights?

"*Congress shall make no law . . . abridging the freedom of speech, or of the press.*" With these simple words, the writers of the Constitution created one of the pillars of our democratic system of government—the First Amendment guarantee of every American's right to the free exchange of ideas, beliefs, and political debate. Most students support their right to express themselves without fear of government reprisal. However, over the years questions have arisen about whether limits should be imposed on our right to free expression when the exercise of that right imposes hardship or pain on others. What happens when the right of one person to state his or her beliefs conflicts with the rights of others to be free from verbal abuse? What happens when free expression runs counter to community and university values? At what point does the perceived degree of offensiveness warrant censorship? Are campus speech codes appropriate? Are they a violation of free speech? And who decides what is acceptable speech? In this unit, we look at the controversial issue of censorship and speech codes on campus.

The free and open exchange of ideas is critical to the goals of higher education. However, when the ideas expressed are racist, sexist, or otherwise offensive toward specific groups on campus, do universities and colleges have the right to censor and punish that form of speech? This chapter takes a look at this issue in depth, presenting multiple points of view.

CRITICAL THINKING

1. What does the female professor mean when she says to the male professor, "they're loaded for white male"? Based on the expressions of the audience, what is likely to happen next?
2. How does this cartoon relate to the issue of free speech on campus? Explain.
3. What point is the cartoonist trying to make with this cartoon? Is it funny? Why or why not?

"Good luck with your lecture, Eric—they're loaded for white male."

Muzzling Free Speech

Harvey A. Silverglate

Harvey Silverglate is a partner at the law firm of Silverglate & Good in Boston. He is the coauthor, with Alan Charles Kors, of *The Shadow University: The Betrayal of Liberty on America's Campuses* (1998). Together with Kors, he founded The Foundation for Individual Rights (FIRE) a nonprofit organization that addresses individual liberty and rights issues on campus. This article was published in the October 2002 issue of the *National Law Journal,* written with Joshua Gewolb, a special projects coordinator at FIRE.

CONNECTING TO THE TOPIC

In an effort to curtail criticism of campus speech codes, some colleges and universities have designated "free speech zones" on campus where students may assemble, speak, and protest. In most cases, students must request permission in advance from the administration to use these zones. Harvey Silverglate argues that such zones do not solve the issue of restricted speech. Instead, he asserts, they have a "chilling effect" on campus discourse and are a dangerous threat to ideals of free speech.

WORDS IN CONTEXT

unfettered: free from restrictions or bonds
de facto: exercising power or serving a function without being legally or officially established
verboten: (German) forbidden
draconian: exceedingly harsh; very severe
arbitrary: determined by chance, whim, or impulse, and not by necessity, reason, or principle
injunction: a court order prohibiting a party from a specific course of action
unbridled: unrestrained or uncontrolled
peripheral: located in, or constituting an outer boundary; not at the center, but on the outskirts
precipitously: abruptly; hastily

1 In the last five years, free speech zones have become the trendiest weapon in campus administrators' war on free expression. More than 20 colleges and universities have established speech-zone systems relegating protests, demonstrations and all other forms of student speech to a handful of places on campus. This past June, the University of Houston (UH) joined a growing number of colleges and universities that have turned their campuses into censorship zones while restricting unfettered expression to a few tiny "free speech zones."

2 The speech-zones movement presents a major threat to the ideals of free thought and free inquiry to which colleges and universities should be devoted. Free expression, however, means freedom to choose where and when and to whom to speak, not just what to say.

3 College administrators have used every trick in the book to try to limit student speech: Content-based speech codes were the weapon of choice against "offensive" speech on campuses in the early 1980s, but universities were forced to abandon these codes after courts uniformly struck them down. Since then, administrators have used racial and sexual harassment rules to create de facto speech codes. Though these rules have had a chilling effect on campus discourse, recent court opinions finding it unconstitutional to classify as "harassment" speech that is merely offensive (but not physically threatening), reduce the utility of such rules in suppressing speech.

4 College speech zones are the rage because they have not yet faced a court test. When they do, however, they will almost certainly be declared unconstitutional on public campuses. The law requires that government infringements on First Amendment rights be narrowly tailored to accomplish a specific, legitimate purpose—which speech zones are not. Public universities can restrict the "time, place and manner of speech" to avoid disturbing, say, sleeping or studying students, but regulations aimed at forcing students to shut up or move to where they won't be heard and seen are constitutionally verboten.

5 Ironically, UH established its draconian new speech-zone system almost immediately after a court ruled that its previous policy was unconstitutional. The old policy allowed free expression everywhere on campus, but gave Dean William Munson authority to relegate "potentially disruptive" events to four designated areas. In March, the university allowed a large anti-abortion traveling exhibit on the main campus green. The display proved uneventful. But when a second student group, the Pro-Life Cougars, sought to bring the

exhibition back for a second run in June, Munson refused permission, citing its potential disruptiveness.

6 The Pro-Life Cougars students sued. On June 24, the U.S. District Court for the Southern District of Texas declared Munson's actions and UH's speech policy unconstitutional. The court held that the lack of objective standards in UH's policy invited arbitrary prior restraints, and issued a preliminary injunction ordering UH to let the Cougars erect their display and barring the university from imposing restrictions on speech in the plaza.

7 The next day, UH's president established the new, more restrictive, zone policy, limiting free speech events on campus to the four zones previously designated for potentially disruptive speech. Students must now register 10 days in advance for even minor protests. Spontaneous demonstrations are relegated to one additional area where amplified sound and signs mounted on sticks are prohibited. Exceptions are only at the dean's discretion.

8 The new policy appears to seek to avoid the unbridled-discretion problem that was fatal to its predecessor. But the administration apparently has not noted the court's warning that even a content-neutral regulation of speech in a public forum must be narrowly tailored to serve a significant government interest and must leave open ample alternative channels of communication. Simply put, there is no legitimate government interest in moving speech from the heart of campus to more peripheral areas.

9 Though free speech zones are on the rise at some universities, several schools, including Penn State and the University of Wisconsin, have revoked their freshly minted zone regulations. In May, speech-zone opponents convinced West Virginia University to liberalize a policy that restricted free expression to two classroom-sized areas. The school is now testing a new policy that, though it does not go far enough, lets small groups stage protests anywhere on campus, at any time, without advance permission.

10 It will take determined advocacy to keep speech zones from invading the rest of America's colleges and universities. But the recent successes at West Virginia University and elsewhere suggest that the censorship zone movement may burn out as precipitously as it has caught fire. There is a growing recognition, especially by students and civil libertarians, that our entire country is a free speech zone, and that our campuses of higher education, of all places, cannot be an exception. ◆

CONSIDERING THE ISSUES

1. Have you ever participated in or witnessed a demonstration on campus? What was the demonstration about? Was it restricted to a particular area? Could the participants speak freely, or were they restricted in what they could say?
2. Should leaders of controversial groups be allowed to speak on campus? For example, should a person with extremist views, such as someone from the Ku Klux Klan or the PLO, be allowed to speak? What about staunchly pro-life and pro-choice groups? Anti-war demonstrators? Who decides what is extremist? Students? Administration? What do you think?

CRAFT AND CONTENT

3. Summarize Silverglate's argument in one paragraph. Include the key points of his discussion and his concluding observations.
4. What is Silverglate's opinion of college administrators? Identify areas of his essay that use "us" and "them" rhetoric.

CRITICAL THINKING

5. What are "free speech zones"? What purpose do they serve? Are they a fair concession to campus free speech or a violation of the First Amendment? Explain.
6. In paragraph 3, Silverglate states, "College administrators have used every trick in the book to try to limit student speech." What "tricks," according to the author, have they used? Why does Silverglate object to limiting student speech? Has your own campus administration employed any of the speech codes he describes?

WRITING ABOUT THE ISSUES

7. Silverglate cites several universities that have employed free speech zones, including the University of Houston, Penn State, and West Virginia University. Research the arguments for and against free speech zones as expressed in university publications available online at each of these universities. Write a short essay summarizing your research. If your own campus has a free speech zone, include it in your discussion.

8. Imagine that a condition of acceptance to your school involved your signing an agreement that you would refrain from using racist, sexist, or offensive language on campus or face suspension or expulsion. Weighing the social benefits against the restrictions of your freedom of expression, write a paper in which you explain why you would or would not sign such an agreement.

Hate Cannot Be Tolerated

Richard Delgado

Richard Delgado is a law professor at the University of Pittsburgh and author of *Understanding Words That Wound* (2004). One of the leading commentators on race in the United States, Delgado has appeared on many television news programs, including *Good Morning America*, NPR, and PBS. His articles have appeared in the *New York Times*, the *Washington Post*, the *Wall Street Journal*, and *USA Today*, and one of his many books was nominated for a Pulitzer Prize. This opinion/editorial article appeared in *USA Today* on March 3, 2004.

CONNECTING TO THE TOPIC

Speech codes and harassment policies have been adopted by many U.S. colleges and universities in an effort to stop racist, sexist, or other types of offensive language. The rationale is that racial and other offensive slurs are violent verbal assaults that interfere with students' rights. Many civil liberties activists, students, college faculty, and administrators fear that such codes violate First Amendment rights. Who decides what is offensive language and what is not? Should "hate speech" be protected, or can it lead to violence? Are there limits to free speech in favor of greater good and greater safety for the campus body?

WORDS IN CONTEXT

epithet: abusive, disdainful, or condescending word or phrase
elicit: to provoke or draw out
revile: to assault or attack with abusive language

evolution: in biology, the gradual change in the genetic composition of a species over generations, resulting in the improvement of existing species or the development of new ones

hone: to focus on or advance toward a target or goal

1 Anonymous vandals scrawl hate-filled graffiti outside a Jewish student center. Black students at a law school find unsigned fliers stuffed inside their lockers screaming that they do not belong there. At a third campus, a group of toughs hurls epithets at a young Latino student walking home late at night.

2 In response to a rising tide of such incidents, some colleges have enacted hate-speech codes or applied existing rules against individuals whose conduct interferes with the educational opportunities of others. Federal courts have extended "hostile environment" case law to schools that tolerate a climate of hate for women and students of color.

3 Despite the alarm these measures sometimes elicit, nothing is wrong with them. In each case, the usual and preferred response—"more speech"—is unavailable to the victim. With anonymous hate speech such as the flier or graffiti, the victim cannot talk back, for the hate speaker delivers the message in a cowardly fashion. And talking back to aggressors is rarely an option. Indeed, many hate crimes began just this way: The victim talked back—and paid with his life.

4 Hate speech is rarely an invitation to a conversation. More like a slap in the face, it reviles and silences. College counselors report that campuses where highly publicized incidents of hate speech have taken place show a decline in minority enrollment as students of color instead choose to attend schools where the environment is healthier.

5 A few federal courts have declared overly broad hate-speech codes unconstitutional, as well they should. Nothing is gained by a rule so broad it could be construed as forbidding the discussion of controversial subjects such as evolution or affirmative action.

6 But this is not what most people mean by hate speech, nor are colleges barred from drafting narrow rules that hone in on the conduct they wish to control. And when they do, courts are very likely to find in their favor. Recent Supreme Court rulings striking down laws upholding affirmative action and approving punishment for cross-burning show that the court is not unaware of current trends. Society is becoming

more diverse. Reasonable rules aimed at accommodating that diversity and regulating the conduct of bullies and bigots are to be applauded—not feared. ◆

CONSIDERING THE ISSUES

1. Does the saying "sticks and stones may break my bones, but names will never hurt me" apply to racist and hate speech? Have you ever witnessed or experienced a verbal assault based on race or gender? What was the impact, if any, on you? How did you react?
2. In your opinion, when racist or hate speech is used on campus, should it be ignored or dealt with formally? If you feel racist or hate speech should be banned from campus, do you think *all* such speech should be prohibited in *any* situation, or only in public forums? Explain your point of view.

CRAFT AND CONTENT

3. This piece is called an opinion editorial that allows the writer to offer an opinion or viewpoint on an issue. Summarize Delgado's opinion in this editorial. What is his position on hate speech and on campus speech codes, and why?
4. Delgado identifies several "cowardly" methods people use to promote hate speech. What are they? Why does Delgado feel such speech is cowardly? Does he object to the speech itself, or the method of delivery, or both?

CRITICAL THINKING

5. What reasons does Delgado offer for banning hate speech from campus and from general public discourse? Do you agree? Explain.
6. Do you think hate speech deserves First Amendment protection? If not, why? If so, can you think of any circumstances when hate speech should be protected? Explain.
7. Delgado observes that "hate speech is rarely an invitation to a conversation." Why do you think he makes this comment? To what free speech argument is he referring? Explain.

WRITING ABOUT THE ISSUES

8. Many legal scholars view restrictions on hate speech as a form of censorship and contrary to the democratic spirit of pluralism and tolerance. Write a paper in which you argue that hate speech should be protected if we are to remain a legitimate democracy.
9. Taking an opposing view expressed in the last assignment, write a paper in which you argue that hate speech should be banned. In your discussion, explain what types of hate speech should be banned, and why. How would bans on speech be enforced?

Free Speech Sucks! . . . But Censorship Sucks Even More

Denise Chaykun

Denise Chaykun is a senior at Bucknell University in Lewisburg, Pennsylvania. She is deputy editor of the *Counterweight,* a publication of the Bucknell Conservatives Club, where this editorial was published in the March 27, 2003, issue. She appeared on the cover of the May 25, 2003, issue of the *New York Times Magazine* with a section titled "The Young Hipublicans: What Campus Conservatives Learned from the 60's Generation" by John Colapinto, of Young America's Foundation.

CONNECTING TO THE TOPIC

In recent years, many colleges and universities across the nation have implemented rules and speech codes restricting or banning words and expressions that may prove hurtful, offensive, or insulting to others, especially to minority groups and women. Few people would argue that racist and sexist speech is good speech. But does that mean that such speech should be banned entirely? Who decides what constitutes offensive speech? Are speech codes restricting the free flow of ideas? In the next essay, a student attending a school with a speech code explains why she feels that restricting free speech is a bad idea.

WORDS IN CONTEXT

reprehensible: deserving rebuke or censure
partisan: devoted to or biased in support of a party, group, or cause, as in *partisan politics*
eradication: abolishment; elimination
abolitionist: one who advocates for the abolishment of slavery
audacity: boldness, unhindered by a sense of propriety or convention
status quo: the existing condition or state of affairs

1 Free speech can really suck sometimes. If not for the First Amendment, there are so many awful things that we would never have to bother with—like the absolutely reprehensible and downright wrong Ku Klux Klan. In this ideal world, we could outlaw all gatherings of the KKK. This elimination of speech doesn't have to be a partisan sort of thing, either. We could also choose to get rid of all speech that calls for the eradication of the white race and any kind of comment that really makes people feel uncomfortable—no more insults, no more criticizing each other's religions, none of this offensive speech business.

2 If only it were that easy. As logical as it may seem to get rid of certain kinds of speech, it's happened before and hasn't worked too well. Remember that Galileo guy? The one who said that the universe didn't revolve around the Earth? The things he said were really offensive—he totally rocked medieval people's world views. He was threatening Christian norms, and since they didn't have to deal with speech they didn't like, they could imprison him for life.

3 Something similar also happened with abolitionists before the Civil War. They had the audacity to say that black people were, well, people—not property. Again, this offensive speech didn't have to be tolerated—the South barred abolitionist material from the mail and Congress imposed the "gag rule." Since everyone was so sure that those crazy abolitionists were wrong, it was okay to make laws that kept them from helping black people succeed.

4 There were also rules sort of like that back in kindergarten—for example, "Don't be mean." Was it always wrong to insult someone? There was a kid in my kindergarten class who got in trouble for calling the class bully a butthead, for example. While that's never the best choice of words for a kindergartener, he was right, wasn't he?

5 Wouldn't you know that we even have some great rules and scenarios like that here? Like the kid who made fun of a dean on the AIM [AOL instant messenger] last year and got taken to the Community Judicial Board for it? That certainly wasn't nice of him. I think he hurt the dean's feelings. Thank goodness that we don't have the freedom to make fun of others, lest the administration's "AIM stalking" go to waste.

6 I think you get the point. Allowing free speech always sucks for someone. If free speech had been allowed in the cases I've mentioned, medieval people would have had to deal with the concept that maybe the universe didn't revolve around them, the South might have had to given up on slavery a bit sooner, the kindergarten bully would have had to hear the truth about himself, and the deans would have had to deal with students making fun of them on AIM. It would really suck to be them.

7 The tough part about this is that all of those restrictions were made with good intentions. Speech can hurt feelings, change the status quo, or even lead to changing someone's point of view. Sometimes these effects can be good, but not always.

8 With this in mind, how are we going to be able to make rules that keep these things from happening?

9 Well, for starters, the Supreme Court has put some pretty good limitations on free speech. According to the Supreme Court, there can be restrictions on "time, place, and manner"—when we speak, where we speak, and how we speak. So with these rules in mind we can all sleep peacefully in our dorms at night. Other than perhaps yelling "fire" (assuming there was one), yelling in a dorm hall at 3 a.m. is unacceptable. Three in the morning is an unacceptable time. A dorm hall is an unacceptable place. Yelling is an unacceptable manner. These rules can be applied to most sorts of extremely obnoxious behavior.

10 Harassment is another form of unprotected speech. As a legal matter, harassment is a behavior done to cause substantial emotional distress to someone. Sexual harassment, behavior that results in unreasonable interference with work performance or creates a severe and pervasively hostile environment, also fits into this category of unprotected speech.

11 So these are the legal restrictions on speech. I think they're pretty good. They make sense, but they don't restrict *what* you say. You can express any sort of idea as long as you do it in an acceptable manner.

12 We're still left with the fact that you can use speech to do all sorts of awful things to people. And because of this we're left with two options. We can accept that people are going to be mean and upset us

sometimes, or we can try to keep this from happening. While it would be great to keep this from happening in lots of cases, what about those times when those upsetting things are true? Based on history, it doesn't seem like anyone can objectively be sure that there is no worth in having a certain idea expressed.

13 Hey, my life would be a lot easier if Bucknell added conservatives to the group of people you can't insult. But then again, how am I sure I'm right? While it might be upsetting or annoying to get hate mail from readers, shouldn't you have the opportunity to try to convince me that I'm wrong? Maybe I am wrong, and if I am, I hope that someone can show me why I am. That's the fair and right thing to have the freedom to do.

14 So Bucknell has also been faced with the dilemma of whether to protect feelings or ideas and has chosen feelings. I can understand why. Feelings matter. But we're a university—we should be all about ideas. If we allow free speech, there's nothing saying that there can't be more speech that opposes whatever may have been offensive or hurtful. If we do this we then all have the opportunity to learn from each other.

15 So we have a choice: we can choose to protect feelings or ideas. Hurt feelings can be mended by ideas, but lost ideas might never be recovered. With this in mind, I propose that we protect ideas.

CONSIDERING THE ISSUES

1. Chaykun recalls rules that governed how students were allowed to speak to each other in grade school. Do you recall any speech codes or rules about acceptable speech from your childhood? Were any reasons given for why some words or phrases were unacceptable? How did you learn about "incorrect" speech?
2. In her essay, Chaykun observes that many opinions that are unpopular often turn out to be true. Can you think of any unpopular opinions that follow this principle? What made the opinions unpopular? How were people treated for expressing unpopular opinions? Have you ever expressed a viewpoint that opposed popular opinion? Explain.

CRAFT AND CONTENT

3. Chaykun cites four examples of how some individuals have had their free speech curtailed. List these examples and explain why

you think they are either effective or ineffective support for her argument.

4. Who is Chaykun's audience for this essay? In what ways does her writing reflect her expectations of her audience? Consider her use of language, tone, and style in your response.

CRITICAL THINKING

5. In her opening paragraph, Chaykun comments that the elimination of speech "doesn't have to be a partisan sort of thing, either." What does she mean? Who supports free speech and who encourages greater control?
6. In paragraph 12, Chaykun wonders if true statements should still be censured if they are upsetting. What do you think? Is it permissible in your opinion to say something harsh or upsetting if it is true? Who decides what is true or not? What about unpleasant opinions? Explain.
7. What restrictions are there on free speech that are not protected by the First Amendment? Chaykun feels that these restrictions are "pretty good" (paragraph 11). What do you think?

WRITING ABOUT THE ISSUES

8. In paragraph 13, Chaykun notes that her life would be a lot easier if her college "added conservatives to the group of people you can't insult." Most speech codes do not cite specific groups of people that are protected by them. What does Chaykun's statement imply about who we feel is protected by speech codes, and who is not? Is a racist or sexist remark worse than saying "conservatives are stupid" or "men are jerks"? Write a short essay exploring how speech codes protect certain groups of students more than others, and whether such protection is justifiable due to the nature of the offensive speech.
9. Chaykun argues that students have a choice—they can choose to protect feelings or ideas. In your own words, write a response to her statement, explaining what you would choose to protect—feelings or ideas—and why.

Difficult Conversations

Dorothy Rabinowitz

Dorothy Rabinowitz is an editorial writer for the *Wall Street Journal*, in which this editorial was printed on November 19, 2002.

CONNECTING TO THE TOPIC

The next two articles take a close look at a controversial and well-publicized call for a campus speech code at Harvard Law School in 2002. In November of 2002, following some racial incidents earlier that year on campus, the Black Law Students Association (BLSA) demanded that the administration come up with a "racial harassment policy." While the administration seemed to support the BLSA's requests, protests against violations of free speech were heard from campus and across the country. "Racial harassment" policies, it was argued, were merely another name for a campus speech code. Should Harvard Law School enforce a speech code? Or should all speech, even objectionable, hurtful speech, be protected under the First Amendment?

WORDS IN CONTEXT

travails: hard work, especially when involving painful effort
rigors: harsh or trying circumstances; hardships
discomfiting: uncomfortable
renowned: famous, well-known, or acclaimed
Socratic method: a teaching technique in which the instructor does not give information directly but instead asks a series of questions, with the result that the student comes either to the desired knowledge by answering the questions or to a deeper awareness of the limits of knowledge
emulate: to imitate
torrents: heavy, uncontrolled outpouring
pall: gloomy effect or atmosphere
empathy: identification with and understanding of another's situation, feelings, and motives
elude: escape understanding
determinative: acting as a determining factor

covenant: in law, agreement, contract, or suit to recover damages for violation of agreement or contract
pedagogic: pertaining to teaching or instruction methods
tort: in law, a civil suit for damage, injury, or willful wrongful acts not involving breach of contract
stigmatize: to mark with infamy or disgrace
implicit: implied or understood although not directly expressed

1 In 1973, film audiences were captivated by "The Paper Chase," a drama about the travails of a first-year student at Harvard Law School. His performance as the mercilessly demanding Professor Kingsfield secured an Oscar for John Houseman, led to a television series based on the film, and left Americans and a good part of the rest of the world with a vivid impression of the fearful intellectual rigors of life at Harvard Law.

2 Current Harvard Law students may have a hard time reconciling this picture with the realities of life at their school today, a time, after all, when a Kingsfield would surely face accusations that he had created a discomfiting learning environment for one group or another. Certain of the newer aspects of life and learning at Harvard Law would also have come as a surprise, to put it mildly, to its renowned longtime dean, the late Erwin Griswold.

3 "Look to the right of you, look to the left of you," the famously tough Griswold was known to advise first-year students: "One of you isn't going to be here by the end of the year." The students had entered a world—and this was still true as recently as the 1980s—in which intellectual rigor, skill in logic and harsh argumentation were prized. Harvard had pioneered the Socratic method of case studies emulated by all other law schools: a combative intellectual exercise requiring students to counter torrents of relentless questions designed to drive them into a corner, much like the kind the devilish Kingsfield asked. And much like those they might encounter from justices of an appellate court.

4 At Harvard Law today, skill in hard combative argument is no longer prized, nor even considered quite respectable. Indeed, first-year law students can hardly fail to notice the pall of official disapproval now settled over everything smacking of conflict and argument. That perception can only have been strengthened by a new program for freshmen called "Managing Difficult Conversations."

5 In the lesson books provided, students learn the importance of empathy. "Emotions need to be acknowledged and understood before people can problem solve," another lesson teaches. In a book by the program's chief creators we learn that "A Difficult Conversation Is Anything You Find It Hard to Talk About." Not the sort of wisdom that would have taxed the minds of the students. Still, the purpose of the three-hour sessions did elude one otherwise accepting attendee, who reports that the discussion leaders seemed to circle around specific issues, and that he had the feeling there was a real subject here not yet clear or acknowledged.

6 He was not the only one wondering about the substance of these meetings. The freshman had just gained entry to the most elite of the nation's law schools. For upward of $32,000 a year tuition, he could learn that a difficult conversation is anything a person finds hard to talk about, and that "logic/reason" has to be combined with "emotions and personal experience" in order to be persuasive. He would not have learned, at such a session, that all the negotiating strategies, all the emphases on emotion and personal history and subtext being advanced at these workshops, was exactly opposite of what legal training was supposed to teach. He would not learn here that the law deals in objective truth that it is concerned with fact. That what is said is determinative, not what is left unsaid, not subtexts, not emotions, expressed or other, not personal history.

7 The student's feeling that the sessions concerned more than the art of difficult conversations was correct. In March, a freshman summarizing a court decision on racial covenants had put his class notes on the Web, which included two references to "Nigs"—abbreviations that caused an uproar. The offender, a Filipino from Hawaii, apologized profusely. Another first-year law student weighed in next, this one from Poland. In an anonymous, extremely unpleasant e-mail, he claimed the right to use the N-word, in the interests of free speech. He, too, apologized.

8 The Harvard Black Law Students Association responded with declarations charging the Law School administrators with willful inaction in the face of "racial outrages." High on their list of perpetrators was senior law professor Charles Nesson, who had offered, as a kind of pedagogic exercise, a mock trial of the anonymous e-mailer, with himself as defense counsel. Arguing that this was an outrage even at a mock trial, the BLSA demanded that Mr. Nesson be barred from teaching mandatory first-year classes.

9 Professor David Rosenberg was similarly named as a perpetrator of racial outrages. "Marxists, feminists and the blacks had contributed nothing to torts," he is alleged to have told his class. From the context of the class discussion it was clear that the reference to "the blacks" was to the school of legal scholars, known as the Crits—critics whose viewpoints were based on radical black and feminist perspectives, who had, in Mr. Rosenberg's view, contributed nothing to tort law. This explanation was unacceptable to the BLSA, which demanded that he, too, be barred from teaching mandatory first-year classes, and that the administration publicly reprimand him (along with Mr. Nesson) in the Harvard Law Bulletin and the Harvard Crimson.

10 The answer from law school dean Robert Clark was a model of responsiveness. The Nesson course would be taught by an assistant dean—Mr. Nesson having volunteered, publicly, to remove himself. As for Mr. Rosenberg, his classes would be tape-recorded, so that students who felt he might insult them need not suffer the discomfort of sitting in his class.

11 Dean Clark next announced plans for a "Committee on Healthy Diversity," along with suggestions that a racial harassment policy might be enacted at the school. There was to be, in addition, "a responsive training program for incoming students and faculty." So did it happen that first-year Harvard law students found themselves in workshops on managing difficult conversations.

12 One senior member of the faculty marveled that the school was now training law students to stigmatize conflict. Just before his own class went off to attend the workshops, he slipped them all pieces of paper—these filled with quotes from Supreme Court justices' opinions holding that free speech is supposed to invite dispute.

13 Boston attorney Harvey Silverglate, who tracks assaults on free speech at universities, describes the workshops as "an exercise in thought reform disguised as an effort to help students improve their negotiation skills." Dean Todd Rakoff, the program's overseer, stands foursquare behind it, nonetheless. The students needed these skills for their careers, he argues. As to free speech, "We are absolutely in favor of uninhibited debate, in a workable fashion."

14 Why the school's administration yielded to the pressure to punish two senior professors charged with racism, one because of a misunderstanding of his meaning, another because of an attempt to turn an ugly episode into an educational one—instead of standing by them—remains

unexplained. Nor has anyone in that administration explained why, instead of a rational assessment of these hysterically inflated incidents, the school's dean was moved to give instant implicit assent to the strange notion that racism was running riot at Harvard Law. Both of these subjects would, of course, make for difficult conversations. ◆

CONSIDERING THE ISSUES

1. Have you ever felt uncomfortable in class or while participating in an online class newsgroup because of something a professor or student said? What were the circumstances and how did you react? If this has never happened, can you think of any circumstances that might make you feel uncomfortable in class? Explain.
2. Rabinowitz describes a program for incoming freshman law students called "Managing Difficult Conversations." Did you attend anything similar at your own freshman orientation? Does a class such as Rabinowitz describes sound like a good idea to you? Why or why not?

CRAFT AND CONTENT

3. Rabinowitz quotes dean Todd Rakoff, "We are absolutely in favor of uninhibited debate, in a workable fashion." Why do you think she chose this quote? What is Rakoff saying? In light of the disciplinary action of professors and students at Harvard Law School, is the administration encouraging uninhibited debate? Explain.
4. What is Rabinowitz's position on a campus speech code or harassment policy at Harvard Law School? Identify the sentence or sentences that reveal her opinion of this issue.

CRITICAL THINKING

5. In paragraph 4 of her editorial, Rabinowitz states that at Harvard Law School, it seems as if "skill in hard combative argument is no longer prized." Is her argument valid? Would a speech code,

in addition to rules curtailing free speech, harm students of the law when they face the real world? Explain.

6. In your opinion, did Harvard Law School dean Robert Clark overreact when confronted by the demands of the BLSA? Do you think the censure of professors Rosenberg and Nesson was fair? What about the students who started the episode? Explain your viewpoint.

WRITING ABOUT THE ISSUES

7. Rabinowitz expresses the concern that if professors fear upsetting students with controversial issues and sensitive topics, education as a whole will suffer. Explore this idea in your own words, based on your own experiences.
8. Review the incidents that led to the Black Law Students Association demands to the administration to create and enforce a campus racial harassment policy and speech code. (For more information on the BLSA's demands and the incidents leading up to it, review the archives of Harvard Law School's student newspaper, the *Record*, at www.hlrecord.org). Are the BLSA's demands reasonable? Or are they an infringement of free speech?

Censor This?

Austin W. Bramwell

Austin W. Bramwell is a graduate of Harvard Law School. This letter to his school newspaper was printed in November 2002, during the controversy described in the previous editorial by Dorothy Rabinowitz. Bramwell's writing has also appeared in the *National Review*.

CONNECTING TO THE TOPIC

In November 2002, during his third year at Harvard, Bramwell wrote this letter to the editor of the law school's student newspaper, the *Record*, expressing his concern over violations of First Amendment rights.

WORDS IN CONTEXT

hyperbolic: prone to exaggeration for effect
petty: unimportant; insignificant
contumely: insolent or arrogant remark or act
obloquy: condition of disgrace suffered as a result of vilification; ill repute
ostracism: banishment or exclusion from a group as the result of great disgrace
augment: to make something greater, as in size, extent, or quantity
univocally: speaking as one; having one voice or opinion
imprimatur: mark of official approval
presumption: act of assuming or accepting something as true
systemic: to or affecting the entire body or an entire organism

To the Editor:

Like many, I am concerned that a speech code would chill valuable speech on campus. In particular, I wonder whether Diversity Committee members would discipline the author of any of the following opinions:

1. Only the most hyperbolic imagination could believe that racism remains a problem at Harvard. Indeed, the threat of being called a racist does more to chill speech on campus than the use of racial slurs.

2. However uncouth the two racist incidents of last spring, most adults, to say nothing of aspiring attorneys, learn to withstand such petty contumely. Even if they can't, the incidents did not merit public demonstrations, months of campus angst, petitions, demands from the administration, and, now, a speech code.

3. The two students responsible for the racist incidents of last spring have already suffered public obloquy, ostracism, discipline from the administration, withdrawn job offers, and may have had their legal careers ruined. A regime which visits even more punishment upon others like them verges on cruelty.

4. The effect, if not the purpose, of "Diversity Fairs," "Ethnic Counselors," and other programs of "Sensitivity Training" is to augment racial differences and exacerbate racial tensions. If the administration really wanted to promote understanding between races, it would eliminate all such programs and add no more.

5. African-Americans at Harvard are far more likely to have their speech chilled by fellow African-Americans than anyone else, as the savage

treatment that Clarence Thomas receives attests. Given that groups like BLSA reinforce the assumption that African-Americans speak univocally, an administration serious about encouraging African-Americans to speak up would withdraw its imprimatur from BLSA and all other ethnic student groups.

6. African-Americans may very well feel disproportionately intimidated at Harvard Law School, but that is more likely a function of affirmative action, which creates a presumption that blacks on campus are less qualified, than systemic racism on campus.

7. BLSA's habit last spring of capitalizing the first letter of "black" in its literature has undeniably racialist overtones. Certainly no group could get away with calling whites "Whites."

I welcome any thoughts on which of the above opinions, if any, should be silenced. ◆

CONSIDERING THE ISSUES

1. Take a look at the letters to the editor in your own campus newspaper. What issues are discussed? Is writing a letter to the editor a good way to express your views to a large audience? Is it an effective forum for debate? Do you feel free to express yourself freely in your campus newspaper? Why or why not?
2. Bramwell notes that students do a good enough job themselves censuring and "ostracizing" individuals who make offensive, racist, and sexist comments. In light of his statement, do you think students are capable of handling racist/sexist speech on their own? How would you react to a racist remark expressed in class or in an online forum? How do you think students would react as a group? Explain.

CRAFT AND CONTENT

3. What is Bramwell's tone in his letter? Do you think he faced a risk in sending it? Explain.
4. Why do you think Bramwell chose to make his letter a list? Would the impact of his letter be lessened if he had chosen to express his opinion in paragraph form? Explain.
5. Consider the author's voice and use of language in this essay. What sense do you get of Bramwell as an individual? In a paragraph, try to characterize the author based on his writing. Take

into consideration his stand in the letter, his style and tone, and the concerns he cites to support his point of view.

CRITICAL THINKING

6. Bramwell makes some very controversial statements in his letter. Identify one or two of them that you feel are especially noteworthy, and write a response to them expressing your own viewpoint on each.
7. Evaluate Bramwell's points in his letter to the editor of the *Record*. How do his points address the current controversy at Harvard Law School?

WRITING ABOUT THE ISSUES

8. Pretend you are a student attending Harvard Law School. Write a letter to the *Record* in which you respond to Bramwell. You may choose either to refute or to support all or some of his points.
9. Did Bramwell's letter affect your own thinking about the subject of campus free speech and censorship? Write a short essay in which you discuss what influence, if any, his letter had on your opinions on this issue. If it did not influence you at all, explain why.

Policy Statement on Discriminatory Harassment

Emory University

CONNECTING TO THE TOPIC

Do colleges and universities have a moral obligation to protect free speech or ensure a peaceful, respectful learning environment for all students? Many schools have opted for the latter, and have come down hard on speech code offenders. One student at the University of Pennsylvania faced disciplinary action for calling a group of rowdy sorority sisters a bunch of "water buffalo." A student group at Gonzaga University had to fight against a letter going into its personal file for posting fliers that included "discriminatory" language announcing a book reading. The fliers used the word "hate"—part of the title of the speaker's book, *Why the Left Hates America.* Recently, the English department at Harvard University found itself in the awkward situation of having to postpone a poetry reading by an Irish poet because some faculty and students objected to his political views. The next item is a reprint of Emory University's policy statement on discriminatory harassment. In what ways is this statement, and others like it adopted by colleges and universities across the country, ambiguous? What does it protect? What does it censure?

WORDS IN CONTEXT

foreseeable: known beforehand
epithet: scornful, abusive, or condescending word or phrase
explicitly: expressed clearly
implicitly: implied
pretext: an excuse

Effective as of January 27, 2004

1 It is the policy of Emory University that all employees and students should be able to enjoy and work in an educational environment free from discriminatory harassment. Harassment of any person or group of persons on the basis of race, color, national origin, religion, sex, sexual orientation, age, disability, or veteran's status is a form of discrimination specifically prohibited in the Emory University community. Any employee, student, student organization, or person privileged to work or study in the Emory University community who violates this policy will be subject to disciplinary action up to and including permanent exclusion from the University.

2 Discriminatory harassment includes conduct (oral, written, graphic, or physical) directed against any person or group of persons because of race, color, national origin, religion, sex, sexual orientation, age, disability or veteran's status and that has the purpose or reasonably foreseeable effect of creating an offensive, demeaning, intimidating, or hostile environment for that person or group of persons. Such conduct includes, but is not limited to, objectionable epithets, demeaning depictions or treatment, and threatened or actual abuse or harm.

3 In addition, sexual harassment includes unwelcome sexual advances, requests for sexual favors, and other verbal or physical conduct of a sexual nature when:

- submission to such conduct is made either explicitly or implicitly a term or condition of an individual's employment or a student's status in a course, program, or activity.
- submission to or rejection of such conduct by an employee or student is used as the basis for employment or academic decisions affecting that employee or student.
- such conduct has the purpose or effect of unreasonably interfering with an employee's work performance or a student's academic performance or creating an intimidating, hostile, or offensive employment, educational, or living environment.

4 All University Vice Presidents, Deans, and Division and Department Chairpersons should take appropriate steps to disseminate this policy statement and inform employees and students of procedures for lodging complaints. All members of the student body, faculty, and staff are expected to assist in implementing this policy.

5 The scholarly, educational, or artistic content of any written, oral, or other presentation or inquiry shall not be limited by this Policy. It is the intent of this paragraph that academic freedom be allowed to all members of the academic community. Accordingly, this provision shall be liberally construed but shall not be used as a pretextual basis for violation of this Policy.

6 Any student or employee with a complaint of discriminatory harassment should contact the Vice President of Equal Opportunity Programs to obtain information on the procedure for handling such complaints. Any questions regarding either this policy statement or specific fact situation should be addressed to the Emory University Office of Equal Opportunity Programs. ◆

CONSIDERING THE ISSUES

1. Does your college or university have a speech code? Locate your student handbook and look up your school's policies on harassment.
2. Do you think censure is an effective way to prevent offensive speech? Does it stop such speech? Does stopping the speech stop the attitudes and opinions behind it, or is that not the issue? Why or why not?

CRAFT AND CONTENT

3. After reading this policy statement, do you understand it? Are there any areas that are confusing or difficult to read? If you were a student at Emory, would you know what language was considered unacceptable? Explain.
4. Who is bound by this policy statement? What would happen if someone violated it? Explain.

CRITICAL THINKING

5. Do harassment codes such as this one violate students' First Amendment rights? Why or why not?
6. Do you think Emory's policy is a good one? Explain why you agree or disagree with it, and why.

WRITING ABOUT THE ISSUES

7. Write a letter to the editor of your school newspaper advocating for restricted or unlimited speech on campus. In your letter, explain why you have adopted this position, and provide supporting material for your argument. How do you think your letter would be received by the student body at your school? Explain.

VISUAL CONNECTIONS

Silencing Free Speech

The *Counterweight* is a student-run, nonpartisan publication published by the Bucknell University Conservatives Club. It is "dedicated to promoting the free exchange of ideas in an environment where meaningful debate and ideological diversity are often lacking." It seeks to serve the Bucknell community by "infusing it with the ingredients necessary for a balanced educational experience . . . includ[ing] conservative, libertarian, and classical liberal thought." The *Counterweight* vowed to reprint Bucknell's speech code in every issue until "the administration does the right thing and eliminates it." As of the printing of this book, Bucknell's speech code is still in place.

CONNECTING TO THE TOPIC

Student-run newspapers and campus magazines often serve as the voice of the student body, or at least a segment of it. Take a look at some of your own campus newspapers and magazines. On what issues do they report? Do they promote a particular agenda or embrace a particular point of view? Do you think they are free to "promote the free exchange of ideas" or are they hampered by campus speech codes?

the
counterweight
the other half of your "balanced" education
Volume 3 Issue I
October 6, 2003
FREE SPEECH
You don't have it

CONSIDERING THE ISSUES

1. Consider how this photograph relays a message to the viewer. What can you determine about campus speech codes based upon what you see in the photo? What "shape" is the tape on the young woman's mouth? What does this symbol mean? What if the woman was gagged? Explain.
2. If you saw this magazine cover on your own campus newsletter or magazine, would you be led to read the article? Why or why not?

CRITICAL THINKING

3. How does this magazine cover make you feel, and why? Explore the implications of this photograph and the ways it is designed to elicit a response from the viewer.
4. Freedom of speech is a fundamental right that many Americans hold sacred. Does it surprise you that many college campuses restrict free speech? Explain.

TOPICAL CONNECTIONS

GROUP PROJECT

1. Imagine that you have been chosen as members of a student committee asked to draft a speech code for your university or college. As a group, draft such a code. Consider students' rights to free speech, what constitutes hate speech, and what limits can be placed on hate speech. Write a prologue to your code explaining and supporting its tenets.

WEB PROJECTS

2. Several authors in this chapter observe how some students are fighting speech codes on their campuses. Visit the Foundation for Individual Rights in Education, Inc. (FIRE) Web site at www.thefire.org/index.php and review the cases it is currently fighting. Select one case that you find particularly

compelling and state your own position on the issue. Research the issue as much as possible, reviewing student newspapers, any administrative commentary, and press received in local newspapers.

3. In a January 2003 article in *Boston* magazine, "The Thought Police," Harvey Silverglate states that the First Amendment should protect your right to say what you wish, but that you are not immune to what happens as a result of your speech. You may be subjected to anger, public shunning, and social pressure, but you should not be officially punished for your language. Write a response to Silverglate expressing your own opinion on this assessment of the First Amendment. You may review the article at *Boston* magazine's Web site at www.bostonmagazine.com.

FOR FURTHER INQUIRY

4. In 1996, Robert B. Chatelle, cochair of the Political Issues Committee National Writers Union, wrote a letter to Wesleyan University President Douglas Bennet to express concern about a Wesleyan student who had been suspended by the university's student judicial board for violating the Wesleyan speech code. Read Chatelle's argument at http://users.rcn.com/kyp/schools/bennet2.html. After determining for yourself both sides of the conflict, write your own views in an essay. Support yourself using information from the readings in this unit, as well as from your own personal experience.

5 Should Gay Marriage Be Legal?

The issue of gay marriage has been hotly argued as some states ban, and others begin to permit, same-sex marriage. The Commonwealth of Massachusetts made headlines at the end of 2003 when its highest court ruled 4 to 3 that same-sex marriage was permissible under its state constitution. Several years earlier, the state of Vermont raised conservative eyebrows when it legally endorsed same-sex civil unions.

Despite all the media coverage implying that many people support same-sex marriage, a December 2003 *New York Times* poll reported that 55 percent of Americans support an amendment to the U.S. Constitution mandating that marriage be between a man and a woman. Support for such an amendment includes people who are supportive of gay rights in general. And many religious leaders have openly declared that while they do not endorse discrimination against homosexuals, the institution of marriage is between a man and a woman—period.

Much of the debate hinges on how we define marriage—is it a partnership between two loving, consenting adults, or a sanctified or legal union between a man and a woman? Many arguments circle around the issue of love—if two people love each other, goes the argument, they should be allowed to marry. Opponents to this view contend that marriage is more than about love—it has traditionally been a legal and social bond between a man and a woman, foremost to support the upbringing of children. To redefine this definition of marriage would be to undermine the institution itself and threaten the American family. This chapter includes several different viewpoints on the issue of same-sex marriage and gay civil unions. Should couples of the same gender be legally allowed to marry? What problems and benefits might result?

CRITICAL THINKING

1. Who are the people in the cartoon? What topic are they discussing, and why?
2. What is the "joke" in this cartoon? How does it connect to the unit's theme on gay marriage? Explain.
3. On what is the man basing his argument? Can the viewer infer the comments the other man made? Explain.

The 'M-Word': Why It Matters to Me

Andrew Sullivan

Andrew Sullivan is a senior editor for the *New Republic*, a magazine of cultural and political opinion. He is gay, conservative, and a Roman Catholic. His 1996 book, *Virtually Normal: An Argument About Homosexuality*, argues that the best way to tackle antigay prejudice is to shape public laws and policies extending the same rights and protections to all U.S. citizens, regardless of sexual orientation. His latest book is *Love Undetectable: Notes on Friendship, Sex, and Survival* (1998). The essay reprinted here first appeared in the February 10, 2004, issue of *TIME* magazine.

CONNECTING TO THE TOPIC

The issue of homosexual marriage has been hotly argued in recent years, as some states ban and others begin to permit same-sex marriage. Supporters of gay marriage argue that it reduces sexual promiscuity, promotes stronger family units, is healthier for same-sex partners, and legitimizes relationships both socially and legally. Critics of homosexual marriage argue that marriage should be between a man and a woman, and permitting homosexual marriages would render marriage itself meaningless. Is marriage a bond between two loving adults who wish to make a lifelong commitment to each other, regardless of gender? Should it be legal for same-sex couples to marry? Is it a right?

WORDS IN CONTEXT

instill: to introduce by gradual, persistent efforts; implant
elude: to escape the understanding or grasp of
anathema: one who is cursed, loathed, or shunned
negation: the opposite or absence of something regarded as actual, positive, or affirmative
neurotic: prone to excessive anxiety and emotional upset
persevere: to remain constant to a purpose, idea, or task in the face of obstacles
atheist: one who disbelieves or denies the existence of God or gods
alleviate: to make (pain, for example) more bearable
euphemism: the substituting of a mild or vague term for one considered blunt or offensive

1 What's in a name?

2 Perhaps the best answer is a memory.

3 As a child, I had no idea what homosexuality was. I grew up in a traditional home—Catholic, conservative, middle class. Life was relatively simple: education, work, family. I was brought up to aim high in life, even though my parents hadn't gone to college. But one thing was instilled in me. What matters is not how far you go in life, how much money you make, how big a name you make for yourself. What really matters is family, and the love you have for one another. The most important day of your life was not graduation from college or your first day at work or a raise or even your first house. The most important day of your life was when you got married. It was on that day that all your friends and all your family got together to celebrate the most important thing in life: your happiness, your ability to make a new home, to form a new but connected family, to find love that puts everything else into perspective.

4 But as I grew older, I found that this was somehow not available to me. I didn't feel the things for girls that my peers did. All the emotions and social rituals and bonding of teenage heterosexual life eluded me. I didn't know why. No one explained it. My emotional bonds to other boys were one-sided; each time I felt myself falling in love, they sensed it, pushed it away. I didn't and couldn't blame them. I got along fine with my buds in a non-emotional context; but something was awry, something not right. I came to know almost instinctively that I would never be a part of my family the way my siblings one day might be. The love I had inside me was unmentionable, anathema—even, in the words of the Church I attended every Sunday, evil. I remember writing in my teenage journal one day: "I'm a professional human being. But what do I do in my private life?"

5 So, like many gay men of my generation, I retreated. I never discussed my real life. I couldn't date girls and so immersed myself in school-work, in the debate team, school plays, anything to give me an excuse not to confront reality. When I looked toward the years ahead, I couldn't see a future. There was just a void. Was I going to be alone my whole life? Would I ever have a "most important day" in my life? It seemed impossible, a negation, an undoing. To be a full part of my family I had to somehow not be me. So like many gay teens, I withdrew, became neurotic, depressed, at times close to suicidal. I shut myself in my room with my books, night after night,

while my peers developed the skills needed to form real relationships, and loves. In wounded pride, I even voiced a rejection of family and marriage. It was the only way I could explain my isolation.

6 It took years for me to realize that I was gay, years later to tell others, and more time yet to form any kind of stable emotional bond with another man. Because my sexuality had emerged in solitude—and without any link to the idea of an actual relationship—it was hard later to reconnect sex to love and self-esteem. It still is. But I persevered, each relationship slowly growing longer than the last, learning in my twenties and thirties what my straight friends found out in their teens. But even then, my parents and friends never asked the question they would have asked automatically if I were straight: so when are you going to get married? When is your relationship going to be public? When will we be able to celebrate it and affirm it and support it? In fact, no one—no one—has yet asked me that question.

7 When people talk about "gay marriage," they miss the point. This isn't about gay marriage. It's about marriage. It's about family. It's about love. It isn't about religion. It's about civil marriage licenses—available to atheists as well as believers. These family values are not options for a happy and stable life. They are necessities. Putting gay relationships in some other category—civil unions, domestic partnerships, civil partnerships, whatever—may alleviate real human needs, but, by their very euphemism, by their very separateness, they actually build a wall between gay people and their own families. They put back the barrier many of us have spent a lifetime trying to erase.

8 It's too late for me to undo my own past. But I want above everything else to remember a young kid out there who may even be reading this now. I want to let him know that he doesn't have to choose between himself and his family any more. I want him to know that his love has dignity, that he does indeed have a future as a full and equal part of the human race. Only marriage will do that. Only marriage can bring him home. ◆

CONSIDERING THE ISSUES

1. In your opinion, should same-sex couples be permitted to legally marry? When you heard about this issue, what was your first reaction? Are you likely to be swayed by hearing different points of view on the subject? Why or why not?

2. Why do people marry? What do they hope to gain by marriage? What does society expect from married couples as compared to unmarried couples?

CRAFT AND CONTENT

3. How does Sullivan's description of his childhood and his troubled adolescence reach out to his reader? Is his story likely to make his audience more sympathetic? To better understand his point of view? Explain.
4. What does Sullivan's title mean? How does it work with his essay's premise? Why does he call marriage "the M-word"?

CRITICAL THINKING

5. Sullivan says, "When people talk about 'gay marriage,' they miss the point. This isn't about gay marriage." What does he mean? If the issue isn't really "gay marriage," does it change the point of the argument?
6. According to Sullivan, why do homosexual couples want to marry—what motivates them? Do heterosexual couples marry for the same reasons as gay couples?

WRITING ABOUT THE ISSUES

7. Gay couples have been more prominent on television programs over the past few years. What images of gay life has television presented to its viewers? How do the images correspond to Sullivan's claims that many gay men and women just want what marriage affords—"social stability, anchors in relationships, and family and financial security"? Write an essay in which you explore the portrayal of gay relationships in the media, and how this portrayal may or may not influence public opinion on the issue of gay marriage.
8. Will legalizing gay marriage increase or decrease the problems involved in gaining the social acceptance gay men and women now encounter in America? What benefits might all gay people receive, whether or not they choose to marry? Do you think that a legal change in marriage will help to change the beliefs of people who now disapprove of homosexuality? Why or why not? Explain.

Same-Sex Marriage

Laurie Essig

Laurie Essig is a professor of sociology at Barnard College in New York. She is the author of *Queer in Russia* (1999). This essay was published in *Salon* magazine's "Mothers Who Think" section, July 10, 2000.

CONNECTING TO THE TOPIC

In the previous essay, Sullivan alludes to the 1999 Vermont ruling sanctioning same-sex civil unions. Civil unions grant legal spousal status to same-sex partners. Despite the media hype, not all gay couples want to get married, even if they were legally able to do so. In fact, quite a few are against the idea of marriage altogether. In the next piece, Laurie Essig wonders why a lesbian woman such as herself in a committed relationship would want to be bound by an institution that is "founded in historical, material, and cultural conditions that ensured women's oppression."

WORDS IN CONTEXT

subjunctive: of, relating to, or being a mood of a verb used for a hypothetical action, or action taking place in a person's mind rather than the external world

Industrial Revolution: the complex of broad socioeconomic changes in the late 18th century, marked by the shift of home-based hand manufacturing to large-scale factory production

Victorians: people who lived during the period of the reign of Queen Victoria of England, during the19th century

infuse: to fill

patriarchal: relating to a social system in which the man is the head of the family with authority over women and children

perversion: departure from what is right or good; inappropriate behavior

alliance: a close association formed to advance common interests or causes

devious: sneaky

promiscuous: having casual sexual relations frequently with different partners

conducive: tending to bring about or contribute to an effect

1 Lately straight relatives and friends have been calling to talk about Vermont and the fact that same-sex "unions" are now legal in that state. They can barely contain their excitement as they ask: "Aren't you just thrilled? You and Liza will go and get married, won't you?"

2 I hate to disappoint them. They so desperately want us to be just like they are, to aspire to nothing more nor less than legal recognition till death do us part. I couch my rejection in subjunctives: "It would be nice if we could be recognized as a family. If we were married, we would save thousands of dollars in insurance bills alone."

3 But the reality is that I don't want to marry Liza (nor she me). In fact, I'm against same-sex marriage for the same reasons I'm against all marriage.

4 Although we like to pretend that marriage is natural and universal, it is an institution founded in historical, material and cultural conditions that ensured women's oppression—and everyone's disappointment. Monogamous, heterosexual marriages were an invention of the Industrial Revolution's emerging middle class. The Victorians created the domestic sphere in which middle-class women's labor could be confined and unpaid. At the same time, by infusing the patriarchal family with the romance of monogamy for both parties, the Victorians reduced sexual pleasure to sexual reproduction. All other forms of sex—homosexuality, masturbation, non-reproductive sex—were strictly forbidden.

5 But in the American culture of the '00s, we like to be paid for our labor and we insist on indulging in our pleasures. That's why a truly monogamous and lifelong marriage today is as rare as a Jane Austen book that hasn't been made into a movie.

6 Now don't go getting your wedding dresses in a twist. I don't care if you're married, had a huge wedding, spent $15,000 on a useless dress and let your father "give you away." I really don't care what personal perversions people partake of in their quest for pleasure.

7 What annoys me is that no one, not even queers, can imagine anything other than marriage as a model for organizing our desires. In the past, we queers have had to beg, cheat, steal and lie in order to create our families. But it's exactly this lack of state and societal recognition that gave us the freedom to organize our lives according to desire rather than convention.

8 Lesbians and gay men have created alliances and households and children together. Lesbians have bought sperm and used it to

devious ends, gay men have explored sex as a public spectacle that is democratically available to all—and we have done this while forming intimate, lifelong allegiances with one another. And yes, many gays and lesbians, including me, have mimicked heterosexual marriage as best we could.

9 But why should those of us who have organized our lives in a way that looks a lot like heterosexual marriage be afforded special recognition by the government because of that? What about people who organize their lives in threes, or fours, or ones? What about my friend who is professionally promiscuous, who for ideological and psychological and sexual reasons has refused to ever be paired with anyone? What about my sister who is straight but has never in her 40-odd years seen a reason to participate in marriage? Which group will gain state recognition next? The polygamous? The lifelong celibate?

10 My point is not that we should do away with marriage but that we should do away with favoring some relationships over others with state recognition and privilege. Religions, not the state, should determine what is morally right and desirable in our personal lives. We can choose to be followers of those religions or thumb our noses at them. But the state has no place in my bedroom or family room, or in yours, either.

11 "Ah," but you say, "the state must recognize monogamous couples as more conducive to stable families and therefore better for children." Hello? Have you noticed that a huge number of marriages end in divorce? Even the supposedly "happy" ones aren't necessarily cheery little islands of serenity. What were your parents like?

12 There is absolutely no evidence that monogamous, state-sanctioned couplings are more stable than other sorts of arrangements. Even if there were such evidence, couples should be recognized by the state only when they decide to become parents. Why should anyone get societal privileges, let alone gifts, when he or she marries for the fourth time at age 68 with no intention of ever becoming a parent?

13 Still, as much as I hate to admit it, I am liberal at heart. If gays and lesbians want to get married, then I don't want to stop them. I just want to lay a couple of ground rules:

14 First, do not expect me to be happy. The legalization of gay marriage does not make me feel liberated as much as it makes me feel depressed. It's sort of like getting excited about gays in the military—until I remember that I don't really care about the military as an institution.

15 Second, under absolutely no circumstances should you expect me to give you a gift for such a decision. If you're insane enough to waste money on tacky clothes and bad cake, I'm not going to underwrite your actions with a toaster oven. ◆

CONSIDERING THE ISSUES

1. In addition to pointing out a high divorce rate, Essig states that even supposedly "happy" marriages are not "islands of serenity." What do we expect from marriage? How would you define a happy marriage? Do you expect it to be an "island of serenity"? Explain.
2. Essig observes that many marriages deemed "happy" ones were far from perfect. She asks readers to think about what their parents were like. Think about your parents' relationship. Were they married to each other while you were growing up? Single? Divorced and married to someone else? Did their relationship influence your view of marriage?

CRAFT AND CONTENT

3. Essig argues that the institution of marriage is far from "natural and universal." On these grounds, she objects to the institution itself. How does she defend her position? What proof does she offer that supports her stance? Explain.
4. Evaluate the author's tone in this essay. For example, what does Essig imply when she assures her audience that they may engage in any "personal perversions" they wish in paragraph 6? Does her tone engage or antagonize her audience? Explain.

CRITICAL THINKING

5. How does Essig field inquiries from her friends and family regarding the subject of marriage? Why doesn't she admit her feelings about marriage up front? Explain.
6. Essig argues, as have some other authors in this unit, that if homosexuals are granted the right to marry, other alternative lifestyle groups may soon demand legal recognition as well. Does this argument seem valid? Why or why not?

WRITING ABOUT THE ISSUES

7. In paragraph 10, Essig states that "religions, not the state, should determine what is morally right and desirable in our personal lives." Write an essay in which you agree or disagree with this position. Consider the broad implications of her statement in your response.
8. A year after she wrote this article, Laurie and Liza were joined in a civil union in Vermont—a decision completely motivated by the fact that they would be "saving thousands of dollars a year in health insurance bills" as a legally joined couple. Two years after their civil union, Laurie and Liza broke up. Read Laurie's description of "My Gay Divorce" in the September 2003 issue of *Legal Affairs* at www.legalaffairs.org/issues/September-October-2003/feature_essig_sepoct03.html. Write a short essay discussing Laurie's decision to undergo a civil union despite her objections described in her original essay. Does her "divorce" reinforce the points she makes in her first essay? Explain.

Gay Marriage—and Marriage

Sam Schulman

Sam Schulman is a New York writer and columnist for the *Jewish World Review.* His work has appeared in the *New York Press,* the *Spectator,* and *Commentary.* Formerly a professor of English at Boston University, he now serves as a publishing consultant to the Columbia University School of Journalism.

CONNECTING TO THE TOPIC

Many opponents of same-sex marriage believe that our culture must preserve the integrity of the marriage bond between a man and a woman. Marriage is, by definition and by essence, between a man and a woman. Anything else is something else. They also express concern that tampering with the institution of marriage will further weaken it. To alter marriage—to change its definition—will have severe social ramifications. The next essay takes a closer look at this perspective. Could gay marriage be harmful to women? To children? Is it even marriage?

WORDS IN CONTEXT

Antigone: in Greek mythology, Antigone performed funeral rites over her brother's body in defiance of her uncle Creon, the King of Thebes, saying that the ancient unwritten law that she perform a funeral rite for her brother was more important than a king's command
paradox: a seemingly contradictory statement that may nonetheless be true
deploy: to bring forth, release, especially for combat
utilitarian: relating to the ethical theory instructing that all action should achieve the greatest happiness for the greatest number of people
degradation: a decline to a lower condition, quality, or level
tangible: possible to treat as fact; real or concrete
liberal: favoring proposals for reform, open to new ideas for progress, and tolerant of the ideas and behavior of others; broad-minded
conservative: favoring traditional views and values; tending to oppose change
anarchic: lacking order and control
domesticate: to make fit for domestic (home) life; tame
promiscuity: the state of behavior involving casual sexual relations, frequently with different partners
delegitimize: to reverse a state or condition that follows established or accepted standards
queue: to line up
dossier: collection of papers about a person or subject
arbitrary: determined by chance, whim, or impulse and not by necessity or reason
incestuous: engaging in sexual relationships with close relatives
prospective: likely and expected to happen
hypothetical: uncertain; possible but unproven
polemics: art or practice of argumentation or controversy
fidelity: faithfulness
inherently: having as an essential characteristic
fallacy: incorrect reasoning or belief
banal: drearily commonplace
procreativity: production of offspring; reproduction
travesty: an imitation; a ridicule

burlesque: a mocking imitation
abridge: to cut short
felicity: happiness
concubinage: a harem; a woman or group of women kept without marriage

1 The feeling seems to be growing that gay marriage is inevitably coming our way in the U.S. Growing, too, is the sense of a shift in the climate of opinion. The American public seems to be in the process of changing its mind—not actually in favor of gay marriage, but toward a position of slightly revolted tolerance for the idea. With honorable exceptions, most of those who are passionately on the side of the traditional understanding of marriage appear to be at a loss for words to justify their passion; as for the rest, many seem to wish gay marriage had never been proposed in the first place, but also to have resigned themselves to whatever happens.

2 I think I understand why this is the case: as someone passionately and instinctively opposed to the idea of homosexual marriage, I have found myself disappointed by the arguments I have seen advanced against it. The strongest of these arguments predict measurable harm to the family and to our arrangements for the upbringing and well-being of children. I do not doubt the accuracy of those arguments. But they do not seem to get at the heart of the matter.

3 To me, what is at stake in this debate is not only the potential unhappiness of children, grave as that is; it is our ability to maintain the most basic components of our humanity. I believe, in fact, that we are at an "Antigone moment." Some of our fellow citizens wish to impose a radically new understanding upon laws and institutions that are both very old and fundamental to our organization as individuals and as a society. As Antigone said to Creon, we are being asked to tamper with "unwritten and unfailing laws, not of now, nor of yesterday; they always live, and no one knows their origin in time." I suspect, moreover, that everyone knows this is the case, and that, paradoxically, this very awareness of just how much is at stake is what may have induced, in defenders of those same "unwritten and unfailing laws," a kind of paralysis.

4 The case for gay marriage enjoys the decided advantage of appealing to our better moral natures as well as to our reason. It deploys two

arguments. The first centers on principles of justice and fairness and may be thought of as the civil-rights argument. The second is at once more personal and more utilitarian, emphasizing the degradation and unhappiness attendant upon the denial of gay marriage and, conversely, the human and social happiness that will flow from its legal establishment.

5 The civil-rights argument goes like this. Marriage is a legal state conferring real, tangible benefits on those who participate in it: specifically, tax breaks as well as other advantages when it comes to inheritance, property ownership, and employment benefits. But family law, since it limits marriage to heterosexual couples over the age of consent, clearly discriminates against a segment of the population. It is thus a matter of simple justice that, in Andrew Sullivan's words, "all public (as opposed to private) discrimination against homosexuals be ended and that every right and responsibility that heterosexuals enjoy as public citizens be extended to those who grow up and find themselves emotionally different."[1] The utilitarian argument is more subtle; just as the rights argument seems aimed mainly at liberals, this one seems mostly to have in mind the concerns of conservatives. In light of the disruptive, anarchic, violence-prone behavior of many homosexuals (the argument runs), why should we not encourage the formation of stable, long-term, monogamous relationships that will redound to the health of society as a whole?

6 The case is elegant, and it is compelling. But it is not unanswerable. And answers have indeed been forthcoming, even if many of them have tended to be couched somewhat defensively. Others, to be sure, attack the Sullivan line more forthrightly. In "What Is Wrong with Gay Marriage,"[2] Stanley Kurtz challenged the central contention that marriage would do for gay men what it does for straights—i.e., "domesticate" their natural male impulse to promiscuity. Kurtz wrote, "In contrast to moderates and 'conservatives' like Andrew Sullivan, who consistently play down [the] difference [between gays and straights] in order to promote their vision of gays as monogamists-in-the-making, radical gays have argued—more knowledgeably, more powerfully, and more vocally than any opponent of same-sex marriage would dare to do—that homosexuality, and particularly male homosexuality, is by its very nature incompatible with the norms of traditional monogamous marriage."

---

1. *Virtually Normal*, 1995
2. *Commentary*, September 2000, pp. 34–41

7 True, Kurtz went on, such radical gays nevertheless support same-sex marriage. But what motivates them is the hope of "eventually undoing the institution [of marriage] altogether," by delegitimizing age-old understandings of the family and thus (in the words of one such radical) "striking at the heart of the organization of Western culture and societies."

8 Nor are radical gays the only ones to entertain such destructive ambitions. Queuing up behind them, Kurtz warned, are the proponents of polygamy ready to argue that their threesomes, foursomes, and other "nontraditional" arrangements are entitled to the same rights as everyone else's. Kurtz is almost certainly correct as to political and legal realities. If we grant rights to one group because they have demanded it—which is, practically, how legalized gay marriage will come to pass—we will find it exceedingly awkward to deny similar rights to others ready with their own dossiers of "victimization." In time, restricting marriage rights to couples, whether straight or gay, can be made to seem no less arbitrary than the practice of restricting marriage rights to one man and one woman. Ultimately, the same must go for even incestuous relationships between consenting adults.

9 A different defense of heterosexual marriage has proceeded by circling the wagons around the institution itself. According to this school of thought, ably represented by the columnist Maggie Gallagher, the essential purpose of that institution is to create stable families. "Most men and women are powerfully drawn to perform a sexual act that can and does generate life," she writes. "Marriage is our attempt to reconcile and harmonize the erotic, social, sexual, and financial needs of men and women with the needs of their partner and their children."[3]

10 Human relationships are by nature difficult enough, Gallagher reminds us, which is why communities must do all they can to strengthen and not to weaken those institutions that keep us up to a mark we may not be able to achieve through our own efforts. For Gallagher, the modest request of gay-marriage advocates for "a place at the table" is thus profoundly selfish as well as utterly destructive—for gay marriage "would require society at large to gut marriage of its central presumptions about family in order to accommodate a few adults' desires."

11 Why do such arguments fail to satisfy? Partly, no doubt, it is because the damage they describe is largely prospective and to that degree

---

3. The *Weekly Standard*, August 4, 2003

hypothetical; and partly, the defensive tone that invariably enters into these polemics may rob them of the force they would otherwise have.

12 To grasp what stands to be undone by gay marriage—we have to distinguish marriage itself from a variety of other goods and values with which it is regularly associated by its defenders and its aspirants alike. Those values—love and monogamous sex and establishing a home, fidelity, childbearing and childrearing, stability, inheritance, tax breaks, and all the rest—are not the same as marriage. True, a good marriage generally contains them, a bad marriage is generally deficient in them, and in law, religion, and custom, even under the strictest of moral regimes, their absence can be grounds for ending the union. But the essence of marriage resides elsewhere, and those who seek to arrange a kind of marriage for the inherently unmarriageable are looking for those things in the wrong place.

13 The largest fallacy of all arises from the emphasis on romantic love. But what exactly does love have to do with marriage, which can follow, precede, or remain wholly independent of that condition? Many people—in ages past, certainly most people—have married for reasons other than sexual or romantic attraction. So what? I could marry a woman I did not love, a woman I did not feel sexually attracted to or want to sleep with, and our marriage would still be a marriage, not just legally but in its essence.

14 The truth is banal, circular, but finally unavoidable: by definition, the essence of marriage is to sanction and solemnize that connection of opposites which alone creates new life. (Whether or not a given married couple does in fact create new life is immaterial.) Men and women can marry only because they belong to different, opposite, sexes. In marriage, they surrender those separate and different sexual allegiances, coming together to form a new entity. Their union is not a formalizing of romantic love but represents a certain idea—a construction, an abstract thought—about how best to formalize the human condition. This thought, embodied in a promise or a contract, is what holds marriage together, and the creation of this idea of marriage marks a key moment in the history of human development.

15 Marriage can only concern my connection to a woman (and not to a man) because marriage is an institution that is built around female sexuality and female procreativity. (The very word "marriage" comes from the Latin word for mother, mater.) It exists for the gathering-in of a woman's sexuality under the protective net of the human or divine

order, or both. This was so in the past and it is so even now, in our supposedly liberated times, when a woman who is in a sexual relationship without being married is, and is perceived to be, in a different state of being (not just a different legal state) from a woman who is married.

16 Because marriage is an arrangement built around female sexuality, women will be the victims of its destruction. And with the success of the gay-liberation movement, it is women themselves, all women, who will be hurt. The reason is that gay marriage takes something that belongs essentially to women, is crucial to their very freedom, and empties it of meaning. In a gay marriage, one of two men must play the woman, or one of two women must play the man. "Play" here means travesty—burlesque. Not that their love is a travesty; but their participation in a ceremony that apes the marriage bond, with all that goes into it, is a travesty.

17 Why should I not be able to marry a man? The question addresses a class of human phenomena that can be described in sentences but nonetheless cannot be. However much I might wish to, I cannot be a father to a pebble—I cannot be a brother to a puppy—I cannot make my horse my consul. Just so, I cannot, and should not be able to, marry a man. If I want to be a brother to a puppy, are you abridging my rights by not permitting it? I may say what I please; saying it does not mean that it can be.

18 What of simple compassion? What do we owe to our fellow-beings who wish, as they might put it, to achieve a happiness they see we are entitled to but which we deny to them? From those of us who oppose gay marriage, Andrew Sullivan demands some "reference to gay people's lives or relationships or needs." But the truth is that many people have many needs that are not provided for by law, by government, or by society at large—and for good reason.

19 Insofar as I care for my homosexual friend as a friend, I am required to say to him that, if a lifelong monogamous relationship is what you want, I wish you that felicity, just as I hope you would wish me the same. But insofar as our lives as citizens are concerned, or even as human beings, your monogamy and the durability of your relationship are, to be blunt about it, matters of complete indifference.

20 That is not because you are gay. It is because, in choosing to conduct your life as you have every right to do, you have stepped out of the area of shared social concern—in the same sense as has anyone, of whatever sexuality, who chooses not to marry. There are millions of lonely people, of whom it is safe to say that the majority are in heterosexual

marriages. But marriage, though it may help meet the needs of the lonely, does not exist because it is an answer to those needs; it is an arrangement that has to do with empowering women to avoid even greater unhappiness, and with sustaining the future history of the species.

21 Marriage is what connects us with our nature and with our animal origins, with how all of us, heterosexual and homosexual alike, came to be. It exists not because of custom, or because of a conspiracy (whether patriarchal or matriarchal), but because, through marriage, the world exists. Marriage is how we are connected backward in time, through the generations, to our Creator (or, if you insist, to the primal soup), and forward to the future beyond the scope of our own lifespan. It is, to say the least, bigger than two hearts beating as one.

22 Severing this connection by defining it out of existence—cutting it down to size, transforming it into a mere contract between chums—sunders the natural laws that prevent concubinage and incest. Unless we resist, we will find ourselves entering on the path to the abolition of the human. The gods move very fast when they bring ruin on misguided men. ◆

CONSIDERING THE ISSUES

1. Schulman warns that to change marriage to include same-sex unions would be to severely undermine the institution itself. Consider your own definition of marriage. How, if at all, does gay marriage fit into your definition?
2. Schulman quotes Maggie Gallagher's statement that sanctioning homosexual marriage "would require society at large to gut marriage of its central presumptions about family in order to accommodate a few adults' desires." In your own words, identify what you think society's "central presumptions about family" are in regard to marriage.

CRAFT AND CONTENT

3. Schulman quotes advocates for and against the issue of same-sex marriage. Does quoting his opposition, such as Andrew Sullivan, undermine or support his argument? Explain.
4. What assumptions does Schulman make about his audience? Their background? Educational level? Religious affiliation? Explain.

CRITICAL READING

5. According to Schulman, why have the arguments against same-sex marriage fallen short? Explain.
6. Schulman identifies two primary arguments made in support of gay marriage. What are they? Identify and summarize them in your own words.
7. Schulman states in paragraph 17 that while we may use words to argue the issue of gay marriage, at the argument's core, it is an impossibility. He can no more be a brother to a puppy than a man can marry another man. What does Schulman mean? Explain.

WRITING ABOUT THE ISSUES

8. Schulman notes that the two primary arguments in support of gay marriage are the civil-rights argument and the utilitarian argument. Select one of these arguments and write a short essay expressing your own point of view on the issue. Refer to points made by Schulman and other authors in your response.
9. Most of the arguments supporting gay marriage note that gay couples are in committed loving relationships and wish to legitimize their relationships with a marriage license. Can you think of other, less idealistic reasons why people marry? Based on these other reasons, including the practical and the shady, could these reasons undermine the movement legalizing homosexual marriage? For example, what if two female heterosexual friends, one employed, the other not, wished to marry for health insurance? Could such alliances be avoided if same-sex marriage were legal? Explain.

Marriage Devalued

Dan Wasserman

Dan Wasserman is a *Boston Globe* staff editorial cartoonist. His cartoons run several times a week in that newspaper. Wasserman's cartoons are also frequently featured in national publications, including *TIME*. He is the author of *We've Been Framed* (1987), a collection covering President Ronald Reagan's two terms in office.

CONNECTING TO THE TOPIC

Massachusetts' highest court ruled in a 4-3 decision in November 2003 that the state's ban on same-sex marriage was unconstitutional, stating, "We declare that barring an individual from the protections, benefits and obligations of civil marriage solely because that person would marry a person of the same sex violates the Massachusetts Constitution." Massachusetts Governor Mitt Romney responded to the ruling by stating, "Marriage is an institution between a man and a woman. I will support an amendment to the Massachusetts Constitution that makes that expressly clear. Of course, we must provide basic civil rights and appropriate benefits to nontraditional couples, but marriage is a special institution that should be reserved for a man and a woman." A few days before the ruling, during the much-publicized debate, the *Boston Globe* ran this editorial cartoon by Dan Wasserman on November 3, 2003.

CRITICAL THINKING

1. Consider Wasserman's cartoon. How are the subjects presented? How does Wasserman portray each character through clothing, manner, words, and typeface?
2. How do you think Sullivan, Kinsley, and Schulman would each respond to this cartoon? Explain.
3. What is the political stance of the cartoonist? What argument is he making in this cartoon? How compelling is his argument, and why?
4. What is the "joke" in this cartoon? What do you need to know in order to understand the joke? Explain.

Abolish Marriage

Michael Kinsley

Michael Kinsley is the founding editor of *Slate*, an online magazine published by Microsoft Corporation. He is also a contributing writer for *TIME* magazine. Kinsley has served in an editorial capacity for several prominent journals, including the *New Republic*, the *Washington Monthly*, and the *Economist*. His writing has appeared in the *New Yorker*, *Vanity Fair*, *Condé Nast Traveler*, and other publications. This editorial appeared in his *Slate* editorial column on July 2, 2003.

CONNECTING TO THE TOPIC

The 2003 Supreme Court decision of Lawrence v. Texas invalidated state anti-sodomy laws, effectively removing the government from interfering with people's sexual choices made in the privacy of their own homes. It was this decision that sparked the flurry of lawsuits advocating for homosexual marriages. In an earlier piece, Andrew Sullivan argued that marriage is a basic human right. On the opposing side of this argument is the dispute that same-sex unions are not natural or moral. Michael Kinsley wonders why, if the government has been kicked out of the bedroom, they are still involved with sanctioning marriage on a legal level at all. He argues that marriage can be whatever it wants to be, for whoever wants it. That would stop all the furor over gay marriage—or would it?

WORDS IN CONTEXT

invalidate: to make something not legally valid
anti-sodomy laws: laws forbidding certain forms of sexual intercourse
dissent: disagreement, as of opinion or belief
mutually: in equal agreement; reciprocal
endorse: to give approval of or support to, especially by public statement or action; sanction
render: to cause to become; make
inexplicable: difficult or impossible to explain or account for
ritualistic: routine; repeated in the same way with little change
Kabuki: popular Japanese drama using stylized movements, dances, and songs
monopoly: a group or entity having exclusive control over an activity
privatize: to change from governmental or public ownership or control to private enterprise
implicate: to involve
bureaucracy: the administrative structure of a large or complex organization
irrelevant: unrelated to the matter being considered
sanction: authoritative permission or approval that makes a course of action valid
amorphous: lacking definite form; shapeless; undefined

1 Critics and enthusiasts of Lawrence v. Texas, [the] Supreme Court decision invalidating state anti-sodomy laws, agreed on one thing: The next argument would be about gay marriage. As Justice Scalia noted in his tart dissent, it followed from the logic of Lawrence. Mutually consenting sex with the person of your choice in the privacy of your own home is now a basic right of American citizenship under the Constitution. This does not mean that the government must supply it or guarantee it. But the government cannot forbid it, and the government also should not discriminate against you for choosing to exercise a basic right of citizenship. Offering an institution as important as marriage to male-female couples only is exactly this kind of discrimination. Or so the gay rights movement argues. Persuasively, I think.

2 Opponents of gay rights may resist mightily, although they have been in retreat for a couple of decades. General anti-gay sentiments are now considered a serious breach of civic etiquette, even in anti-gay circles. The current line of defense, which probably won't hold either, is

between social toleration of homosexuals and social approval of homosexuality. Or between accepting the reality that people are gay, even accepting that gays are people, and endorsing something called "the gay agenda." Gay marriage, opponents argue, crosses this line. It renders homosexuality respectable and, worse, normal. Gays are welcome to exist all they want, and to do their inexplicable thing if they must, but they shouldn't expect a government stamp of approval.

3 It's going to get ugly. And then it's going to get boring. So, we have two options here. We can add gay marriage to the short list of controversies—abortion, affirmative action, the death penalty—that are so frozen and ritualistic that debates about them are more like Kabuki performances than intellectual exercises. Or we can think outside the box. There is a solution that ought to satisfy both camps and may not be a bad idea even apart from the gay-marriage controversy.

4 That solution is to end the institution of marriage. Or rather (he hastens to clarify, Dear) the solution is to end the institution of government-sanctioned marriage. Or, framed to appeal to conservatives: End the government monopoly on marriage. Wait, I've got it: Privatize marriage. These slogans all mean the same thing. Let churches and other religious institutions continue to offer marriage ceremonies. Let department stores and casinos get into the act if they want. Let each organization decide for itself what kinds of couples it wants to offer marriage to. Let couples celebrate their union in any way they choose and consider themselves married whenever they want. Let others be free to consider them not married, under rules these others may prefer. And, yes, if three people want to get married, or one person wants to marry herself, and someone else wants to conduct a ceremony and declare them married, let 'em. If you and your government aren't implicated, what do you care?

5 In fact, there is nothing to stop any of this from happening now. And a lot of it does happen. But only certain marriages get certified by the government. So, in the United States we are about to find ourselves in a strange situation where the principal demand of a liberation movement is to be included in the red tape of a government bureaucracy. Having just gotten state governments out of their bedrooms, gays now want these governments back in. Meanwhile, social-conservative anti-gays, many of them Southerners, are calling on the government in Washington to trample states' rights and nationalize the rules of marriage, if necessary, to prevent gays from getting what they want. The Senate Majority Leader, Bill Frist of Tennessee,

responded to the Supreme Court's Lawrence decision by endorsing a constitutional amendment, no less, against gay marriage.

6 If marriage were an entirely private affair, all the disputes over gay marriage would become irrelevant. Gay marriage would not have the official sanction of government, but neither would straight marriage. There would be official equality between the two, which is the essence of what gays want and are entitled to. And if the other side is sincere in saying that its concern is not what people do in private, but government endorsement of a gay "lifestyle" or "agenda," that problem goes away, too.

7 Yes, yes, marriage is about more than sleeping arrangements. There are children, there are finances, there are spousal job benefits like health insurance and pensions. In all these areas, marriage is used as a substitute for other factors that are harder to measure, such as financial dependence or devotion to offspring. It would be possible to write rules that measure the real factors at stake and leave marriage out of the matter. Regarding children and finances, people can set their own rules, as many already do. None of this would be easy. Marriage functions as what lawyers call a "bright line," which saves the trouble of trying to measure a lot of amorphous factors. You're either married or you're not. Once marriage itself becomes amorphous, who-gets-the-kids and who-gets-health-care become trickier questions.

8 So, sure, there are some legitimate objections to the idea of privatizing marriage. But they don't add up to a fatal objection. Especially when you consider that the alternative is arguing about gay marriage until death do us part.

CONSIDERING THE ISSUES

1. Is marriage, in your opinion, a private affair between individuals and their social and religious preferences, or a public issue that must be sanctioned by state and federal government? Or both? Explain your point of view.
2. Kinsley notes in paragraph 2 that in most social circles, "general anti-gay sentiments are now considered a serious breach of etiquette, even in anti-gay circles." What does Kinsley mean? Do you agree? Does current "social etiquette" influence what you say and how you express your feelings about homosexuality or the issue of gay marriage? Is this trend a positive or negative one? Explain.

CRAFT AND CONTENT

3. What is Kinsley's tone in this piece? Identify some specific phrases or words that serve as examples of his tone and style.
4. Kinsley observes that the debates over abortion, affirmative action, and the death penalty have become more like "Kabuki performances" rather than intellectual exercises. What image does his comparison generate? How are these arguments like "Kabuki"?
5. In paragraph 2, Kinsley puts quotation marks around the words "the gay agenda." What does putting quotes around words or phrases tell the reader about those words? Explain.

CRITICAL THINKING

6. What was Lawrence v. Texas about? Why was gay marriage the natural "next argument" to follow the Supreme Court's decision in Lawrence v. Texas? Explain.
7. Kinsley advocates for the privatization of marriage. How do you think each side of the gay marriage argument would respond to his idea? Explain.

WRITING ABOUT THE ISSUES

8. Write a letter to a minister, rabbi, or other religious leader. Explain why you think he or she should agree to perform a marriage ceremony celebrating the commitment of two close friends—a gay couple. Alternatively, you may write a letter arguing against such a marriage. Assume that you care about your friends, and know that your opinions may cause them pain, but that you still must advise against such a union.
9. In this essay, Kinsley argues that marriage should be a religious or moral undertaking, separate from the state. Making this distinction, he reasons, will settle the issue over legalizing gay marriage. If the government has nothing to formally recognize in the first place, the argument is null. Write an essay in which you agree or disagree, either in whole or in part, with Kinsley, expressing your own point of view. Respond directly to the points he makes in his article.

VISUAL CONNECTIONS

God-Ordained Marriage?

CONNECTING TO THE TOPIC

One argument against gay marriage is that it goes against the biblical definition of marriage as a union between a man and a woman. This photo features young Hawken Runquist as he joins his family members during a rally against the legalization of gay marriage on February 14, 2004, in front of the Clinton County Courthouse in Clinton, Iowa.

CONSIDERING THE ISSUES

1. What is the "God-Ordained" definition of marriage? Does your religious background influence your opinion of the gay-marriage issue? Explain.
2. Have you ever taken part in a protest for a cause you believed in? If so, what was the cause and what was your role in the protest? In your opinion, is the participation of a young child, as in the photo, an effective way to protest this particular issue? Why or why not?

CRITICAL THINKING

3. What argument does the child's sign present against gay marriage? Is this a valid argument on this issue? How might opponents respond to the claim the sign makes?
4. Is it likely that the child in the photo is responsible for the sign's content? Do you think it is an appropriate sign for the child to hold? What can you determine about the child based upon what you see in this photo? Explain.

TOPICAL CONNECTIONS

GROUP PROJECT

1. Should marriage be a political and public institution, or a religious and moral one? Or both? Working in groups of at least four people, list the qualities that marriage draws from each of these areas. After your group has developed a list, divide in half and debate the issue—one side arguing that marriage is a public and legal institution, the other a private or moral one. As debate continues, try to reach a common ground in which both sides agree on certain points. Write down the areas of agreement for a larger class discussion.

WEB PROJECTS

2. In 2001, the Netherlands became the first country in the world to allow same-sex couples to marry. Research the issue of same-sex marriage in the Netherlands at the Dutch Ministry of Justice Web site at www.justitie.nl/english/publications/factsheets/same-sex_marriages.asp and www.justitie.nl/english/Themes/family_law/ index.asp. Based on your Web research, draw connections between the Dutch policy on same-sex marriage and the controversy in the United States. Would the Dutch policy work in the United States? Why or why not?
3. The project above takes a closer look at same-sex marriage in the Netherlands, the first country in the world to legalize gay marriage. Use the Internet to investigate this issue in other countries that are passing laws supporting same-sex unions, such as Canada, Sweden, and England. Or research a country that forbids it.

FOR FURTHER INQUIRY

4. Laurie Essig feels that marriage is an outdated institution that doesn't appropriately fit modern life. Other writers fear that same-sex marriage will "further harm" the already weakened institution of marriage. Does marriage have a place in 21st-century life? Research this issue and present your own point of view.
5. If you could live together with a partner and enjoy the same benefits afforded to married couples, such as health and property insurance, inheritance rights, and retirement benefits, would you still get married? Create a questionnaire on the issue of marriage and living together. Develop between 10 and 12 questions designed to gather information on people's opinions about marriage, living together before marriage, and nonmarried partnerships. Include questions that address the issue of gay marriage. Give the test to at least 20 people (try to survey a wide demographic). In a short essay summarizing your results, write about whether popular opinion believes living together without marriage is better, or worse, than marriage itself. Do your results reveal a shift in social mores?

6 Can Racial Profiling Be Justified?

As a nation of immigrants, the United States comprises many races, ethnic traditions, religions, and languages. Under a common political and legal system, we agree that we have the right to life, liberty, and the pursuit of happiness. Many of us take pride in our differences—what makes us unique from one another. That is what makes America so special. But difference can pose challenges as well. Stereotyping—generalized assumptions about groups of people based on characteristics such as race, ethnic origin, social class, religion, gender, or physical appearance—may marginalize some groups and even persecute them because of their ethnic background. When ethnic stereotyping is used as a law enforcement tool, it is called *racial profiling*.

Racial profiling in the United States began with the first Puritan settlers, who practiced a form of it in their relationships with Native Americans. Each new immigrant group to arrive on America's shores—Irish, Italian, Chinese, German—experienced some form of racial profiling, usually at the hands of the groups that came before them. As America became more ethnically blended, the profiling of some groups decreased and even disappeared. But racial profiling in America remains an issue of controversy and debate for many ethnic groups. The readings in this chapter address the controversy surrounding racial profiling—most specifically of African Americans and, after September 11, individuals who look like they could be from the Middle East.

CRITICAL THINKING

1. What is the man holding? What is the relevance of this object to the message of the cartoon? What must the viewer know about the situation and even the object in order to understand the statement the cartoon is trying to make?
2. Who is depicted in the cartoon? What visual clues does the cartoonist use to identify the person in the cartoon? What visual props are used?
3. What is happening in this cartoon? What issue is being addressed? What do you think is the cartoonist's position on this particular issue? Explain.

Blind Spot

Randall Kennedy

Randall Kennedy is a professor at Harvard Law School, where he teaches courses on the freedom of expression and the regulation of race relations. He is the author of several books, including *Race, Crime, and the Law* (1998), for which he won the 1998 Robert F. Kennedy Book Award. His articles have appeared in many journals, newspapers, and magazines, including the *Nation*, the *New Republic*, and the *American Prospect*. This commentary first appeared in the April 2002 issue of the *Atlantic*.

CONNECTING TO THE TOPIC

Racial profiling is law enforcement's use of race to assess the likelihood of certain types of criminal behavior. Based on statistical assumptions, racial profiling presumes that certain groups of people are more likely to commit—or not to commit—certain crimes. The U.S. Supreme Court has officially upheld the constitutionality of this practice, as long as race is only one of several factors leading to the detainment or arrest of an individual. But while racial profiling may seem to be based on statistics, and may even make police work more efficient, does that mean it is right?

WORDS IN CONTEXT

obfuscate: to cloud or blur
proponent: supporter
scrutiny: examination
unassailable: undeniable; indisputable
presumptive: founded on probability
illicit: not sanctioned by custom or law; unlawful
rigorous: strict; hard
empirical: verifiable or provable by means of observation or experiment
speculative: given to conjecture; supposed
rhetoric: the language of a particular subject
affirmative action: a policy or a program that seeks to correct past discrimination through measures to ensure equal opportunity, as in education and employment

trumpet: to sound or proclaim loudly
fanatical: motivated by excessive, irrational zeal
subordinating: making less important

1 What is one to think about "racial profiling"? Confusion abounds about what the term even means. It should be defined as the policy or practice of using race as a factor in selecting whom to place under special surveillance: if police officers at an airport decide to search Passenger A because he is twenty-five to forty years old, bought a first-class ticket with cash, is flying cross-country, and is apparently of Arab ancestry, Passenger A has been subjected to racial profiling. But officials often prefer to define racial profiling as being based solely on race; and in doing so they are often seeking to preserve their authority to act against a person partly on the basis of race. Civil-rights activists, too, often define racial profiling as solely race-based; but their aim is to arouse their followers and to portray law-enforcement officials in as menacing a light as possible.

2 The problem with defining racial profiling in the narrow manner of these strange bedfellows is that doing so obfuscates the real issue confronting Americans. Exceedingly few police officers, airport screeners, or other authorities charged with the task of foiling or apprehending criminals act solely on the basis of race. Many, however, act on the basis of intuition, using race along with other indicators (sex, age, patterns of past conduct) as a guide. The difficult question, then, is not whether the authorities ought to be allowed to act against individuals on the basis of race alone; almost everyone would disapprove of that. The difficult question is whether they ought to be allowed to use race at all in schemes of surveillance. If, indeed, it is used, the action amounts to racial discrimination. The extent of the discrimination may be relatively small when race is only one factor among many, but even a little racial discrimination should require lots of justification.

3 The key argument in favor of racial profiling, essentially, is that taking race into account enables the authorities to screen carefully and at less expense those sectors of the population that are more likely than others to contain the criminals for whom officials are searching. Proponents of this theory stress that resources for surveillance are scarce, that the dangers to be avoided are grave, and that reducing these dangers helps

everyone—including, sometimes especially, those in the groups subjected to special scrutiny. Proponents also assert that it makes good sense to consider whiteness if the search is for Ku Klux Klan assassins, blackness if the search is for drug couriers in certain locales, and Arab nationality or ethnicity if the search is for agents of al Qaeda.

4 Some commentators embrace this position as if it were unassailable, but under U.S. law racial discrimination backed by state power is presumptively illicit. This means that supporters of racial profiling carry a heavy burden of persuasion. Opponents rightly argue, however, that not much rigorous empirical proof supports the idea of racial profiling as an effective tool of law enforcement. Opponents rightly contend, also, that alternatives to racial profiling have not been much studied or pursued. Stressing that racial profiling generates clear harm (for example, the fear, resentment, and alienation felt by innocent people in the profiled group), opponents of racial profiling sensibly question whether compromising our hard-earned principle of antidiscrimination is worth merely speculative gains in overall security.

5 A notable feature of this conflict is that champions of each position frequently embrace rhetoric, attitudes, and value systems that are completely at odds with those they adopt when confronting another controversial instance of racial discrimination—namely, affirmative action. Vocal supporters of racial profiling who trumpet the urgency of communal needs when discussing law enforcement all of a sudden become fanatical individualists when condemning affirmative action in college admissions and the labor market. Supporters of profiling, who are willing to impose what amounts to a racial tax on profiled groups, denounce as betrayals of "color blindness" programs that require racial diversity. A similar turnabout can be seen on the part of many of those who support affirmative action. Impatient with talk of communal needs in assessing racial profiling, they very often have no difficulty with subordinating the interests of individual white candidates to the purported good of the whole. Opposed to race consciousness in policing, they demand race consciousness in deciding whom to admit to college or select for a job.

6 The racial-profiling controversy—like the conflict over affirmative action—will not end soon. For one thing, in both cases many of the contestants are animated by decent but contending sentiments. Although exasperating, this is actually good for our society; and it would be even better if participants in the debates acknowledged the simple truth that their adversaries have something useful to say. ◆

CONSIDERING THE ISSUES

1. We have all heard of racial profiling, but what does it mean to you? Is it something you have experienced yourself? Have you, or has anyone you know, been subjected to a situation in which you were singled out because of how you looked? Explain.
2. Do you think racial profiling has contributed to distrust among certain groups of people against the police? How might such distrust impact law enforcement overall? Explain.

CRAFT AND CONTENT

3. Summarize Kennedy's argument and conclusion into one paragraph. You may wish to identify his key points in each paragraph before developing your summary.
4. Kennedy notes in paragraph 5 that supporters of racial profiling are willing to impose a "racial tax" on profiled groups. What does he mean by racial tax? Explain.

CRITICAL THINKING

5. What is "racial profiling"? What challenges do we face in trying to define it?
6. How can racial profiling work counter to the aims of law enforcement, both in the community and in the courtroom?

WRITING ABOUT THE ISSUES

7. Kennedy notes that while racial profiling is wrong, so is affirmative action, which he claims is just another form of profiling. If we are to be truly "colorblind," he argues, we must be so universally. What do you think? Does he make a valid point? Write an essay summarizing your opinion on both racial profiling and affirmative action, and then explain why you believe they are either similar or different.
8. Young people often complain that they are watched more closely in stores (shoplifting) or while driving (inexperienced operators) or while hanging out in groups (gang activity) than other people simply because of their age and the way they look. Consider the

validity of other kinds of profiling, based on criteria such as age, gender, income, profession, and fashion. What criminal assumptions might accompany different groups of people? If racial profiling is wrong, as Kennedy contends, is it also wrong to profile people based on other criteria? Why or why not?

What Looks Like Profiling Might Just Be Good Policing

Heather Mac Donald

Heather Mac Donald is a fellow at the Manhattan Institute and the author of *The Burden of Bad Ideas: How Modern Intellectuals Misshape Our Society* (2000) and *Are Cops Racist? How the War Against the Police Harms Black Americans* (2003). This article first appeared in the *Los Angeles Times* on January 19, 2003.

CONNECTING TO THE TOPIC

Despite media hype implying the contrary, on a national level, we have actually witnessed a decline in crime over the last decade. During this same period, however, tension and mistrust between the police and urban communities where crime is at its worst has risen, especially in issues connected to race. But are police racially profiling people in certain communities, or are they merely responding to where the crime is? If a witness claims that a Latino man robbed a bank, should police stop men who are obviously not Latino in their efforts to find the robber? If they do stop Latino men who fit the description, are they racially profiling him? In the next piece, Heather Mac Donald wonders if the outcry against racial profiling will make the job of the police even harder.

WORDS IN CONTEXT

perennial: recurrent; repeating
ipso facto: by the fact itself; by that very fact
contextual: pertaining to circumstances in which an event occurs
benchmark: to measure

disparity: difference; inequality
compounding: additional; collective
arbitrarily: by whim or impulse, and not by necessity or reason
contraband: illegal or stolen items
predominate: to be of or have greater quantity
prevalence: wide or common existence
antagonize: to incur the dislike of; to provoke hostility
endemic: common in or peculiar to a particular region or people
bigotry: state of being prejudiced against or intolerant of other groups

1 Los Angeles' perennial critics of the cops are going to have to decide: Do they want policing that mirrors the demographics of the city or goes after criminals? They cannot have it both ways.

2 Recently released data compiled by the Los Angeles Police Department as part of a federal consent decree show that the city's officers are more likely to ask black and Latino drivers to step out of their cars after stopping them than their white counterparts. Once out of their cars, members of these minorities are more likely to be patted down or searched. Ipso facto, say the critics, L.A. cops discriminate against minorities.

3 Not so fast. To the charge that the police have "too many" law enforcement interactions with minorities, the question must always be: "Too many" compared to what? To compare stop, search and arrest data to demographics, as cop critics would have us do, is absurd. The police don't formulate their crime strategies based on census findings; they go where the crime is.

4 What's more, an officer's decision to ask a person to step out of a car or to search that person is triggered by behavioral and contextual cues—nervousness, threatening behavior, resemblance to a suspect, absence of a license and car registration, tinted windows, among others—that are not even remotely captured by demographics.

5 To benchmark police activity, one must start, at a bare minimum, with the rate of lawbreaking among various groups, for it is ultimately criminal behavior and its consequences that drive police actions. Any disparities in crime rates will have compounding effects throughout the law enforcement system.

6 For example, last year a man with a gold tooth was robbing and viciously beating up pedestrians in Mid-City. Victims identified him as either a dark-skinned Latino or a light-skinned African American.

Accordingly, if an officer made a traffic stop in the area and noticed that the driver had a gold tooth and was black or Latino, the driver probably would have been asked to step out of his car, frisked and possibly even taken to the station house for a line-up. Some 15 men were stopped before a bike officer caught the actual criminal jaywalking.

7 Those 15 brief detentions went into the LAPD database, but the racial disparities they suggest are misleading. If criminal activity is not evenly distributed across the population, investigatory stops and searches will fall heaviest on individuals who are members of groups who commit most of the crime.

8 In Los Angeles, crime rates are in fact lopsided. In 2001, blacks committed 41% of all robberies, according to victims' descriptions given to the LAPD, though they constitute only 11% of the city's population. Robbery victims named whites, who make up 30% of the population, 4% of the time, while Latinos, 46% of the population, were identified as the assailant in 45% of such crimes. The figures for aggravated assault and rape are similarly skewed. Only if the police searching for the gold-toothed robber had arbitrarily stopped some whites could they have avoided contributing to racially disproportionate data.

9 Multiply this problem tens of thousands of times, and you will understand why police data look as they do. Furthermore, if criminals are disproportionately black and Latino, so will be parolees and probationers. Police can search parolees and probationers after stopping them to make sure that they are complying with the terms of their release and not carrying contraband. Without doubt, a portion of the searches in the LAPD data represents multiple encounters with this particular population, though the data are too crude to identify how large it is.

10 And where is criminal activity taking place? Nearly half of all homicides in 2001 occurred in South-Central, and slightly more than half of them were gang-related, according to the Police Department. It stands to reason that homicide investigators will spend a disproportionate amount of time there, where African Americans and Latinos predominate. It is not racism that sends them there; it is the incidence of crime. Would cop bashers prefer that officers investigating a murder on Western Avenue go to Brentwood for the sake of racial balance?

11 Once in South-Central, the police will probably look for homicide suspects among gang members. If a cop spots a driver flashing gang signs after running a red light, the man will probably be asked to step out of his car when stopped and, if exhibiting suspicious behavior, frisked. Police

investigating a murder spree by the Aryan Brotherhood in the Foothill Division would do the same if they spotted a white driver behaving similarly.

12 Rates of lawbreaking are just the start of what's needed to analyze police activity. Many other details—including patterns of police deployment, relative number of young people in various populations, locations of high-profile crimes and prevalence of illegal immigrants lacking driver's licenses—are also important.

13 The reemergence of racial-profiling charges following the release of the LAPD data could not have come at a worse moment for the city. The many law-abiding residents in crime-plagued neighborhoods are crying out for protection from the escalating violence. Go to any police-community meeting in a crime-ridden area and the most frequent complaint you will hear is "Why aren't there more cops getting dealers and gangbangers off the streets?" rather than "Why are you profiling us?"

14 Sure, some L.A. officers antagonize civilians with their unnecessarily aggressive attitudes, and the department must teach them communications skills and courtesy. But that is a far different problem than endemic officer racism.

15 Still, if critics keep accusing officers of bigotry for trying in good faith to do their jobs, it will be all the harder for them to fight crime. ◆

CONSIDERING THE ISSUES

1. Have you ever been pulled over by a police officer for a traffic violation? What was the experience like? If not, what would you expect to happen, and how do you think you would react?
2. What expectations and assumptions do we have in how we should be treated by others? How do we react when our expectations are not met? Should such considerations be taken into account when reviewing issues connected to racial profiling? Why or why not?

CRAFT AND CONTENT

3. Evaluate the evidence Mac Donald uses to support her argument. First, identify facts, statements, and observations she offers as proof to support her argument. Then assess how compelling this proof is in supporting her point.
4. What does Mac Donald mean in her opening paragraph that critics of the cops "cannot have it both ways"? Explain.

CRITICAL THINKING

5. Mac Donald notes in her opening comments that Los Angeles' "critics" of the cops may be drawing false conclusions from the LAPD data. Who do you think these critics are? Based on her essay, can you tell?
6. In paragraph 8, Mac Donald cites statistical data on criminal activity based on race. Review this paragraph. Based on the information in this paragraph alone, what conclusions might you draw from it? Do these conclusions change when considered in the larger context of the issue of racial profiling? Why or why not?

WRITING ABOUT THE ISSUES

7. In your opinion, if statistical evidence proved that certain racial groups were indeed more likely to engage in criminal activities in certain areas, do you think racial profiling is justifiable? Why or why not? Explain your point of view.
8. How do you think Kennedy and Mac Donald would respond to Alton Fitzgerald White's experience described later in this chapter? Based on the essays of these three people, and drawing from their specific statements, create a fictitious debate between Kennedy and Mac Donald, using White's arrest as the subject for the debate. Was White the object of racial profiling? Was his only offense having the "wrong face"?

Are You a Terrorist, or Do You Play One on TV?

Laura Fokkena

Laura Fokkena's writing has been published in a variety of newspapers and magazines in the United States and the Middle East, including *HipMama* and *Home Education Magazine*. This essay first appeared in the November 2002 edition of *PopPolitics*.

CONNECTING TO THE TOPIC

Sometimes stereotypes can be more than simply insulting, they can interfere with the daily lives of the people victimized by them. As Laura Fokkena observes in the next essay, Hollywood has long cast people from the Middle East as terrorists. This stereotype wasn't helped by the tragic events of September 11. The perpetuation of the Arab-as-terrorist stereotype has caused Fokkena, who is American, and her husband, who is Egyptian, to face the scrutiny of airport security, to be kept off flights, and to be eyed with suspicion merely because he resembles the same ethnicity as the Muslim extremists who committed acts of terrorism. As Fokkena explains, for some people, racial profiling—on the street or on the screen—is nothing new.

WORDS IN CONTEXT

baritone: a deep voice, between a bass and a tenor
unadulterated: pure
mammoth: enormous; huge
decry: to openly condemn
savvy: shrewd understanding
eradicate: to remove; to erase
albeit: although
mediocre: of inferior quality
nuance: degree of difference
incommunicado: unreachable; unable to communicate
egregious: markedly offensive or insulting
subordinating: rendering less important
purported: professed
affirm: to declare true
marginalized: relegated to the edge; not part of the mainstream
impromptu: unplanned

1 Several years ago I came home from work one night to find my Egyptian husband and his Jordanian friend up past midnight watching *Aladdin.* Our daughter—then a toddler and the rightful owner of the video—had gone to bed hours earlier and left the two of them to enjoy their own private cultural studies seminar in our living room.

2 "Oh, God, now the sultan's marrying her off!" cried Jordanian Friend. "It's barbaric, but hey, it's home," quipped my husband, repeating lyrics from the film while rolling his r's in a baritone imitation of an accent he's never had.

3 I admit it: I purchased Disney crap. In my own defense, I try to avoid all strains of happily-ever-after princess stories. But, other than a few grainy videos that you can order from, say, Syria, *Aladdin* is one of the rare movies with an Arab heroine available for the 2-to-6-year-old set. And so I had taken my chances with it.

4 My husband preferred to tell my daughter bedtime stories taken straight out of *1,001 Nights*, before they'd been contorted at the hands of Hollywood. (Tales of Ali Baba's clever servant Morghana are far more feminist than the big screen version of *Aladdin* ever was.) For my daughter's sake, I think this is wonderful. But it's also disappointing to see yet another example of unadulterated Middle Eastern literature trapped in Middle Eastern communities, told in whispers to children at bedtime, while the world at large is bombarded with a mammoth distorted Hollywood version replete with hook-nosed villains, limping camels, a manic genie and Jasmine's sultan dad who is (of course) a sexist.

5 While Native Americans, Asian Americans and numerous other ethnic groups have had significant success in battling racist and inaccurate media images of their communities, Muslims and Middle Easterners are just beginning to decry stereotypical portrayals of Arabs and Islam. In April, following another crisis in the West Bank, Edward Said wrote a short piece, published in both the American and Arab press, stressing the importance of media savvy. "We have simply never learned the importance of systematically organizing our political work in this country on a mass level, so that for instance the average American will not immediately think of 'terrorism' when the word 'Palestinian' is pronounced."

6 After Sept. 11, an astonishing number of films and television programs were cancelled, delayed or taken out of production due to unfortunate coincidences between their violent plotlines and, well, reality. It went without saying that all this mad scrambling was for the benefit of a nation momentarily unwilling to see the fun in shoot-em-up action adventures, and that it was not—at least in the case of movies with Middle Eastern characters—indicative of a sudden dose of sensitivity towards anti-Arab stereotyping.

7 But apparently Hollywood has either declared the grieving period over, or has decided that what we need most right now are more escapist

fantasies of Americans kicking the asses of aliens and foreigners. A number of films initially pushed back have since been released (some, like *Black Hawk Down* and *Behind Enemy Lines* were actually moved up), and television series that were hastily rewritten to eradicate any terrorist references have now been rewritten again, this time to highlight them.

8 This first became obvious back in March 2002, when CBS was bold enough to broadcast *Executive Decision* (albeit opposite the Oscars). *Executive Decision*, originally released in 1996, is a mediocre thriller that depicts Muslim terrorists hijacking a 747 en route to Washington, D.C. Like most films in its genre, wild-eyed Arabs are foiled by the technological, intellectual and ultimately moral superiority of Americans.

9 *Executive Decision* has since appeared repeatedly on various cable networks, along with *True Lies* (1994), *The Siege* (1998) and *Not Without My Daughter* [1991]. NBC's *The West Wing* has written a fictional Arab country into its plotline (and assassinated its defense minister); *Law and Order* opened this year's season with the story of an American convert to Islam who murders a women's rights activist. Islam is treated with varying degrees of nuance in each of these works, but it is always approached as a dilemma to be overcome—one always needs to do something about these troublesome Muslims—rather than folded unproblematically into the background, the way Josh and Toby's Judaism is presented on *The West Wing*, or the way Betty Mahmoody's Christianity is portrayed in *Not Without My Daughter*.

10 According to a recently released report from Human Rights Watch, the federal government received reports of 481 anti-Muslim hate crimes in 2001, 17 times the number it received the year before. It also noted that more than 2,000 cases of harassment were reported to Arab and Muslim organizations. The Bush administration and the Department of Justice have responded on the one hand by condemning hate crimes against the Muslim and Middle Eastern community, and on the other by rounding up Muslims and Middle Easterners for questioning. Most notoriously, the FBI and Justice Department announced last fall their intent to schedule "interviews" with 5,000 men of Arab descent between the ages of 18 and 33. More than 1,000 men were detained indefinitely and incommunicado in the aftermath of Sept. 11, most of them on minor visa charges.

11 Yet racial profiling and ethnic stereotyping are nothing new to Americans of Middle Eastern descent. Hollywood has long used images of bumbling, accented Arabs and Iranians as shorthand for "vile enemy," depicting them as stupid (witness the terrorist lackey in *True*

Lies who forgets to put batteries in his camera when making a video to release to the press), yet nevertheless deeply threatening to all that is good and right with America. So ingrained is the image of Arab-as-terrorist that Ray Hanania, an Arab-American satirist, titled his autobiography *I'm Glad I Look Like a Terrorist* ("almost every TV or Hollywood Arab terrorist looks like some uncle or aunt or cousin of mine. The scene where Fred Dryer [of TV's *Hunter*] pounces on a gaggle of terrorists in the movie *Death Before Dishonor* [1987] looks like an assault on a Hanania family reunion").

12 Nowhere is this game of Pin The Bomb Threat On The Muslim more obvious than at the airport. A few years ago I flew out of Cairo with my husband and discovered that F.W.A. (Flying While Arab) is no joke. We landed in Paris with a crying baby and were ushered to the back of the line while the airline attendants processed every other passenger. My husband was unconcerned; he was used to the routine. But I was acutely aware of two things: 1) that the baby was on her last diaper; and 2) that diaper was feeling heavy.

13 Our turn finally came a good three hours later, whereupon we spent another 45 minutes having our carry-on luggage examined and re-examined, answering the same questions again and again, and waiting while security checked and re-checked their computer database. All this over a graduate student from Egypt, married to an American citizen, during a time when world politics were calm enough that Bill Clinton's main preoccupation was rubbing lipstick smudges off his fly.

14 As it happened, most of the French airline workers were on strike that week (imagine that!) so we were sent to an airport hotel for the night and told we could take our connecting flight to D.C. the next day. While the other Americans and Europeans on our flight took the opportunity to spend a free night in Paris, my husband was instructed not to leave the hotel. I suppose the baby and I could have taken our crisp blue passports and gone into the city without him, but the thought of taking advantage of my American citizenship—something I'd just been born into by chance, mind you—while he stayed behind watching bad French television in the hotel lounge was too much to take.

15 Of course, it would be a mistake to assume that the most egregious offenses of racial profiling take place at the airport. The Council on American-Islamic Relations reports that half of the discrimination complaints it received in 2001 were work-related, and there has been a leap in the number of outright hate crimes, including at least three murders, since Sept. 11.

16 The *Atlantic Monthly* featured an essay by Randall Kennedy, a Harvard law professor [in which he] compared racial profiling to its "alter ego," affirmative action. "Supporters of profiling, who are willing to impose what amounts to a racial tax on profiled groups, denounce as betrayals of 'color blindness' programs that require racial diversity," he wrote. "A similar turnabout can be seen on the part of many of those who support affirmative action. Impatient with talk of communal needs in assessing racial profiling, they very often have no difficulty with subordinating the interests of individual white candidates to the purported good of the whole."

17 Kennedy's piece reaches no conclusions—other than to affirm the need for the debate in the first place—but I see no contradiction here. When workers are paid unequally for doing equivalent work, union organizers naturally argue that all workers should be paid what the highest-earning worker is paid, a process called "leveling up." Both the opposition to racial profiling and the support of affirmative action are about leveling up.

18 In both cases, marginalized groups who have suffered from stereotyping and injustice are asking to be considered full-fledged participants in our culture, to be given the same benefit of the doubt that white people have been given for centuries. Membership has its privileges, including job promotions, tenure, the ability to speed in a school zone and get off with a warning, and impromptu nights in Paris cafés. Whether one considers these things rights or luxuries, they are the aspects of citizenship that make one feel both accepted in and loyal to one's community and culture.

19 Some, like Ann Coulter—a columnist so out of touch even *The National Review* fired her—call those who complain about such matters "crazy," "paranoid," "immature nuts" and (my favorite) "ticking time bombs." Though most people would find her language over-the-top, there are many people who agree with the sentiment: that an increase in security, even if it means engaging in racial profiling, is a necessary evil in these dark times.

20 Lori Hope, in a "My Turn" column published in *Newsweek* last spring, worried that in alerting a flight attendant of a suspicious-looking traveler ("He was olive-skinned, black-haired and clean-shaven, with a blanket covering his legs and feet"), she might have "ruined an innocent man's day" when the man was removed from the flight. Nevertheless, she said, "I'm not sure I regret it . . . it's not the same world it was half a lifetime ago."

21 And for her, it probably isn't. But for the thousands of people who have been falsely associated with a handful of extremists for no reason

other than their ancestry or their religion, for those who have been targeted not for their crimes but for color of their skin, not a whole lot has changed.

22 The assumption in all these discussions is that getting kicked off a plane is merely a hassle. Granted, no one should be hassled because of their race or ethnicity, but c'mon, be reasonable. This is just a little annoyance we're talking about, the way watching the mad professor getting chased around by psychotic Libyans in *Back to the Future* is "fun," "just a joke," you know, like someone in blackface. National security is the real issue. Anyone who can't see that must have something to hide.

23 But those who argue that it's an inevitable necessity should look to countries like Egypt, where racial and religious profiling as a manner of combating Islamic extremism is obviously unworkable. Ethnic stereotyping, whether by Hollywood or by the FBI, solidifies the wedge between what we call "mainstream" culture and those who are perceived to be on the outside of it. "Ruining an innocent man's day" isn't the point, just as the hassle of moving to a different seat on the bus wasn't the point for Rosa Parks. Didn't we hammer all this out 40 years ago? ◆

CONSIDERING THE ISSUES

1. Fokkena notes that immediately following the attacks, many movie studios delayed the release of violent films, especially ones featuring Arabs as the bad guys. In light of the events of September 11, what new obstacles do Arab Americans face in dispelling the film stereotype Fokkena describes?
2. Think about your own family's sense of ethnic or racial identity. What are the origins of some of your family's values, traditions, and customs? Have these customs ever been questioned by people who did not understand them? What assumptions do you think other people may have about your family?

CRAFT AND CONTENT

3. Evaluate Fokkena's connection between racial profiling and affirmative action. In what ways are they similar, and how are they different.
4. What does Fokkena allude to in her final sentence? Why does she end her essay with this reference?

CRITICAL THINKING

5. In what ways has Hollywood promoted the stereotype of Arabs as terrorists? What do you think of this stereotype? Is it art imitating life? Is it unfair? Explain.
6. In paragraph 20, Fokkena refers to an essay written by Lori Hope that appeared in *Newsweek*. Read about the Lawyers Committee for Civil Rights suit www.lccr.com/khan.doc against the airline that ejected a passenger from the flight on the recommendation of another passenger. Do you think Hope was correct in voicing her concerns? What about the airline? Explain.

WRITING ABOUT THE ISSUES

7. Fokkena opens her essay with a reference to Disney's *Aladdin*, a movie she purchases because it featured an Arab heroine. Consider the ways Hollywood influences our cultural perspectives of race and ethnicity. Write an essay exploring the influence, however slight, film and television has had on your own perception of race. If you wish, interview other students for their opinions on this issue and address some of their observations in your essay.
8. Fokkena comments that Ann Coulter was a columnist "so out of touch even the *National Review* fired her." Read her controversial column at www.townhall.com/opinion/columns/anncoulter/2001/09/14/160244.html. Respond to her column in your own words.

Ragtime, My Time

Alton Fitzgerald White

Alton Fitzgerald White is an actor best known for his performances in the Broadway plays *Smokey Joe's Café* and *Ragtime*, in which he played the starring role of Coalhouse Walker Jr. He performed for former president, Bill Clinton and his wife, Senator Hillary Rodham Clinton. He has released two CDs, *How Do I Feel* and *Ecstasis*, and has written a book of poetry, *Uncovering the Heart Light*. This article was first published in the October 11, 1999, issue of the *Nation*.

CONNECTING TO THE TOPIC

As Americans, we are raised to believe in the values of justice and freedom. We believe that we are entitled to certain rights, opportunities, and protections as citizens. But what happens when we feel our rights have been violated by the very system supposed to uphold them? As this personal account by a young Broadway actor attests, the damage can be deep, undermining not only our feelings of justice, but our entire perspective of how we fit into society.

WORDS IN CONTEXT

naïve: innocent, unsuspecting of harm
ovation: enthusiastic, prolonged applause

1 As the youngest of five girls and two boys growing up in Cincinnati, Ohio, I was raised to believe that if I worked hard, was a good person and always told the truth, the world would be my oyster. I was taught to be courteous and polite. I was raised a gentleman and learned that these fine qualities would bring me one very important, hard-earned human quality: Respect!

2 While respect is indeed something one has to earn, consideration is something owed to every human being, even total strangers. On Friday, June 16, 1999, when I was wrongfully arrested while trying to leave my building in Harlem, my perception of everything I had learned as a young man was forever changed—not only because of the fact that I wasn't given even a second to use any of the wonderful manners and skills my parents had taught me as a child, but mostly because the police, who I'd always naïvely thought were supposed to serve and protect me, were actually hunting me.

3 I had planned the day to be a pleasant one. The night before was not only payday but also I received a rousing standing ovation after portraying the starring role of Coalhouse Walker Jr. in *Ragtime* on Broadway. It is a role I've worked very hard for professionally, and emotionally as well. A role that requires not only talent but also an honest emotional investment, including the morals and lessons I learned as a child.

4 Coalhouse Walker Jr. is a victim (an often misused word but in this case the true definition) of overt racism. His story is every black man's nightmare. He is hard-working, successful, talented, charismatic, friendly and polite. Perfect prey for someone with authority and

not even a fraction of those qualities. The fictional character I portrayed on Thursday night became a part of my reality on Friday afternoon. Nothing in the world could have prepared me for it. Nothing I had seen on television. Not even stories told to me by other black men who had suffered similar injustices.

5 Most Fridays for me mean a trip to the bank, errands, the gym, dinner and then to the theater. On this particular day, I decided to break my usual pattern of getting up and running right out of the house. Instead, I took my time, slowed down my pace and splurged by making myself some homemade strawberry pancakes. It was a way of spoiling myself in preparation for my demanding, upcoming four-show weekend. Before I knew it, it was 2:45, and my bank closes at 3:30, leaving me less than forty-five minutes to get to midtown on the train. I was pressed for time but in a relaxed, blessed state of mind. When I walked through the lobby of my building, I noticed two light-skinned Hispanic men I'd never seen before. Not thinking much of it, I continued on to the vestibule, which is separated from the lobby by a locked door.

6 As I approached the exit, I saw people in uniforms rushing toward the door. I sped up to open it for them, especially after noticing that the first of them was a woman. My first thought was that they were paramedics, seeing as many of the building's occupants are retired and/or elderly. It wasn't until I had opened the door and greeted the woman that I recognized that they were the police. Within seconds I was told to "hold it" because they had received a call about young Hispanics with guns. I was told to get against the wall. I was searched, stripped of my backpack (which was searched repeatedly), put on my knees, handcuffed and told to be quiet when I tried to ask any questions.

7 With me were three other innocent black men. They had been on their way to their U-Haul, parked on the side of the building. They were moving into the apartment beneath me and were still glowing from the tour I'd given them of the beautiful historic landmark building. I had just bragged to them about how safe it was and how proud I was to have been living there for over five years. And now here the four of us were being told to get on our knees, handcuffed and not allowed to say a word in our defense. As a matter of fact, it was one of these gentlemen who got off his knees, still handcuffed, and unlocked the door for the policemen to get into the lobby where the two strangers were. Instead of being thanked or even acknowledged, we were led out the door past our neighbors, who were all but begging the police in our defense.

8 We were put into cars with the two strangers and taken to the 33rd Precinct at 165th and Amsterdam. The police automatically linked us to them with no questions and no regard for our character or our lives. No consideration was given to where we were going or what we were in need of doing before they came into our building. Suppose I had an ailing relative upstairs in my apartment waiting for me to return with her emergency remedy? Or young children who were told Daddy is running to the corner store for milk and will be right back? These three gentlemen weren't even allowed to lock their apartment or check on the U-Haul full of their personal belongings.

9 After we were lined up in the station, the younger of the two Hispanic men was immediately identified as an experienced criminal, and drug residue was found in a pocket of the other. I now realize how naïve I was to think the police would then uncuff me, apologize for their terrible mistake and let me go. Instead, they continued to search my backpack repeatedly, questioned me and put me in jail with the criminals.

10 The rest of the nearly five-hour ordeal was like a horrible dream, putting me in a surreal state of shock. Everything from being handcuffed, strip-searched, taken in and out for questioning, to being told that they knew exactly who I was and my responsibility to the show and that in fact they knew they already had whom they wanted, left me in absolute disbelief.

11 When I asked how they could keep me there, or have brought me there in the first place with nothing found and a clean record, I was told it was standard procedure. As if the average law-abiding citizen knows what that is and can dispute it. From what I now know, "standard procedure" is something that every citizen, black and white, needs to learn, and fast. Even though they knew I was innocent, they made me feel completely powerless. All for one reason. Why do you think? Here I was, young, pleasant and successful, in good physical shape, dressed in clean athletic attire. I was carrying a backpack, containing a substantial paycheck and deposit slip, on my way to the bank and to enjoy a well-deserved great day. Yet after hours and hours I was sitting at a desk with two officers who not only couldn't tell me why I was there but seemed determined to find something on me, to the point of making me miss my performance.

12 *It was because I am a black man!*

13 I sat in that cell crying silent tears of disappointment and injustice with the realization of how many innocent black men are convicted for no reason. When I was handcuffed, my first instinct had been to pull away

out of pure insult and violation as a human being. Thank God I was calm enough to do what they said. When I was thrown in jail with the criminals and strip-searched, I somehow knew to put my pride aside, be quiet and do exactly what I was told, hating it but coming to terms with the fact that in this situation I was powerless. I was a victim. They had guns!

14 Before I was finally let go, exhausted, humiliated, embarrassed and still in shock, I was led to a room and given a pseudo-apology. I was told that I was at the wrong place at the wrong time. My reply? "I was where I live."

15 As a result, what I learned growing up in Cincinnati has been shattered. Life will never be the same. ◆

CONSIDERING THE ISSUES

1. What assumptions do you have regarding our legal system? Do you believe that you will be treated fairly if approached by a law enforcement officer? That you are innocent until proven guilty? Or do you expect to be hassled or even harassed? Explain.
2. Review the U.S. Constitution's Bill of Rights (try the Cornell University Web site at www.law.cornell.edu/constitution/constitution.billofrights.html. What rights does it defend? How much are your expectations of liberty and justice connected to this document?

CRAFT AND CONTENT

3. How does White use emotions and feelings to convey his experience to the reader? What personal information does he offer to explain his point of view? Cite some specific examples where personal details about his day or his feelings help convey his point to his audience.
4. In paragraph 11, White describes his physical appearance. How does he describe himself? Why does he relay this information to the reader? Explain.

CRITICAL READING

5. Why were White and the other men in the lobby arrested by the police? What was the charge? On what grounds did the police

arrest them? After the real criminals were identified, why were they retained?

6. White states in several places in his essay that he felt his arrest was connected solely to his race. In your opinion, was this indeed a case of racial profiling, or of mistaken identity? Or could it be a bit of both? Explain.
7. White clearly feels that he was unfairly judged by the officers involved in his arrest based on the color of his skin. What does he feel was most violated by his experience? How does his reaction resonate with the reader? Explain.

WRITING ABOUT THE ISSUES

8. How do you feel after reading this essay? Are there particular points in White's narrative that seem especially compelling or disturbing? Did you find yourself becoming involved in his narrative? Write a letter to the editor of the *Nation* expressing your own feelings about White's experience.
9. Read about White's lawsuit against the New York City police department for wrongful arrest at www.nyclu.org/white_complaint.html. After reading the document posted on the New York Civil Liberties Union Web site, write a response to it as if you were a member of a jury. If you wish, you may further research this issue on the Internet for more information.

Racial Profiling Goes Beyond Black and White

Sasha Polakow-Suransky

Sasha Polakow-Suransky is a journalist and a fellow at the *American Prospect* magazine. He has been published in the *Chronicle of Higher Education* and the *Brown Alumni Magazine*, and has presented at the American Educational Research Association. This article was published in *Africana*, November 2001, two months following the terrorist attacks of September 11.

CONNECTING TO THE TOPIC

Many people immediately equate racial profiling with discrimination against African Americans and Latinos. But racial profiling takes many forms and affects many different groups. This reality was made very apparent after the terrorist attacks on September 11. Suddenly, the focus of racial profiling shifted to Arab Americans and people who looked like they could be from the Middle East. Even groups who had experienced racial profiling firsthand endorsed its use in law enforcement, as the next essay reveals.

WORDS IN CONTEXT

perniciousness: harmfulness; destructiveness
bolstered: supported; held up
glib: offhanded; not thoughtful
ingrained: firmly established; deep-seated
qualitatively: relating to or concerning quality
comparable: of similar characteristics; equal to
egregious: conspicuously bad or offensive
beleaguered: harassed
reciprocate: to return

1 Eric Hotchandani, a 20-year-old University of California-Santa Barbara student, boarded a packed rush-hour train on the evening of September 21. When the train emptied out, he took the first open seat, next to a middle-aged black man in a suit, and began reading his newspaper. The black man stared at him coldly.

2 "How're you doing?" Hotchandani greeted him.

3 "Not so good anymore," the man replied.

4 "Why is that?" Hotchandani asked.

5 "Look who's sitting next to me," the man snapped back.

6 Hotchandani was taken aback. "Just go ahead and spell this one out for me," he said.

7 The man turned to him and asked, "Where were you born?"

8 Although shocked by the question, Hotchandani answered. "I was born in Brazil, but I have this Indian side to me, which darkens my skin and probably makes you think I'm a terrorist," he said.

9 The black man seemed surprised. "Sorry, I thought you were from the Middle East," he said. But Hotchandani was not satisfied.

10 "Let's go ahead and assume that I was," he said to the man, raising his voice. "What happened in New York on September 11 was done by an extreme group of Muslims who don't represent Islam or people of my skin color. I'm not here to inflict harm on anyone. I'm just minding my own business."

11 "I'm not going to let you do any harm to me," the black man retorted. "I just don't feel comfortable with you sitting next to me."

12 To the shock and dismay of many African American leaders, polls released in the weeks following September 11 indicate that the views expressed by this black man on a Bay Area train are not uncommon. A Zogby International poll conducted between September 25 and October 8 showed that African American approval of racially profiling Arab-Americans reached a peak of 60% on September 30, compared to 45% among the overall population. The statistics later leveled out with African Americans showing a 45% approval rating by October 8, virtually in line with the 41% figure for other racial groups. Similarly, an October 25 Africana.com poll found that 34% of respondents thought it was "okay" for US law enforcement to racially profile Arabs.

13 These results have provoked a range of reactions. Urban League President Hugh Price is disturbed. "We should see in these polls' findings more evidence of the perniciousness of racial profiling itself, no matter how it's seemingly bolstered by glib or urgently declared rationalizations," he said. "These polls show that whenever people speak in favor of racial profiling, they always favor its use against some other group, not theirs."

14 Others, such as Henry L. Taylor, a University of Buffalo Professor of Architecture and Urban Planning, claim that the results are not representative of general black attitudes because they are based solely on immediate fears of terrorism. "A lot of people, African Americans included, have not looked at the civil implications of these questions," said Taylor. "Right now we're in a time period where anything that looks like it will preserve the security of a nation is going to be embraced."

15 While the statistics indicating widespread black approval of Arab racial profiling can certainly be attributed in part to a knee-jerk reaction after September 11, there are deeper causes as well. Syndicated columnist Earl Ofari Hutchinson points to religious intolerance and ingrained distrust of Muslims within the African American community. Complex issues such as the presence of Arab-owned convenience

stores in predominantly black neighborhoods and the tension between the two communities play into this equation as well. As Hutchinson contends, "Many [blacks] still view all Muslims with the same mix of caution, distrust and hostility, as many white Americans do."

16 While such views may be widespread, they are largely based on a false premise. In fact, the majority of Arabs in the United States are not Muslims, they are Syrian and Lebanese Christians. According to the Arab-American Institute, 77 percent of Arabs in America are Christians and only 23 percent practice Islam. Another little known fact further complicates matters: the majority of American Muslims are not Arabs. Statistics from the Council on American-Islamic Relations reveal that most Muslims in the US are of African or South Asian descent—only 25 percent are Arab.

17 Hutchinson concludes his column, "When the Profiled Become Profilers," by observing that black support for the racial profiling of others could very well backfire: "Bush has implored Americans to return life back to normalcy. Unfortunately, those blacks who approve racial profiling against Muslims run the grave risk of making sure that racial profiling could be part of that normalcy, and with them once more the prime targets."

18 NAACP leaders have expressed similar dismay. "It is unfortunate that it would be African Americans that have suffered this kind of terror and profiling at the hands of the police . . . to then support this type of profiling," says Buffalo NAACP President Frank Mesiah.

19 But *New York Daily News* columnist Stanley Crouch disagrees. Crouch insists that racial profiling of blacks is qualitatively different than the current profiling of Arabs. While pulling over black motorists involves police officers' frequently incorrect assumptions about who might commit a crime, Crouch claims that profiling Arabs is not comparable.

20 "The Arabs-in-America question removes us from the area of speculation and abstract theories about individual freedom," he argues. "We have had war declared on us by a spider at the center of a web of terrorist cells. Followers of that spider are hiding in the Arab-American community."

21 And finally there are some in the African American community who are simply relieved that someone else is the target for once, as a group of black and Latino teenagers in Brooklyn told the *New York Times*. "The police would probably racially profile everyone that's here . . . But now they don't really bother us. They, like, stop everyone that has Middle Eastern features. They stop them. They ask them questions like that," said Louis Johnson, an 18-year-old whose parents are from Trinidad.

22 "We've become a little more at ease with the policemen," agreed Johnson's Latino friend, Miqueo Rawell-Peterson, 17. "We realize what they've done. Now we look at them more as heroes, instead of—I guess, what you'd say, enemies."

23 But while black and Latino teenagers enjoy their reprieve from racial profiling, a series of complaints has emerged from profiling's newfound targets. In the post-September 11 climate, "driving while black" has become "flying while brown" and the most egregious cases to emerge involve men who look "Middle Eastern" being kicked off airplanes after passing through security. All in all, over a dozen men have been denied the right to board or been removed from planes.

24 In Orlando, two Pakistani businessmen invited to attend a conference by the US Department of Commerce were kicked off a US Airways flight on September 17, despite the fact that they showed a letter of invitation from the US consul. The same day, in San Antonio, Ashraf Kahn was ejected from a Delta flight and, as a result, missed his brother's wedding in Pakistan. In Minneapolis, Kareem Alasady and two companions were not allowed to board a Northwest flight on September 20.

25 In Tampa, Mohamed el-Sayed, a US citizen born in Egypt, was barred from boarding a United flight to Washington. United has also kicked several other men off its flights in recent weeks; in Phoenix, Iraqi-American businessman Younadam Youkhana and his companions were forced off a United flight to Chicago, and in Boston, businessman Muhammad Ali was removed, questioned extensively and cleared by law enforcement, and still not allowed to re-board his United flight to Washington.

26 Worse yet, Ali Khadraoui, an American citizen originally from Algeria, was strip-searched and detained by French police after being kept off of his United flight home to Washington from Paris. Finally, in Seattle, Vahid Zohrehvandi, an Iranian-American engineer and part-time employee of American Airlines, was kicked off a flight operated by his own employer. He was not allowed to fly home to Dallas until the airline found a pilot who agreed to fly with a "Middle Eastern" man on board.

27 The US Code states clearly, "An air carrier or foreign air carrier may not subject a person in air transportation to discrimination on the basis of race, color, national origin, religion, sex, or ancestry." Secretary of Transportation Norman Mineta, himself a victim of Japanese internment during World War II, has vowed to enforce the law. "Protecting the civil rights of our passengers is essential to maintaining the security of our nation, because those civil rights are essential to our most

fundamental values," he declared. "There have been times in our history as a nation when that has been forgotten. I am committed, and the administration is committed, to ensuring that it is never forgotten again."

28 Poll results aside, some Middle Eastern Americans, and others singled out because they look like Arabs, have found that more African Americans seem supportive than suspicious. [One reported that he even] received a sympathetic reception from a black flight attendant in first class, who expressed his empathy by offering the beleaguered coach passenger some champagne.

29 And when confronted with the hostile black man on the Bay Area train, Eric Hotchandani seized the opportunity to speak out, and found a sympathetic audience.

30 "Do you want me to go to the back of the train? Do we have to redo Rosa Parks all over again?" Hotchandani asked the man who had expressed discomfort at his presence, as the whole train grew silent, looking on. "To me you are beyond ignorant. I'm sure you've experienced some sort of racism considering that you're black. If you knew anything about your own history you wouldn't be doing this. I can't believe you're reciprocating this kind of hate—you're kicking me down when you've been kicked before."

31 A black man in his mid-20s seated near the two men broke the silence.

32 "At first I thought this guy was joking with you," he said, addressing Hotchandani. "Please don't think all black people think like this."

33 The middle aged black man did not respond. At the next stop, he gathered his belongings and left the train. The passengers clapped as he stepped off. ◆

CONSIDERING THE ISSUES

1. In your opinion, do you consider racial profiling ever justifiable? If so, under what circumstances? If not, why?
2. In the days following September 11, did you consider the race or ethnicity of the people around you? If you are or look like you could be of Middle Eastern descent, did you notice any differences in the way people treated you? Explain.

CRAFT AND CONTENT

3. Evaluate how the author presents and supports the thesis of his essay. First, identify his thesis, and then analyze the supporting

elements he uses to prove his point. Does the author allow for alternative points of view? Does he try to see multiple sides of the issue? Explain.

4. How does the case of Eric Hotchandani serve to support Polakow-Suransky's argument? Is Hotchandani even from the Middle East? What is the irony of his situation on the train? How does he handle it?

CRITICAL THINKING

5. Eric Hotchandani asks the man on the train if they have to "do Rosa Parks all over again?" Who is Rosa Parks? What did she do? Why does Hotchandani refer to her? What effect did naming her probably have on the other people on the train? Explain.
6. In paragraph 13, Urban League president Hugh Price is quoted, "polls show that whenever people speak in favor of racial profiling, they always favor its use against some other group, not theirs." What are the sociological implications of this statement? What does it reveal about the motivation behind racial profiling in general?
7. Henry L. Taylor notes that racial profiling by African Americans against people who looked Middle Eastern followed in the immediate aftermath of a terrorist attack involving Middle Eastern men. Therefore, the "civil implications" of the situation were not evaluated—people were reacting from the gut. Is this understandable? Justifiable? Explain.

WRITING ABOUT THE ISSUES

8. Henry Taylor notes that while racial profiling of any group is not admirable or right, it sometimes can be a knee-jerk reaction to specific events such as those connected with September 11. Explore the psychology of such reactions from your own perspective.
9. How would you have reacted if you were in Eric Hotchandani's situation? What would you have said? Would you have left? Moved? Reacted with anger? Write a fictitious dialogue between yourself and the man on the train, being honest to your temperament and personality.

VISUAL CONNECTIONS

Pulling Teeth

The American Civil Liberties Union (ACLU) was founded in 1920. Since its beginning, the nonprofit, nonpartisan ACLU has grown from a small group of civil liberties activists to an organization of nearly 400,000 members with offices in almost every state. The ACLU's mission is to fight civil liberties violations wherever and whenever they occur. It is also active in national and state government arenas and is dedicated to upholding the Bill of Rights.

CONNECTING TO THE TOPIC

In October of 2001, as part of a larger campaign to bring attention to the issue of racial profiling in New Jersey, the ACLU ran this advertisement to raise awareness and inform victims of their rights. The ad features Dr. Elmo Randolph, a New Jersey dentist and a plaintiff in a racial profiling case in that state.

Randolph, an African American man, says he has been pulled over approximately 100 times over a five-year period without ever receiving a ticket. In the ad, Dr. Randolph describes his experience with the police, stating that "the police searched my car and I had to prove to the troopers that being an African-American man in a nice car doesn't mean that I am a drug dealer or car thief." Deborah Jacobs, executive director of the ACLU of New Jersey, said of the ad, "We want to send a message to the victims about their rights, and to the state about its obligations." This ad ran in the October 29, 2001, edition of the *Newark Star-Ledger*.

Getting the New Jersey State Police to Stop Racial Profiling is like Pulling Teeth.

Dr. Elmo Randolph, Dentist

"My name is Elmo Randolph and I am a dentist. Within a five year period, **I was pulled over by New Jersey State Troopers approximately 100 times** without ever receiving a ticket. The police searched my car and I had to prove to the troopers that being an African-American man in a nice car doesn't mean that I am a drug dealer or a car thief.

This kind of stereotyping is called **racial profiling, and it's wrong.** The State of New Jersey has admitted to racial profiling and has admitted that It's ongoing, but has yet to make amends to victims like me who are left with nothing but **fear of police and fear of driving on the Turnpike.**

The ACLU represents me. It may be able to help you, too. Please **CALL 1-877-6-PROFILE** or go to **aclu.org** to report your citation, stop or search to the ACLU and to seek assistance with any claim you have."

Paid for by the ACLU

CONSIDERING THE ISSUES

1. What words are treated differently within the body text, and why? What is the effect of having certain words in bold or a larger typeface than others?
2. How does the headline of the ad connect to the ad's content and message? Explain.

CRITICAL THINKING

3. In this ad, Elmo Randolph states that he has been pulled over "approximately 100 times without ever receiving a ticket." What is the audience likely to infer from this statement?
4. Consider the photograph used in this ad. How is Dr. Randolph dressed? Where is he sitting? In what environment is he placed? Would this ad be as effective if Randolph was younger? Less professionally dressed? Explain.
5. A January 8, 2003, follow-up story in the *New Jersey Star-Ledger* reported that Randolph received a $75,000 settlement for his lawsuit against the state. The story notes, "Randolph said his story began soon after he bought his first BMW. Over the course of a decade, he estimated he was pulled over on North Jersey roads 50 to 100 times." In your opinion, did the ACLU skew the information in its ad? Does it matter if it gets an important point across? Explain.

TOPICAL CONNECTIONS

GROUP PROJECTS

1. Working in a group of 3 or 4 people, develop a definition of racial profiling drawing from information provided in the article, your own interpretations, and from online research. After preparing your definition, write a position statement on racial profiling for your own school's public safety department.

2. In the aftermath of the attacks of September 11, 2001, many individuals who were or looked like they might be from the Middle East were questioned on airplanes, stopped by security officials, and even shunned by neighbors in their own communities, as the situation in the preceding essay describes. The general consensus, however, was that, under the circumstances, such suspicions were justified, putting a new spin on the debate over racial profiling. In small groups, discuss this issue and come up with your own position on racial profiling in times of crisis.

WEB PROJECTS

3. The argument of whether racial profiling should be permitted during periods of high terrorist alert is highly charged. Look up these two editorials on the *Washington Post*'s Web site (www.washingtonpost.com) with different viewpoints on this issue: "You Can't Fight Terrorism with Racism" and "Give Grandma a Pass; Politically Correct Screening Won't Catch Jihadists." After reading each piece, write an editorial responding to either or both authors expressing your viewpoint.
4. What is the government's official position on racial profiling? Visit the U.S. Department of Justice Web site and read the "Racial Profiling Fact Sheet" posted online at www.usdoj. gov/opa/pr/2003/June/racial_profiling_fact_sheet.pdf. Review the entire fact sheet. What exceptions does the government make concerning racial profiling, and why? Identify any areas of the document that you find questionable or particularly compelling and explain why.

FOR FURTHER INQUIRY

5. Visit the ACLU's Web site on racial equality at www.aclu .org/RacialEquality/RacialEqualityMain.cfm and review their information on racial profiling. What are the most pressing issues concerning racial profiling today? Select an issue or case described on the ACLU Web site and research it in greater depth. Write a short essay summarizing the situation or issue, and your position on it.

7 Are Designer Humans in Our Future?

That discussion every parent dreads—the talk about the birds and the bees—may get even harder to answer in the not-too-distant future. Reproductive technology is moving toward what was once the realm of science fiction. It is now possible for us to clone animals and, presumably, ourselves. With the mapping of the human genome, there is the selective possibility of creating "perfect" children. In light of these dramatic scientific breakthroughs, parents might need more than a biology textbook to answer Junior's question "Where did I come from?"

This chapter examines some of the current discussions regarding human cloning and genetic engineering for reproductive purposes. What is the controversy all about? Is it likely that humans will be cloned? If so, what would they be like? Do people have unrealistic expectations such as creating a replica of a dead loved one? Will human cloning solve the reproductive problems of infertile couples and allow them to have children? Can we use cloning technology to improve human life—making stronger, healthier children for the future?

CRITICAL THINKING

1. Identify the visual clichés in this cartoon. How do these conventional images tell the viewer what is happening in the cartoon? Explain.
2. What is the meaning of the woman's question to her doctor? Is such a comment a possibility in the future? Explain.

Baby, It's You and You and You

Nancy Gibbs

Nancy Gibbs is a senior editor at *TIME* magazine, where she divides her time between writing major stories on national affairs and domestic policy issues and editing various sections of the magazine. She has taught a seminar, "Politics and the Press," at Princeton University. In addition to being published in *TIME* and other magazines and journals, Gibbs' work is included in the *Princeton Anthology of Writing*. This article is an abridged version of the original, which was published in the February 19, 2001, issue of *TIME*.

CONNECTING TO THE TOPIC

When researchers at Roslin Institute in Scotland announced that they had cloned a sheep in 1997, no one could have prepared them for the calls and letters from people eager to clone their loved ones. Said Ian Wilmut, one of the scientists who created Dolly, the first cloned sheep, "Such pleas are based on a misconception that cloning of the kind that produced Dolly confers instant, exact replication—a virtual resurrection." As anyone who has taken college biology knows, we are more than our DNA—we are products of our environment, beginning with the first divisions of fetal cells. Nevertheless, many people are indeed interested in human cloning, and one sect, the Raelians, has even claimed (unproven) to have done just that. Will cloned humans be the next step in human reproduction? Can they help alleviate the pain of losing a loved one? Will the practice of human cloning force us to reconsider what it means to be human?

WORDS IN CONTEXT

narcissist: one who harbors excessive love or admiration of oneself
consortium: a joint venture
consensus: an opinion or position reached by a group as a whole
euthanize: to end the life of an individual to prevent extreme suffering
condemnation: state of being condemned

1 Before we assume that the market for human clones consists mainly of narcissists who think the world deserves more of them or neo-Nazis who dream of cloning Hitler or crackpots and mavericks and mischief

makers of all kinds, it is worth taking a tour of the marketplace. We might just meet ourselves there.

2 Imagine for a moment that your daughter needs a bone-marrow transplant and no one can provide a match; that your wife's early menopause has made her infertile; or that your five-year-old has drowned in a lake and your grief has made it impossible to get your mind around the fact that he is gone forever. Would the news then really be so easy to dismiss that around the world, there are scientists in labs pressing ahead with plans to duplicate a human being, deploying the same technology that allowed Scottish scientists to clone Dolly the sheep several years ago?

3 All it took was that first headline about the astonishing ewe, and fertility experts began to hear the questions every day. Our two-year-old daughter died in a car crash; we saved a lock of her hair in a baby book. Can you clone her? My husband had cancer and is sterile. Can you help us?

4 The inquiries are pouring in because some scientists are ever more willing to say yes, perhaps we can. A well-known infertility specialist, Panayiotis Zavos of the University of Kentucky, announced that he and Italian researcher Severino Antinori were forming a consortium to produce the first human clone. Researchers in South Korea claim they have already created a cloned human embryo, though they destroyed it rather than implanting it in a surrogate mother to develop. Cover stories in *Wired* and the *New York Times Magazine* tracked the efforts of the Raelians, a religious group committed to, among other things, welcoming the first extraterrestrials when they appear. They intend to clone the cells of a dead 10-month-old boy whose devastated parents hope, in effect, to bring him back to life as a newborn. The Raelians say they have the lab and the scientists, and—most important, considering the amount of trial and error involved—they say they have 50 women lined up to act as surrogates to carry a cloned baby to term.

5 Given what researchers have learned since Dolly, no one thinks the mechanics of cloning are very hard: take a donor egg, suck out the nucleus, and hence the DNA, and fuse it with, say, a skin cell from the human being copied. Then, with the help of an electrical current, the reconstituted cell should begin growing into a genetic duplicate. "It's inevitable that someone will try and someone will succeed," predicts Delores Lamb, an infertility expert at Baylor University. The consensus among biotechnology specialists is that within a few years—some scientists believe a few months—the news will break of the birth of the first human clone.

6 At that moment, at least two things will happen—one private, one public. The meaning of what it is to be human—which until now has involved, at the very least, the mysterious melding of two different people's DNA—will shift forever, along with our understanding of the relationship between parents and children, means and ends, ends and beginnings. And as a result, the conversation that has occupied scientists and ethicists for years, about how much man should mess with nature when it comes to reproduction, will drop onto every kitchen table, every pulpit, every politician's desk. Our fierce national debate over issues like abortion and euthanasia will seem tame and transparent compared with the questions that human cloning raises.

7 By day, Randolfe Wicker, 63, runs a lighting shop in New York City. But in his spare time, as spokesman for the Human Cloning Foundation, he is the face of cloning fervor in the U.S. "I took one step in this adventure, and it took over me like quicksand," says Wicker. He is planning to have some of his skin cells stored for future cloning. "If I'm not cloned before I die, my estate will be set up so that I can be cloned after," he says, admitting, however, that he hasn't found a lawyer willing to help. "It's hard to write a will with all these uncertainties," he concedes. "A lot of lawyers will look at me crazy."

8 As a gay man, Wicker has long been frustrated that he cannot readily have children of his own; as he gets older, his desire to reproduce grows stronger. He knows that a clone would not be a photocopy of him but talks about the traits the boy might possess: "He will like the color blue, Middle Eastern food and romantic Spanish music that's out of fashion." And then he hints at the heart of his motive. "I can thumb my nose at Mr. Death and say, 'You might get me, but you're not going to get all of me,'" he says. "The special formula that is me will live on into another lifetime. It's a partial triumph over death. I would leave my imprint not in sand but in cement."

9 This kind of talk makes ethicists conclude that even people who think they know about cloning—let alone the rest of us—don't fully understand its implications. Cloning, notes ethicist Arthur Caplan of the University of Pennsylvania, "can't make you immortal because clearly the clone is a different person. If I take twins and shoot one of them, it will be faint consolation to the dead one that the other one is still running around, even though they are genetically identical. So the road to immortality is not through cloning."

10 At the moment, the American public is plainly not ready to move quickly on cloning. In a *TIME*/CNN poll, 90% of respondents thought

it was a bad idea to clone human beings. "Cloning right now looks like it's coming to us on a magic carpet, piloted by a cult leader, sold to whoever can afford it," says ethicist Caplan. "That makes people nervous."

11 And it helps explain why so much of the research is being done secretly. We may learn of the first human clone only months, even years, after he or she is born—if the event hasn't happened already, as some scientists speculate. The team that cloned Dolly waited until she was seven months old to announce her existence. Creating her took 277 tries, and right up until her birth, scientists around the world were saying that cloning a mammal from an adult cell was impossible. "There's a significant gap between what scientists are willing to talk about in public and their private aspirations," says British futurist Patrick Dixon. "The law of genetics is that the work is always significantly further ahead than the news. In the digital world, everything is hyped because there are no moral issues—there is just media excitement. Gene technology creates so many ethical issues that scientists are scared stiff of a public reaction if the end results of their research are known."

12 All it will take, some predict, is that first snapshot. "Once you have a picture of a normal baby with 10 fingers and 10 toes, that changes everything," says San Mateo, Calif., attorney and cloning advocate Mark Eibert, who gets inquiries from infertile couples every day. "Once they put a child in front of the cameras, they've won." On the other hand, notes Gregory Pence, a professor of philosophy at the University of Alabama at Birmingham and author of *Who's Afraid of Human Cloning?*, "if the first baby is defective, cloning will be banned for the next 100 years."

13 "I wouldn't mind being the first person cloned if it were free. I don't mind being a guinea pig," says Doug Dorner, 35. Dorner has known since he was 16 that he would never be able to have children the old-fashioned way. A battle with lymphoma left him sterile, so when he and Nancy started thinking of having children, he began following the scientific developments in cloning more closely. The more he read, the more excited he got. "Technology saved my life when I was 16," he says, but at the cost of his fertility. "I think technology should help me have a kid. That's a fair trade."

14 How do the Dorners imagine raising a cloned child, given the knowledge they would have going in? "I'd know exactly what his basic drives were," says Doug. The boy's dreams and aspirations, however, would be his own, Doug insists. "I used to dream of being a fighter pilot," he recalls, a dream lost when he got cancer. While they are at it, why

not clone Doug twice? "Hmm. Two of the same kid," Doug ponders. "We'll cross that bridge when we come to it. But I know we'd never clone our clone to have a second child. Once you start copying something, who knows what the next copies will be like?"

15 In fact the risks involved with cloning mammals are so great that Wilmut, the premier cloner, calls it "criminally irresponsible" for scientists to be experimenting on humans today. Even after four years of practice with animal cloning, the failure rate is still overwhelming: 98% of embryos never implant or die off during gestation or soon after birth. Animals that survive can be nearly twice as big at birth as is normal, or have extra-large organs or heart trouble or poor immune systems. Dolly's "mother" was six years old when she was cloned. That may explain why Dolly's cells show signs of being older than they actually are–scientists joked that she was really a sheep in lamb's clothing. This deviation raises the possibility that beings created by cloning adults will age abnormally fast.

16 "We had a cloned sheep born just before Christmas that was clearly not normal," says Wilmut. "We hoped for a few days it would improve and then, out of kindness, we euthanized it, because it obviously would never be healthy." Wilmut believes "it is almost a certainty" that cloned human children would be born with similar maladies. Of course, we don't euthanize babies. But these kids would probably die very prematurely anyway. Wilmut pauses to consider the genie he has released with Dolly and the hopes he has raised. "It seems such a profound irony," he says, "that in trying to make a copy of a child who has died tragically, one of the most likely outcomes is another dead child."

17 A world in which cloning is commonplace confounds every human relationship, often in ways most potential clients haven't considered. For instance, if a woman gives birth to her own clone, is the child her daughter or her sister? Or, says bioethicist Kass, "let's say the child grows up to be the spitting image of its mother. What impact will that have on the relationship between the father and his child if that child looks exactly like the woman he fell in love with?" Or, he continues, "let's say the parents have a cloned son and then get divorced. How will the mother feel about seeing a copy of the person she hates most in the world every day? Everyone thinks about cloning from the point of view of the parents. No one looks at it from the point of view of the clone."

18 "The short answer to the cloning question," says ethicist Caplan, "is that anybody who clones somebody today should be arrested. It

would be barbaric human experimentation. It would be killing fetuses and embryos for no purpose, none, except for curiosity. But if you can't agree that that's wrong to do, and if the media can't agree to condemn rather than gawk, that's a condemnation of us all." ◆

CONSIDERING THE ISSUES

1. Do you think genetic technology could be eroding our definitions of what it means to be human? Could the way we view ourselves, and our sense of identity, change because of this new technology? Why or why not?
2. Would you opt to clone a loved one if you knew that it could be successfully done without any risks? If so, whom would you clone? If not, why?

CRAFT AND CONTENT

3. What reasons does Gibbs list for why people are interested in human cloning? How are the expectations of the general population different from the expectations of the scientific world?
4. Gibbs includes examples of real people who would like to clone themselves. How do these people come across to the reader? Are readers likely to be sympathetic to these people?
5. In paragraph 13, Doug Dorner states that he "wouldn't mind being a guinea pig." Would the donor of the cells used to create a human clone be the "guinea pig"? Or is the clone the "guinea pig"?

CRITICAL THINKING

6. Ian Wilmut observes that there is a tragic twist to parents' desire to clone their dead children—that the success rate is so miniscule, they are more likely to end up with another dead child. Should parents be able to pursue this option? Is any chance, no matter how remote, worthy of the risk? Why or why not?
7. Gibbs observes that many people who support human cloning seem to do so without considering the point of view of the clone. How do the examples she provides of people who favor cloning support this viewpoint?

WRITING ABOUT THE ISSUES

8. In 1997, the National Bioethics Advisory Council recommended against human cloning because of the dangers it presented to the child born of such reproductive technology. In 2000, researchers reported that Dolly's cells appeared to age faster than normal. Through online and library research, track Dolly's development. If Dolly were human, what biological problems would she face? Based on your research, can you make a recommendation for or against human cloning at this time?
9. Research the cloning claims of the Raelians and their efforts to clone a human being. After the announcement of the cloning of Dolly, Rael, the founder of the Raelian movement, founded Clonaid, a company offering human cloning services (www.clonaid.com). Visit the Clonaid Web site. Are their efforts dangerous? Noble? Write a short news article on the most recent activities of Clonaid using the voice of an impartial journalist.

Me, My Clone, and I

Jonathan Colvin

Jonathan Colvin is a freelance technical writer who lives in Vancouver, British Columbia, Canada. This article first appeared in the May 2000 issue of the *Humanist.*

CONNECTING TO THE TOPIC

Since the cloning of Dolly the sheep was announced in 1997, the issue of human cloning has been one of great debate. Some ethicists argue that human cloning may prove reckless and irresponsible, endangering future generations and creating questionable quality of life for the cloned person. Other people contend that much of the opposition to human cloning stems from a "yuck factor"—the idea simply makes us uncomfortable, like many new technologies that are now widely accepted. Are human clones in our genetic future? Will human cloning be just one more reproductive option? Should it be?

WORDS IN CONTEXT

amalgam: a combination of diverse elements; a mixture
concur: to be of the same opinion; to agree
impromptu: performed with little or no preparation
narcissism: excessive love or admiration of oneself
genotype: genetic makeup
nurture over nature: *nature versus nurture* is the phrase used to describe the debate that humans are formed by nature, i.e., heredity or biological make up, or nurture, i.e., environment and external experience
serendipitous: relating to a fortunate accidental discovery
esoteric: confined to a small group, a select few
intrinsic: relating to the essential nature of a thing; inherent

1 Clone. To many people the word has sinister overtones; it's a disturbing amalgam of flesh and technology. Most people believe that human cloning should be illegal, and most governments are moving to concur.

2 Interested in this near-unanimous sentiment, I carried out my own impromptu survey of friends and strangers. Most said they agreed with the prohibition of human cloning. But when I asked them to explain exactly why they thought it should be illegal, the poll became much more revealing.

3 Many mumbled about the dangers of "cloning Hitler" or creating a subclass of slaves. Others brought up the specter of basketball teams full of identical seven-foot-tall players. A smaller, more thoughtful percentage believed it would be unnatural or the ultimate in narcissism. In general, however, public attitudes toward human cloning seem to be based on a diet of science-fiction B-movies and paperbacks. But should human cloning be feared, as the next Frankenstein's monster of genetic engineering?

4 While undoubtedly fascinating, few people would perceive identical twins to be the least bit sinister. And yet identical twins are in fact natural clones, formed from the same egg and sharing the same genotype. If natural clones are not to be feared, why should we fear the deliberate ones?

5 Many of the attitudes concerning human cloning are reminiscent of the arguments against in vitro fertilization in the 1960s, when accusations of "playing God" and interfering with nature were common. Today, however, "test tube" babies are celebrated for their own individuality

and as people in their own right. Exactly, say opponents of cloning. Babies born in vitro are unique individuals; clones are photocopies of people who already exist. What will happen to individuality if we can stamp out copies of ourselves like so many cookies on a tray?

6 Interestingly, many of those who make this argument also tend to emphasize nurture over nature and deny that our genes determine ourselves—whether it be IQ, athletic ability, or our favorite ice cream flavor. But these arguments contradict each other. For if nurture triumphs over nature, then a clone will be an individual as unique as any other, determined for the most part by the environment in which she or he was reared.

7 Perhaps the most weighty argument against cloning is that, by eliminating the mixing of genes that occurs during conventional reproduction, human biodiversity will be diminished and human evolution will cease. It is the serendipitous mixing of genes that produces the Einsteins and Mozarts of the world; take away this process and surely the potential for new genius will cease. However, the fact is that human biological evolution for all intents and purposes has become insignificant compared to cultural evolution.

8 At this point, it is appropriate that I reveal the source of my interest in this subject. For the truth is, I wish to clone myself. Before my gate is stormed by villagers wielding branding irons, let me explain why.

9 I am thirty-two years old and have cystic fibrosis, an inherited genetic disease that prohibits those who suffer from it from conceiving children and usually kills by the mid-thirties. My dream is to clone myself, repair my clone's genetic defect, and give him the opportunity to fulfill the potential that has been denied to me by a cruel quirk of nature.

10 Perhaps my clone will climb Mount Everest, single-handedly sail around the world, or simply marry and raise a family without the fear that his children will be prematurely fatherless and his wife a widow. The clone will not be me, but perhaps he will be who I could have been.

11 With the coming genetic revolution, we will be directing our own evolution rather than relying on a natural (and sometimes disastrous) lottery to do it for us. And surely cloning will remain an esoteric and unusual method of reproduction, with most people choosing to do it the old-fashioned (and far more pleasurable) way. But should government be able to tell me what I can or cannot do with what is, after all, an intrinsic part of what and who I am?

12 Criminalizing an activity may be easier than answering the thorny philosophical questions raised by it. But before government rushes to outlaw my dream, it should at least seriously consider whether the opposition to human cloning is based on real dangers. ◆

CONSIDERING THE ISSUES

1. Are so many people opposed to human cloning because it poses legitimate risks, or because it is intellectually upsetting? What do you think is at the root of their objections? Do you have any of your own? Explain.
2. Would you clone yourself or a loved one for any reason—such as to save a living child, or even yourself? Explain why or why not.

CRAFT AND CONTENT

3. Colvin notes that 30 years ago, we asked the same questions about test tube babies and in vitro fertilization (IVF) that we are asking now about human cloning. Yet now IVF is considered acceptable by most people. Is this an effective means of supporting his argument that human cloning is acceptable? Is it the same thing in principle? Explain.
4. Colvin adopts a conversational tone in this piece. Who is his audience? How does his tone affect how readers accept, or do not accept, his argument?

CRITICAL THINKING

5. Colvin reasons in paragraph 4 that created clones should be accepted the same way natural clones (identical twins) are. He wonders why created clones would be more feared than identical twins. Respond to his observation with your own opinion, and what you understand about human nature.
6. Why does Colvin want to clone himself? Do you think the reasons he expresses are valid? Is it realistic to expect that his clone would be the person he could not be? Despite his comments to the contrary, do you think he expects his clone to be a replica of himself, only without his disease? Explain using references from his essay.

WRITING ABOUT THE ISSUES

7. To find out why most people are against human cloning, the author decides to conduct an impromptu survey, asking *why* people are against the idea. Conduct your own survey. Based on the comments made by people opposed to human cloning, write a short essay about the reasons they were against it. Respond to some of their reasons, expressing your own opinions.
8. In his closing paragraph, Colvin comments that "before government rushes to outlaw my dream, it should at least seriously consider whether the opposition to human cloning is based on real dangers." Is this argument valid when applied to human life? How would you respond to this statement?

The Genetic Bill of Rights

The Board of Directors of the Council for Responsible Genetics

Founded in 1983, the Council for Responsible Genetics (CRG) is a nonprofit, nongovernmental organization based in Cambridge, Massachusetts. CRG aims to "foster public debate about the social, ethical and environmental implications of genetic technologies." This "bill of rights" was posted in Spring 2000 by CRG.

CONNECTING TO THE TOPIC

The Council for Responsible Genetics drafted the Genetic Bill of Rights in order to introduce "a global dialogue on the fundamental values that have been put at risk by new applications of genetics." The council explains that the Genetic Bill of Rights is a basic set of common principles that are "essential for creating a framework for understanding the ethical, legal, social and environmental implications of biotechnology." While this document has not been adopted by any official government agency, the CRG hopes that it will assist in the process of regulation and governance of new genetic technologies.

WORDS IN CONTEXT

indigenous: native; being a member of the original inhabitants of a particular place
expropriation: deprivation of possession
eugenic: the practice of hereditary improvement of the human race through controlled selective breeding
gestated: conceived and carried to term

Preamble

Our life and health depend on an intricate web of relationships within the biological and social worlds. Protection of these relationships must inform all public policy.

Commercial, governmental, scientific and medical institutions promote manipulation of genes despite profound ignorance of how such changes may affect the web of life. Once they enter the environment, organisms with modified genes cannot be recalled and pose novel risks to humanity and the entire biosphere.

Manipulation of human genes creates new threats to the health of individuals and their offspring, and endangers human rights, privacy and dignity.

Genes, other constituents of life, and genetically modified organisms themselves are rapidly being patented and turned into objects of commerce. This commercialization of life is veiled behind promises to cure disease and feed the hungry.

People everywhere have the right to participate in evaluating the social and biological implications of the genetic revolution and in democratically guiding its applications.

To protect our human rights and integrity and the biological integrity of the earth, we, therefore, propose this Genetic Bill of Rights.

The Genetic Bill of Rights

All people have the right to preservation of the earth's biological and genetic diversity.

All people have the right to a world in which living organisms cannot be patented, including human beings, animals, plants, microorganisms and all their parts.

All people have the right to a food supply that has not been genetically engineered.

All indigenous peoples have the right to manage their own biological resources, to preserve their traditional knowledge, and to protect these from expropriation and bio-piracy by scientific, corporate or government interests.

All people have the right to protection from toxins, other contaminants, or actions that can harm their genetic makeup and that of their offspring.

All people have the right to protection against eugenic measures such as forced sterilization or mandatory screening aimed at aborting or manipulating selected embryos or fetuses.

All people have the right to genetic privacy including the right to prevent the taking or storing of bodily samples for genetic information without their voluntary informed consent.

All people have the right to be free from genetic discrimination.

All people have the right to DNA tests to defend themselves in criminal proceedings.

All people have the right to have been conceived, gestated, and born without genetic manipulation.

CRITICAL THINKING

1. What is a "bill of rights"? Why is it written and what does it seek to protect? What motivated the creation of this document? In what ways does the document reflect current issues connected to human cloning and genetic enhancement and testing?
2. From whose perspective is this Genetic Bill of Rights written? Do you think that Jonathan Colvin, author of "Me, My Clone, and I," would agree with it? Why or why not?

WRITING ABOUT THE ISSUES

3. Draft your own genetic bill of rights. Referring to the CRG document as a prototype, list your articles, and any preamble you wish to preface it, expressing your own position on the issue of genetic enhancement and human cloning.
4. Is there such a thing as "genetic identity"? Should we have such a right? How could our genetic identity be violated? Write an essay exploring the concept of genetic identity and what it might mean for the future.

The Last Human

Gregory Stock

Gregory Stock is director of the Program on Medicine, Technology, and Society at the University of California School of Medicine at Los Angeles. He is the author of several books, including *Metaman: The Merging of Humans and Machines into a Global Superorganism* (1993) and *The Book of Questions* (1987). The following essay is an excerpt from the introduction of Stock's latest book, *Redesigning Humans: Our Inevitable Genetic Future* (2002).

CONNECTING TO THE TOPIC

With advances in DNA technology, we may be confronting the most difficult decisions ever to face humanity. While many ethicists worry that this technology may irrevocably alter the human genome and humanity as we now define it, others argue that if we have the ability, why not use it? Is genetic enhancement inevitable? Is the question no longer whether we should use DNA technology to improve human lives, but rather when we will use it?

WORDS IN CONTEXT

***Homo sapiens*:** modern species of humans
transcend: to be greater than, as in intensity or power; to surpass
***in vitro* fertilization (IVF):** a form of assisted reproduction in which eggs taken from a donor's body are fertilized with sperm in a lab and placed into a recipient's uterus; the fertilized eggs are expected to implant and develop into a fetus
Prometheus: in Greek mythology, a Titan who stole fire from Olympus and gave it to humankind
incredulous: skeptical or disbelieving
germ line: alterations of the fertilized egg so that the genetic changes will be copied into every cell of the future adult, including reproductive cells, and passed to all future generations
potent: powerful
cadre: a tightly knit group of zealots active in advancing the interests of a particular group
feasible: possible

metabolic: pertaining to the chemical processes occurring within a living cell or organism that are necessary for the maintenance of life
physiological: in accord with or characteristic of the normal functioning of a living organism
daunting: discouraging
aesthetic: of or concerning the appreciation of beauty
manifestations: obvious or visible signs
dubious: uncertain
bravado: defiant behavior

1 We know that *Homo sapiens* is not the final word in primate evolution, but few have yet grasped that we are on the cusp of profound biological change, poised to transcend our current form and character on a journey to destinations of new imagination.

2 At first glance, the very notion that we might become more than "human" seems preposterous. After all, we are still biologically identical in virtually every respect to our cave-dwelling ancestors. But this lack of change is deceptive. Never before have we had the power to manipulate human genetics to alter our biology in meaningful, predictable ways.

3 Bioethicists and scientists alike worry about the consequences of coming genetic technologies, but few have thought through the larger implications of the wave of new developments arriving in reproductive biology. Today, *in vitro* fertilization is responsible for fewer than 1 percent of births in the United States; embryo selection numbers only in the hundreds of cases; cloning and human genetic modification still lie ahead. But give these emerging technologies a decade and they will be the cutting edge of human biological change.

4 These developments will write a new page in the history of life, allowing us to seize control of our evolutionary future. Our coming ability to choose our children's genes will have immense social impact and raise difficult ethical dilemmas. Biological enhancement will lead us into unexplored realms, eventually challenging our basic ideas about what it means to be human.

5 Some imagine we will see the perils, come to our senses, and turn away from such possibilities. But when we imagine Prometheus stealing fire from the gods, we are not incredulous or shocked by his act. It is too characteristically human. To forgo the powerful technologies that

genomics and molecular biology are bringing would be as out of character for humanity as it would be to use them without concern for the dangers they pose. We will do neither. The question is no longer whether we will manipulate embryos, but when, where, and how.

6 The arrival of safe, reliable germline technology will signal the beginning of human self-design. We do not know where this development will ultimately take us, but it will transform the evolutionary process by drawing reproduction into a highly selective social process that is far more rapid and effective at spreading successful genes than traditional sexual competition and mate selection.

7 The road to our eventual disappearance might be paved not by humanity's failure but by its success. Progressive self-transformation could change our descendants into something sufficiently different from our present selves to not be human in the sense we use the term now. Such an occurrence would more aptly be termed a pseudoextinction, since it would not end our lineage. Unlike the saber-toothed tiger and other large mammals that left no descendants when our ancestors drove them to extinction, *Homo sapiens* would spawn its own successors by fast-forwarding its evolution.

8 Some disaster, of course, might derail our technological advance, or our biology might prove too complex to rework. But our recent deciphering of the human genome (the entirety of our genetic constitution) and our massive push to unravel life's workings suggest that modification of our biology is far nearer to reality than the distant space travel we see in science fiction movies. Moreover, we are unlikely to achieve the technology to flit around the galaxy without being able to breach our own biology as well. The Human Genome Project is only a beginning.

9 Many bioethicists do not share my perspective on where we are heading. They imagine that our technology might become potent enough to alter us, but that we will turn away from it and reject human enhancement. But the reshaping of human genetics and biology does not hinge on some cadre of demonic researchers hidden away in a lab in Argentina trying to pick up where Hitler left off. The coming possibilities will be the inadvertent spinoff of mainstream research that virtually everyone supports. Infertility, for example, is a source of deep pain for millions of couples. Researchers and clinicians working on *in vitro* fertilization don't think much about future human evolution, but nonetheless are building a foundation of expertise in conceiving, handling, testing, and implanting human embryos, and this will one day be the basis for the

manipulation of the human species. Already, we are seeing attempts to apply this knowledge in highly controversial ways: as premature as today's efforts to clone humans may be, they would be the flimsiest of fantasies if they could not draw on decades of work on human IVF.

10 Similarly, in early 2001 more than five hundred gene-therapy trials were under way or in review throughout the world. The researchers are trying to cure real people suffering from real diseases and are no more interested in the future of human evolution than IVF researchers. But their progress toward inserting genes into adult cells will be one more piece of the foundation for manipulating human embryos.

11 Not everything that can be done should or will be done, of course, but once a relatively inexpensive technology becomes feasible in thousands of laboratories around the world, and a sizable fraction of the population sees it as beneficial, it *will* be used.

12 The best gauge of how far we will go in manipulating our genetics and that of our children is not what we say to pollsters, but what we are doing in those areas in which we already can modify our biology. On August 2, 1998, Marco Pantani cycled along the Champs Elysees to win the eighty-fifth Tour de France, but the race's real story was the scandal over performance enhancement—which, of course, means drugs.

13 The banned hormone erythropoietin was at the heart of this particular chapter in the ongoing saga of athletic performance enhancement. By raising the oxygen-carrying capacity of red blood cells, the drug can boost endurance by 10 to 15 percent. Early in the race, a stash of it was found in the car of the masseur of the Italian team Festina—one of the world's best—and after an investigation the entire team was booted from the race. A few days later, more erythropoietin was found, this time in the possession of one of the handlers of the Dutch team, and several of its cyclists were kicked out. As police raids intensified, five Spanish teams and an Italian one quit in protest, leaving only fourteen of the original twenty-one teams.

14 The public had little sympathy for the cheaters, but a crowd of angry Festina supporters protested that their riders had been unfairly singled out, and the French minister of health insisted that doping had been going on since racing began. Two years later in a courtroom in Lille, the French sports icon Richard Virenque, five-time winner of the King of the Mountains jersey in the Tour de France, seemed to confirm as much when the president of the court asked him if he took doping products. "We don't say doping," replied Virenque. "We say we're 'preparing for the race.'"

15 The most obvious problem with today's performance-enhancing drugs—besides their being a way of cheating—is that they're dangerous. And when one athlete uses them, others must follow suit to stay competitive. But more than safety is at issue. The concern is what sports will be like when competitors need medical pit crews. As difficult as the problem of doping is, it will soon worsen, because such drugs will become safer, more effective, and harder to detect.

16 Professional sports offers a preview of the spread of enhancement technology into other arenas. Sports may carry stronger incentives to cheat, and thus push athletes toward greater health risks, but the non-sporting world is not so different. A person working two jobs feels under pressure to produce, and so does a student taking a test or someone suffering the effects of growing old. When safe, reliable metabolic and physiological enhancers exist, the public will want them, even if they are illegal. To block their use will be far more daunting than today's war on drugs. An anti-drug commercial proclaiming "dope is for dopes" or one showing a frying egg with the caption "your brain on drugs" would not persuade anyone to stop using a safe memory enhancer.

17 Aesthetic surgery is another budding field for enhancement. When we try to improve our appearance, the personal stakes are high because our looks are always with us. Knowing that the photographs of beautiful models in magazines are airbrushed does not make us any less self-conscious if we believe we have a smile too gummy, skin too droopy, breasts too small, a nose too big, a head too bald, or any other such "defects." Surgery to correct these non-medical problems has been growing rapidly and spreading to an ever-younger clientele. Public approval of aesthetic surgery has climbed some 50 percent in the past decade in the United States. We may not be modifying our genes yet, but we are ever more willing to resort to surgery to hold back the most obvious (and superficial) manifestations of aging, or even simply to remodel our bodies. Older women who have subjected themselves to numerous face-lifts but can no longer stave off the signs of aging are not a rarity. But the tragedy is not so much that these women fight so hard to deny the years of visible decline, but that their struggle against life's natural ebb ultimately must fail. If such a decline were not inevitable, many people would eagerly embrace pharmaceutical or genetic interventions to retard aging.

18 The desire to triumph over our own mortality is an ancient dream, but it hardly stands alone. Whether we look at today's manipulations of our bodies by face-lifts, tattoos, pierced ears, or erythropoietin, the same

message rings loud and clear: if medicine one day enables us to manipulate our biology in appealing ways, many of us will do so—even if the benefits are dubious and the risks not insignificant. To most people, the earliest adopters of these technologies will seem reckless or crazy, but are they so different from the daredevil test pilots of jet aircraft in the 1950s? Virtually by definition, early users believe that the possible gains from their bravado justify the risks. Otherwise, they would wait for flawed procedures to be discarded, for technical glitches to be worked through, for interventions to become safer and more predictable.

19 In truth, as long as people compete with one another for money, status, and mates, as long as they look for ways to display their worth and uniqueness, they will look for an edge for themselves and their children. People will make mistakes with these biological manipulations. People will abuse them. People will worry about them. But as much could be said about any potent new development. No governmental body will wave some legislative wand and make advanced genetic and reproductive technologies go away, and we would be foolish to want this. Our collective challenge is not to figure out how to block these developments, but how best to realize their benefits while minimizing our risks and safeguarding our rights and freedoms. ◆

CONSIDERING THE ISSUES

1. Stock comments that we may be facing a "pseudoextinction" of the human race as we consider ways to apply genetic technology to enhance our DNA. If humans were to use genetic engineering to alter their DNA, would they still be human, or something else?
2. Stock argues that if genetic technology were available to make people stronger or younger, people would use it, risks and ethics aside. If you could use genetic engineering to make yourself be a better athlete or more beautiful or youthful, would you use it? Why or why not?

CRAFT AND CONTENT

3. How does Stock feel about genetic engineering? Summarize his argument in a paragraph.

4. Stock uses the case of cyclists doping with erythropoietin during the 1998 Tour de France as a parallel to what is likely to happen with genetic engineering. How effective is this example? Does it serve as a good indicator of what humans will do to achieve and succeed? Explain.

CRITICAL THINKING

5. Stock states, "Biological enhancement will lead us into unexplored realms, eventually challenging our basic ideas about what it means to be human" (paragraph 4). What does he mean? What are the implications of this statement? Does it seem frightening? Exciting? Explain.
6. Stock makes a reference to Hitler's eugenics plan to create a master race. Could DNA technology be abused this way? Theoretically, could a dictator use genetic engineering to create smarter, stronger citizens?

WRITING ABOUT THE ISSUES

7. Stock predicts that in 30 years, unlike the space program, we will be actively using genetic technology to "manipulate ourselves." Write an exploratory essay in which you predict what genetic technology might be used for in actual practice 30 years from now.
8. Stock notes bioethicists have argued against genetic enhancement because it may create a point of no return, irrevocably altering the human race. Write a response to Stock from the viewpoint of such a bioethicist. Refer to points made in other essays in your response.

Enough

Bill McKibben

Bill McKibben is a scholar in residence at Middlebury College. He is a regular contributor to many publications, including the *New York Review of Books*, the *New York Times*, and the *Atlantic*. He is the author of many books, most recently *Maybe One*, *Long Distance: A Year of Living Strenuously*, and *Enough*, from which this essay was excerpted.

CONNECTING TO THE TOPIC

In the preceding essay, Gregory Stock extolled the promise of genetic engineering. In the next piece, Bill McKibben takes a grim perspective on the issue. He warns that we are approaching the transformation of our species as if we were "sleepwalking." Unless we open our eyes and take a good hard look at what genetic technology means for the future of the human race, we will soon reach a point of no return. We must consider the implications before it is too late. Will genetic enhancement mark the extinction of the human race as we know it?

WORDS IN CONTEXT

arbitrary: determined by chance, whim, or impulse
unambiguous: clear
cipher: one having no influence or value; a nonentity
nanotechnology: the science and technology of building electronic circuits and devices from single atoms and molecules
irradiated: exposed to radiation
mitochondria: spherical or elongated organelle in the cytoplasm of nearly all eukaryotic cells, containing genetic material and many enzymes important for cell metabolism, including those responsible for the conversion of food to usable energy

1 For the first few miles of the marathon, I was still fresh enough to look around, to pay attention. I remember mostly the muffled thump of several thousand pairs of expensive sneakers padding the Ottawa pavement—an elemental sound, like surf, or wind. But as the race wore on, the herd stretched into a dozen flocks and then into a long string of solitary runners. Pretty soon each of us was off in a singular race, pitting one body against one will. By the halfway point, when all the adrenaline had worn off, the only sound left was my breath rattling in my chest. I was deep in my own private universe, completely absorbed in my own drama.

2 Now, this run was entirely inconsequential. For months I'd trained with the arbitrary goal of 3 hours and 20 minutes in my mind. Which is not a fast time: it's an hour and a quarter off the world record. But it would let a forty-one-year-old into the Boston Marathon. And given how fast I'd gone in training, I knew it lay at the outer edge of possible.

So it was a worthwhile target, a number to live with through one early-morning run after another, a number to multiply and divide against the readouts on the treadmill display when downpours kept me in the gym. It's rare enough in my life to have a goal so concrete and unambiguous.

3 By about, say, mile 23, two things were becoming clear. One, my training had worked. I'd reeled off one 7:30 mile after another. Two, my training wouldn't get me to the finish by itself. My legs were starting to slow and wobble, my knees and calves were hard pressed to lift and push at the same pace as an hour earlier. I could feel my goal slipping away, my pace dropping. With every hundred yards the race became less a physical test and more a mental one, game spirit trying to rally sagging flesh before sagging flesh could sap game spirit and convince it the time had come to walk. Someone stronger passed me, and I slipped onto her heels for a few hundred crucial yards, picking up the pace. The finish line swam into my squinted view, and I stagger-sprinted across. With 14 seconds to spare.

4 A photographer clicked a picture, as he would of everyone who finished. I was a cipher to him—a grimacing cipher, the 324th person to cross, an unimportant finisher in an unimportant time in an unimportant race. In the picture you can see the crowd at the finish, looking right past me toward the middle distance, waiting for their mom or dad, son or daughter to hove into sight. It mattered not at all what I had done.

5 But it mattered to *me*. When it was done, I had a clearer sense of myself, of my power and my frailty. For a period of hours, and especially those last gritty miles, I had been absolutely, utterly *present*, the moments desperately, magnificently clarified. As meaningless as it was to the world, that's how meaning*ful* it was to me. I met parts of myself I'd never been introduced to before, glimpsed more clearly strengths and flaws I'd half suspected. A marathon peels you down toward your core for a little while, gets past the defenses we erect even against ourselves. That's the high that draws you back for the next race, a centering elation shared by people who finished an hour ahead and two hours behind me. And it must echo in some small way what runners have always felt—the Tarahumara Indians on their impossible week-long runs through the canyons of Mexico, the Masai on their game trails. Few things are more basic than running.

6 And yet it is entirely possible that we will be among the last generations to feel that power and that frailty. Genetic science may

soon offer human beings, among many other things, the power to bless their offspring with a vastly improved engine. For instance, scientists may find ways to dramatically increase the amount of oxygen that blood can carry. When that happens, we will, though not quite as Isaiah envisioned, be able to run and not grow weary.

7 This is one small item on the long list of "improvements" that the proponents of human genetic engineering envision, and one of the least significant comers of human life they propose to alter. But it serves as a decent template for starting to think about all the changes they have in mind, and indeed the changes that may result from a suite of other new engineering marvels like advanced robotics and nanotechnology.

8 Consider sports. Attempts to alter the human body are nothing new in sports, ofcourse. It's been more than a century since Charles-Edouard Brown-Sequard, the French physiologist called "the father of steroids," injected himself with an extract derived from the testicle of a guinea pig and a dog.[1] Athletes have been irradiated and surgically implanted with monkey glands; they have weight-trained with special regimens designed to increase mitochondria in muscle cells and have lived in special trailers pressurized to simulate high altitudes.[2] For endurance athletes, the drug of choice has for the last decade been erythropoietin, or EPO, a man-made version of a hormone released by the kidneys that stimulates the production of red blood cells, so that the blood can carry extra oxygen. With EPO, the red blood cells can get so thick that the blood curdles, turns into a syrupy ooze—in the early days of the drug, elite cyclists started dropping dead across their handlebars, their hearts unable to pump the sludge running through their veins.

9 In 1995, researchers asked two hundred Olympic hopefuls if they'd take a drug that would guarantee them a five-year winning streak and then kill them. Almost half said yes.[3] The Tour de France has been interrupted by police raids time and again; in 2001, Italian officials found what they described as a "mobile hospital" trailing the Giro d'Italia bike race, well stocked with testosterone, human growth hormone, urofillitophin, salbutamol, and a synthetic blood product called HemAssist.[4]

---

1. John M. Hoberman, *Mortal Engines: The Science of Performance and the Dehumanization of Sport* (New York: 1992), p. 72.
2. Ibid., pp. 136, 102; Sharon Begley, "Good Medal Workouts," *Newsweek*, Dec. 17, 2001.
3. Mark Compton, "Enhancement Genetics: Let the Games Begin," *DNA Dispatch*, July 2001.
4. "More Giro Shocks Still to Come," *Pro Cycling*, March 5, 2002.

The British sports commentator Simon Eassom said recently that the only people likely to be caught for steroid abuse were from Third World countries: everyone else could afford new-generation drugs that didn't yet show up on tests.[5] Some sports, like power lifting, have had to give in and set up "drug-free" or "natural" divisions.[6]

10 In other words, you could almost say that it makes no difference whether athletes of the future are genetically engineered—that the damage is already done with conventional drugs, the line already crossed. You could almost say that, but not quite. Because in fact, in the last couple of years, the testing has gotten better. The new World Anti-Doping Agency has caught enough offenders to throw a scare into dirty athletes, and some heart into clean ones. Some distance athletes who had decided to retire because they felt they couldn't compete have gone back into training; a new group of poststeroids shotputters and discus hurlers have proved their point by winning meets with shorter throws than the records of a decade ago.[7] And both athlete and fan remain able to draw the line in their minds: no one thought Ben Johnson's 1988 dash record meant anything once the Olympic lab found steroids in his system. It was erased from the record books, and he was banned from competition. Against the odds, sports just manages to stay "real."

11 But what if, instead of crudely cheating with hypodermics, we began to literally program children before they were born to become great athletes? "Picture this," writes one British journalist. "It is 2016. A 'young couple are sitting in a doctor's waiting room. They know that what they are about to do is illegal, but they are determined. They have come to make their child a world-beating athlete," by injecting their embryo with the patented genes of a champion.[8] Muscle size, oxygen uptake, respiration—much of an athlete's inherent capacity derives from her genes. What she makes of it depends on her heart and mind, of course, as well as on the accidents of where she's born, and what kind of diet she gets, and whether the local rulers believe that girls should be out running.

---

5. Amanda Swift, "The Sports Factor," ABC radio [Australia], July 12, 2001.

6. Ira Berkow, "This Lifter Is Fueled by Natural Power," *New York Times*, Feb. 6, 1994.

7. Rod Osher, "Hot Performances," Time.com, Sept. 6, 1999.

8. Michael Butcher, "Next: The Genetically Modified Athlete," *Guardian*, Dec. 15, 1999.

12 And her genes aren't entirely random: perhaps her parents were attracted to each other in the first place because both were athletes, or because they were not. But all those variables fit within our idea of fate. Flipping through the clinic catalogue for athletic genes does not; it's a door into another world.

13 If it happens—and when that girl grows up to compete–it won't be as if she is "cheating." "What if you're born with something having been done to you?" asks the Olympic dash champion Maurice Greene. "You didn't have anything to do with it."[9] But if that happens, what will be the point of running? "Just what human excellences are we supposed to be celebrating?" asks the medical ethicist Eric Juengst. 'Who's got the better biotech sponsor?"[10] Spectacle will survive, and for many fans that may be enough. But the emptiness will be real.

14 For those of us who will never win a race, it should be easy to nod. But as we move into this new world of genetic engineering, we won't simply lose races, we'll lose racing: we'll lose the possibility of the test, the challenge, the celebration that athletics represents. Forget elite athletes–they drip one drop of sweat for every thousand that roll off the brows of weekend warriors. It's the average human, once "improved," who will have no more reason for running marathons. Say you've reached Mile 23, and you're feeling strong. Is it because of your hard training and your character, or because the gene pack inside you is pumping out more red blood cells than your body knows what to do with? Will anyone be impressed with your dedication? More to the point, will you be impressed with your dedication? Will you know what part of it is you, and what part is your upgrade? Right now we think of our bodies (and our minds) as givens; we think of them as us, and we work to make of them what we can. But if they become equipment—if your heart and lungs (and eventually your character) are a product of engineering—then running becomes like driving. Driving can be fun, and goodness knows there are people who care passionately about their cars, who will come to blows on the question Ford

---

9. Jere Longman, "Getting the Athletic Edge May Mean Altering Genes," *New York Times*, May 11, 2001.

10. Compton, "Enhancement Genetics."

vs. Chevy. But the skill, the engagement, the meaning reside mostly in those who design the machines. No one goes out and drives in honor of a dying sister.

15 Sport is the canary in a miner's cage. It's possible the canary will die; there are those who think, with good reason, that genetic engineering of the human organism may be crude and dangerous, especially at first. But the even greater danger is that the canary will be souped up into an ever perkier, ever tougher, ever "better" specimen. Not a canary anymore, but a parrot, or a golden eagle, or some grand thing we can only guess at. A canary so big and strong that it . . . won't be a canary anymore. It will be something else entirely, unable to carry the sweet tune it grew up singing.

16 No one needs to run in the twenty-first century. Running is an outlet for spirit, for finding out who you are, no more mandatory than art or music. It is a voluntary beauty, a grace. And it turns out to be a fragile beauty. Its significance depends on the limitations and wonders of our bodies as we have known them. Why would you sign up for a marathon if it was a test of the alterations some embryologist had made in you, and in a million others? If 3 hours and 20 minutes was your design spec? We'll still be able to run hard; doubtless we'll even hurt. It's not the personal challenge that will disappear. It's the personal. ◆

CONSIDERING THE ISSUES

1. Twenty years ago, many people were raising serious questions about "test tube" babies and the ethics of *in vitro* fertilization—a practice that most people now find acceptable. Do you think it is likely that we will feel the same way about human genetic engineering? Will it become acceptable as time passes? Why or why not?
2. Would knowing you were genetically enhanced to perform better at sports or mathematics reduce your pride when you excelled in these areas? Imagine your parents explaining that they chose to enhance your genes to make you more athletic or smarter. Would you feel differently about your successes in these areas? Why or why not?

3. McKibben describes how a marathon made him realize things about himself he never knew. "For a period of hours, and especially those last gritty miles, I had been absolutely, utterly *present*, the moments desperately, magnificently clarified. As meaningless as it was to the world, that's how meaning*ful* it was to me." Write a short personal narrative describing a time when you pushed yourself beyond your expectations. What did you learn about yourself, and why?

CRAFT AND CONTENT

4. Why does McKibben choose to open his argument with the story of his first marathon? How does this story frame the points that follow? Is it an effective way to draw in his readers? How does it relate to his thesis? Explain.
5. McKibben comments, "You could almost say that it makes no difference whether athletes of the future are genetically engineered—the damage is already done with conventional drugs, the line already crossed." On what grounds does he disprove this statement?

CRITICAL THINKING

6. If genetic engineering were used to create better athletes, how would it change sports in general? Would people still be impressed by excellence? Would athletes have to undergo genetic screenings before they could compete? Would it create a different "race"—a race of athletes bred for muscle? Discuss.
7. McKibben wonders if the inherent challenge in running a race would disappear if you were genetically engineered to be a stronger runner. "It's not the personal challenge that will disappear. It's the personal." What does he mean?

WRITING ABOUT THE ISSUES

8. McKibben warns that genetic engineering will change what it means to be human—for the worse. But are people likely to

heed his concerns and those of others like him? Imagine that you could go back in time 150 years and warn government leaders that the weapons of war soon to be invented, such as automatic weapons, missiles, gases, mines, and grenades, would result in millions of deaths in a 30-year time period between 1915 and 1945. Do you think they would have banned such technology? Would this have been good for humanity? (Remember that many forms of technology used in modern weaponry are also used in modern medicine.) Explore this idea from your own viewpoint.

9. A deeper issue McKibben raises connected to genetic alteration is that it could irrevocably alter how we feel about ourselves as individuals and how we relate to others. Imagine a world in which there are genetically enhanced individuals who have been made smarter, stronger, or more beautiful than conventionally conceived children. What issues are likely to arise? How would the nonenhanced people function in a world in which there was no hope to ever compete on the same level as the enhanced?

VISUAL CONNECTIONS

The Art of Human Cloning

CONNECTING TO THE TOPIC

This photograph created by Gandee Vasan was a second-place winner in the 2002 Visions of Science contest, a photographic awards program organized by Novartis Pharmaceuticals. The goal of Visions of Science is to highlight "attention-grabbing images that give new insight into the world of science and the workings of nature." Vasan's photograph was part of the "Science Concepts" category of the competition and is a composite of several images combined through Painter and Adobe Photoshop. Adam Hart-Davis, a 2002 competition judge, said of this image, "This cloning fantasy impressed us mainly for its slightly sinister implications." Gandee Vasan is a photographer living in the United Kingdom. His work has appeared in several books.

CONSIDERING THE ISSUES

1. If this image were not titled *human cloning,* would you have automatically assumed that this was its subject matter? How does the title connect to our understanding of the image? What other titles could this image have? Come up with a few alternative titles of your own.
2. How would you react if you found out that you were one of several cloned children created to help infertile couples have a child? Until this point, you had grown up thinking you were just like any other person. Now you discover you are actually a clone. How would you feel? Would you be angry? Accepting? Explain.

CRITICAL THINKING

3. Is human cloning likely to change the way we view children? Why or why not? Frame your answer in terms of how society may view cloned children.
4. Adam Hart-Davis described this image as "slightly sinister." What do you think he found sinister about it? Do you view the photograph in a similar way, or did you have completely different feelings about it when you first viewed it? Explain.

TOPICAL CONNECTIONS

GROUP PROJECTS

1. The year is 2040, and the U.S. government, concerned that tinkering with human DNA could have dire consequences generations from now, has banned the practice of human genetic engineering. However, routine genetic screening, a common health practice, reveals that a young boy has been genetically altered to make him smarter than he normally would have been. His parents are arrested, having admitted to paying for the genetic engineering at a center in Europe. They argue that they obtained this service because they felt it was in the best interest of their child. Your group, a jury, must decide what to do. Do you incarcerate the couple? Fine them? Discuss the case and present your decision to the class as part of a larger discussion.
2. If genetic manipulation could be performed with accuracy and was made available to the general population, what rules should govern its use to prevent a gap between the haves and the have-nots? Develop a set of recommendations considering the points raised by the authors in this unit.

WEB PROJECT

3. Obtain a copy of the President's Council on Bioethics' report on human cloning at its Web site at www.bioethics.gov/reports/cloningreport/index.html. You have been appointed as a member of a commission that must reassess the position drafted by the council in 2002. Research current cloning technology and address the section on children and research in particular. Based on your research, revise the 2002 report and make a recommendation to the president.

FOR FURTHER INQUIRY

4. Both Gregory Stock and Bill McKibben comment on the use of performance-enhancement drugs used by many athletes today. Stock argues that if a safe genetically engineered product were available to make us smarter, more youthful, or have better

memories, we would use them. McKibben contends that such a use obliterates the point of sports altogether. Research the issue of athletes using erythropoietin and other performance drugs. How prevalent is their use? Based on your research, do you think athletes are likely to use genetic enhancing technology if it were likely to improve their performance? Should such a use be banned? Is it preventable? Explain.

8 Can Television Violence Influence Behavior?

Television is the prime mover of modern culture. Over five decades, it has become the country's foremost source of entertainment and news. More than any other medium, television regulates commerce, lifestyles, and social values. But the medium is also the object of considerable scorn. For years, television has been blamed for nearly all our social ills—the rise in crime, juvenile violence, racism, increased sexual promiscuity, drug addiction, and the collapse of the family. In short, it has been cited as the cause of the decline of Western civilization.

The average 20-year-old viewer will have spent nearly three years of his or her life in front of the television set. But what has that 20-year-old spent his or her time watching? From afternoon cartoons to prime-time programs, the shows that tend to attract a child audience are increasingly violent, featuring aggressive superheroes, action-packed fights, bloodshed, and even murder. What influence, if any, does such programming have on young minds? If television can indeed shape society, can it shape children too? This chapter will explore in greater depth the issue of violent television's influence on children.

Does violent television programming influence children to be more violent themselves, and thus, more likely grow into violent adults? Is it the responsibility of parents to monitor what their children see and hear, or should the television industry also be held accountable for its programming? As a society, are we simply becoming insensitive to violence? Are children today more likely to bring guns to school or solve conflicts through violence than children in the past? This chapter takes a look at the possible connections between television and violent behavior in kids.

CRITICAL THINKING

1. What are the visual clichés in this cartoon? How do stock props convey a moment in time to the viewer? Explain.
2. What issues is the cartoonist addressing in this cartoon? Explain.
3. Why are the boy's words to the girl appropriate to the subject matter of the cartoon? Why are they funny?

Violence on Television— What Do Children Learn? What Can Parents Do?

American Psychological Association

Based in Washington, D.C., the American Psychological Association (APA) is a scientific and professional organization that represents psychology in the United States. It promotes the advancement and distribution of psychological knowledge to promote health, education, and public welfare. This fact sheet is available on their Web site: www.apa.org.

CONNECTING TO THE TOPIC

Almost 20 years ago, the National Institute of Mental Health reported that television violence could be dangerous for children. Since then, and despite such warnings, violence on television has significantly increased both in quantity and intensity. Studies indicate that children who watch a lot of violent television programming tend to be less bothered by violence. Other studies reveal that children who watch violent programming are less likely to call for help or intervene when they witness violent acts among their peers. Should the television industry be more responsible for its programming? Is this an issue for parents, or the medium of television itself? And is society as a whole at risk?

WORDS IN CONTEXT

psychology: the study of the mind and behavior
intervene: to interfere; to get involved with
National Institute of Mental Health: a division of the National Institutes of Health (NIH), the federal government's principal biomedical and behavioral research agency. Its mission is to reduce the burden of mental illness and behavioral disorders through research on mind, brain, and behavior.
prosecute: to impose legal punishment
accumulate: gathered in a substantial quantity

"Violent programs on television lead to aggressive behavior by children and teenagers who watch those programs."

1 That was the word from a 1982 report by the National Institute of Mental Health, a report that confirmed and extended an earlier study done by the surgeon general. As a result of these and other research findings, the American Psychological Association passed a resolution in February of 1985 informing broadcasters and the public of the potential dangers that viewing violence on television can have for children.

What Does the Research Show?

2 Psychological research has shown three major effects of seeing violence on television:

- Children may become less sensitive to the pain and suffering of others.
- Children may be more fearful of the world around them.
- Children may be more likely to behave in aggressive or harmful ways toward others.

3 Children who watch a lot of TV are less aroused by violent scenes than are those who only watch a little; in other words, they're less bothered by violence in general, and less likely to see anything wrong with it. One example: in several studies, those who watched a violent program instead of a nonviolent one were slower to intervene or to call for help when, a little later, they saw younger children fighting or playing destructively.

4 Studies by George Gerbner, Ph.D., at the University of Pennsylvania, have shown that children's TV shows contain about 20 violent acts each hour and also that children who watch a lot of television are more likely to think that the world is a mean and dangerous place.

5 Children often behave differently after they've been watching violent programs on TV. In one study done at Pennsylvania State University, about 100 preschool children were observed both before and after watching television; some watched cartoons that had a lot of aggressive and violent acts in them, and others watched shows that didn't have any kind of violence. The researchers noticed real differences between the kids who watched the violent shows and those who watched nonviolent ones.

6 "Children who watch the violent shows, even 'just funny' cartoons, were more likely to hit out at their playmates, argue, disobey class rules, leave tasks unfinished, and were less willing to wait for things than those who watched the nonviolent programs," says Aletha Huston, Ph.D., now at the University of Kansas.

Real-Life Studies

7 Findings from the laboratory are further supported by field studies which have shown the long-range effects of televised violence. Leonard Eron, Ph.D., and his associates at the University of Illinois, found that children who watched many hours of TV violence when they were in elementary school tended to also show a higher level of aggressive behavior when they became teenagers. By observing these youngsters until they were 30 years old, Dr. Eron found that the ones who'd watched a lot of TV when they were eight years old were more likely to be arrested and prosecuted for criminal acts as adults.

A Continuing Debate

8 In spite of this accumulated evidence, broadcasters and scientists continue to debate the link between viewing TV violence and children's aggressive behavior. Some broadcasters believe that there is not enough evidence to prove that TV violence is harmful. But scientists who have studied this issue say that there is a link between TV violence and aggression, and in 1992, the American Psychological Association's Task Force on Television and Society published a report that confirms this view. The report, entitled *Big World, Small Screen: The Role of Television in American Society*, shows that the harmful effects of TV violence do exist.

What Parents Can Do

9 While most scientists are convinced that children can learn aggressive behavior from television, they also point out that parents have tremendous power to moderate that influence.

10 Because there is a great deal of violence in both adult and children's programming, just limiting the number of hours children watch television will probably reduce the amount of aggression they see.

11 Parents should watch at least one episode of the programs their children watch. That way they'll know what their children are watching and be able to talk about it with them.

12 When they see a violent incident, parents can discuss with their child what caused the character to act in a violent way. They should also point out that this kind of behavior is not characteristic, not the way adults usually solve their problems. They can ask their children to talk about other ways the character could have reacted, or other nonviolent solutions to the character's problem.

13 Parents can outright ban any programs that they find too offensive. They can also restrict their children's viewing to shows that they feel are more beneficial, such as documentaries, educational shows and so on.

14 Parents can limit the amount of time children spend watching television, and encourage children to spend their time on sports, hobbies, or with friends; parents and kids can even draw up a list of other enjoyable activities to do instead of watching TV.

15 Parents can encourage their children to watch programs that demonstrate helping, caring and cooperation. Studies show that these types of programs can influence children to become more kind and considerate. ◆

CONSIDERING THE ISSUES

1. Think about the level and frequency of violence in the programs you watch on television. Is violence a common theme? What types of television programs do you like to watch, and why?
2. In this article, the APA provides recommendations to parents, but not to television broadcasters. In your opinion, does control over television's violent content belong at home, or at the network? Explain.

CRAFT AND CONTENT

3. This article was produced by the APA to provide guidance and information for parents on the issue of children and television violence. Does the fact that the APA is a scientific body make its statements seem more credible? What sources of information do we tend to trust, and why?

4. What information does this document convey most strongly? What visual and organizational devices does it use to make certain points stand out? Explain.
5. What authorities and sources does the APA cite to support its point? How do these authorities influence the reader?

CRITICAL THINKING

6. The APA notes that George Gerbner's research indicates that children who watch violent television programs are more likely to think that the world is "a mean and dangerous place." What effect might such a belief have on a child? What about when that child grows up? Explain.
7. According to the APA, what are the real-life ramifications for children who view violent television programming?

WRITING ABOUT THE ISSUES

8. The APA article notes that despite significant evidence indicating that television violence influences children, the issue continues to be debated. Why do you think that is? Why is this issue so controversial?
9. The APA provides some recommendations to parents at the end of its article. Evaluate the practicality and logic of the advice they offer. Respond to each recommendation with your own viewpoint.

Beyond Banning War and Superhero Play

Diane E. Levin

Diane E. Levin is a professor of education at Wheelock College in Boston. Her current research focuses on how to promote children's healthy development, learning, and behavior in violent times. She is the author of and contributor to several books, including *Teaching Young Children in Violent Times: Building a Peaceable Classroom* (1994). This article appeared in the May 2003 issue of *Young Children.* The fully referenced article may be viewed at www.journal.nacyc.org/btj/200305/warandsuperhero.pdf.

CONNECTING TO THE TOPIC

The American Academy of Child and Adolescent Psychiatry has found that TV violence may encourage children to imitate the violence they observe on television. Moreover, children may identify with certain characters featured on violent programming. Usually, imitated violence emerges during "war" or "superhero" play, with "good guys" and "bad guys." Such play can pose challenges for teachers of young children. However, play is one way children learn to work out issues that bother them and things that they find troubling in the adult world. How do teachers balance children's need for play with the need to maintain a safe classroom environment? Is the answer to banish play from the classroom?

WORDS IN CONTEXT

obsess: to be excessively preoccupied
suppress: to forcibly subdue or restrain
therapeutic: having healing effects
cognitive: relating to the process of understanding factual knowledge
salient: conspicuous; prominent; noticeable
generic: general; not specific
replicate: to reproduce or repeat; to copy
diversion: a turning aside; distraction
veteran: experienced; having a great deal of practice in a particular area
circumvent: to go around
guerilla wars: covert, irregular warfare, usually hidden and not immediately obvious, marked by sneak attacks
sustained: of longer duration; enduring
elaborated: developed thoughtfully and carefully with attention to details
one-dimensional: flat and lacking in any depth

1 *"Four-year-old Jules is particularly obsessed. Telling him no guns or pretend fighting just doesn't work. When he's a good guy, like a Power Ranger, or Spiderman, he thinks it's okay to use whatever force is needed to suppress the bad guy, "because that's what a superhero does!" And then someone ends up getting hurt. When we try to enforce a ban, the children say it's not superhero play, it's some other kind of play. Many children don't seem to know more positive ways to play, or they play the same thing over and over without having any ideas of their own. I need some new ideas."*

2 This experienced teacher's account captures the kinds of concerns I often hear from teachers worried about how to respond to war play in their classrooms. Expressions of concern about play with violence tend to increase when violent world events, like 9/11 and the war against Iraq, dominate the news.

3 Play, viewed for decades as an essential part of the early childhood years, has become a problem in many classrooms, even something to avoid. Teachers ask why play is deemed so important to children's development when it is so focused on fighting. Some are led to plan other activities that are easier to manage and appear at first glance to be more productive. Reducing playtime may seem in the short term to reduce problems, but this approach does not address the wide-ranging needs children address through play.

Why Are Children Fascinated with War Play?

4 There are many reasons why children bring violent content and themes into their play. They are related to the role of play in development and learning as well as to the nature of the society in which war play occurs.

5 From both therapeutic and cognitive perspectives, children use play to work out an understanding of experience, including the violence to which they are exposed. Young children may see violence in their homes and communities as well as in entertainment and news on the screen. We should not be surprised when children are intent on bringing it to their play. Children's play often focuses on the most salient and graphic, confusing or scary, and aggressive aspects of violence. It is this content they struggle to work out and understand. Typically, the children who seem most obsessed with war play have been exposed to the most violence and have the greatest need to work it out.

6 Most young children look for ways to feel powerful and strong. Play can be a safe way to achieve a sense of power. From a child's point of view, play with violence is very seductive, especially when connected to the power and invincibility portrayed in entertainment. The children who use war play to help them feel powerful and safe are the children who feel the most powerless and vulnerable.

7 Children's toys give powerful messages about what and how to play. Open-ended toys, like blocks, stuffed animals, and generic dinosaurs, can be used in many ways that the child controls. Highly structured toys, such as action figures that talk and playdough kits with molds to make movie characters, tend to have built-in features

that show children how and what to play. Many of today's best-selling toys are of the highly structured variety and are linked to violent media. Such toys are appealing because they promise dramatic power and excitement. These toys channel children into replicating the violent stories they see on screen. Some children, like Jules, get "stuck" imitating media-linked violence instead of developing creative, imaginative, and beneficial play.

Teachers' Concerns About War Play

8 There are many reasons why teachers are concerned about war play and why they seek help figuring out how to deal with it. Play with violence tends to end up with children out of control, scared, and hurt. Managing aggressive play and keeping everyone safe can feel like a never-ending struggle and a major diversion from the positive lessons we want children to learn.

9 Many veteran teachers say that the bans they used to impose on war play no longer work. Children have a hard time accepting limits or controlling their intense desire or need to engage in the play. And children find ways to circumvent the ban—they deny that their play is really war play (that is, they learn to lie) or sneak around conducting guerilla wars the teacher does not detect (they learn to deceive).

10 Like Jules, some children engage in the same play with violence day after day and bring in few new or creative ideas of their own. Piaget called this kind of behavior imitation, not play. These children are less likely to work out their needs regarding the violence they bring to their play or benefit from more sustained and elaborated play.

11 Seeing children pretend to hurt others is the opposite of what we hope they will learn about how to treat each other and solve problems. Children learn as they play—and what they play affects what they learn. When children are exposed to large amounts of violence, they learn harmful lessons about violence, whether they are allowed to play it in the classroom or not.

12 At the same time, children do not think about the violence they bring into their play in the same way adults do. Jules focuses on one thing at a time; he sees the bad guy as one dimensional without thinking about what makes him bad. He thinks good guys can do whatever hurtful things they want because they are good. Except when he gets carried away and hurts another child, Jules probably does know that at some level his play is different from the real violence he is imitating.

More Important Now Than Ever

13 There is no perfect approach for dealing with children's play with violence in these times. The best strategy is to vastly reduce the amount of violence children see. This would require adults to create a more peaceful world and limit children's exposure to media violence and toys marketed with media violence.

14 Given the state of the world—including the war against Iraq—children now more than ever need to find ways to work out the violence they see. For many, play helps them do so. We have a vital role in helping children meet their needs through play. We must create an approach that addresses the unique needs of children growing up in the midst of violence as well as the concerns of adults about how play with violence contributes to the harmful lessons children learn. ◆

CONSIDERING THE ISSUES

1. Levin begins her article with the case of four-year-old Jules and then asks the question, "Why are children fascinated with war play?" Answer this question based on observations and experiences of your own. As a child, did you engage in violent play such as "cops and robbers," war, G.I. Joe, Power Rangers, or other superhero-related role-playing?
2. At the end of her article, Levin notes that the American war in Iraq has made children more likely to engage in war play as they "work out" things they see on TV. This idea raises the question whether parents should shield their children from the nightly news, just as they might discourage violent children's programs such as Power Rangers or Superman. What do you think? Should children be allowed to view the nightly news?

CRAFT AND CONTENT

3. How does Levin's use of the case of a real child (Jules) help introduce her topic? Is this an effective way to catch the attention of an audience? Why or why not?
4. This essay is organized as a problem/solution—that is, Levin presents a problem in the case of Jules, discusses the issue in larger scope, and then suggests a solution. In your own words,

summarize each of these components—the problem, the discussion, and the solution.

CRITICAL THINKING

5. In paragraph 3, Levin notes that some teachers have reduced or even banned playtime in order to avoid the problem of having children act up and engage in violent play. Why is this solution unlikely to work? Explain.
6. Why is role-playing and imaginative play important for young children? In your opinion, if war play does not harm other children, do you think it is permissible? Should it be discouraged? Why or why not?

WRITING ABOUT THE ISSUES

7. In a short essay, evaluate the solutions Levin offers on how to channel children's desire for war play. Are these solutions likely to work? Why or why not? Can you offer additional solutions? Describe some other possible ideas in a short essay.
8. Are there reasons other than those Levin mentions that children like war play? Write a short essay identifying that some of the reasons children like to play war, drawing from your personal experience and some of the points Levin makes in her article.

Hate Violence? Turn It Off!

Tim Goodman

Columnist Tim Goodman is a television and media critic for the *San Francisco Chronicle,* in which this article first appeared on April 29, 2001.

CONNECTING TO THE TOPIC

Not everyone agrees that television violence is a problem. Some people argue that if you don't like what you see on television, change the channel, or turn it off. The author of the next piece is tired of critics whining that television violence is damaging to children. He says, "vote with your remote" and stop trying to ruin television for everyone else.

WORDS IN CONTEXT

plethora: a superabundance; an excess
censorship: the practice of restricting, suppressing, or removing material that is considered morally, politically, or socially objectionable
scapegoat: one that is made to bear the blame of others
lax: lacking in strictness; overly permissive; negligent
vaunted: boasted; bragged
pap: material lacking real value or substance
prominent: immediately noticeable; conspicuous
ratcheted: to increase or decrease by increments
erode: to wear away
chaos: condition or place of great disorder or confusion

1 Perhaps it's a sign of progress that Americans are becoming just as concerned about violence on television as they are about sex. For years, a barely concealed nipple or a tame bed scene was deemed worse than hundreds of people being brutally shot down on cop shows and the like.

2 Now you can't pick up the paper without some watchdog group denouncing Hollywood for ruining their children's lives with a plethora of violent images nightly. Some kid goes postal at his high school and "Starsky and Hutch" is the root cause.

3 We're getting our priorities right and wrong simultaneously. If sexuality is now not the enemy, great. But to continue to demonize Hollywood for its portrayals of violence is to put our heads in the sand about the world we live in.

4 Worse, it's just plain wrong, reeks of censorship and, in the context of parents worried about their children, it's looking for a scapegoat when lax parenting skills are more to blame.

5 For example, parents have put pressure on their elected officials to "do something" about violence, and the result has been a ratings system that surveys suggest most parents never use. And then there's the vaunted "V-chip," which effectively shifted parental responsibility to the government and doesn't consider the simplest way for everyone to solve this problem: Vote with your remote.

6 Some of us like violence. Some of us like shows that have a gritty realism to them, rather than the glossy pap offered up by most networks. And think of all the people without children who, as grown-ups, choose to watch programming clearly geared to adults. Just because you've given little Jimmy his own TV set upstairs and now you can't stop him from watching "Jackass" on MTV or "Oz" on HBO, don't cry foul and ruin it for the rest of us.

7 This is an old and now increasingly tired defense of art, anti-censorship and the need for parents to take more responsibility for what their children are watching. Don't like it? Don't watch it. There are enough elements in place now—blocking devices, ratings, V-chips, etc.—that to whine about how Hollywood should tone it down (as you allow the blood-and-guts nightly news to waft over dinner) completely misses the point about whose kid it is.

8 Then again, many adults also dislike violence. Fine. Vote with the remote. Go to PBS, the History Channel, Disney—whatever—just stop writing letters to politicians who have already had a chilling effect (thus a watering- and dumbing-down of content) on what we already see.

9 Most recently, there has been a backlash against "The Sopranos," with many people thinking there's been an amping up of the violence and at least two very disturbing episodes filled with violence toward women.

10 First off, yes, those were difficult to watch. But HBO runs a very prominent content advisory at the front of every episode. And, more important, "The Sopranos" is not "Leave It to Beaver," despite near universal acclaim from critics and an almost scary loyalty among viewers.

11 It's just a hunch, but perhaps creator David Chase, sensing this weird, uncomfortable embracing of—let's be honest here—bad people, ratcheted up the violence as a reminder of what exactly it is we're watching.

12 If this moved people out of their comfort zones, they should stop watching. Many have. Others have complained to HBO and some are asking that such behavior be toned down. The short answer to that is this: No. "The Sopranos" is art. As a viewer, your reaction to that art can be anything you want it to be, but restricting it instead of looking away is not the right course.

13 This goes beyond freedom of expression, of course, and those who do not embrace their own freedom to choose other programming. People assume that television has somehow helped erode the social contract that keeps chaos and horror at bay. They blame television for the downfall of the nation's morals.

14 But we have always been a violent country. People were killed at a pretty good clip before television appeared. It's the dark side of our nature, but it didn't come out of the bogeyman's closet 50 years ago.

15 Violence as entertainment, or as a realistic expression of what is really going on in our world, will never appeal to some people. But no one is forcing them to watch. There are dozens of other channels, hundreds of other programs.

16 There's also an off button. Sometimes that gets forgotten.

17 Television is not the problem in our society. It may always be the scapegoat, but it's nothing more than a bastard machine, not half as disturbing as the real thing. ◆

CONSIDERING THE ISSUES

1. Goodman states that pressuring Hollywood to change violent programming "reeks of censorship." Do you agree with Goodman? What do you think censorship means? Are you opposed to censorship of this kind? Why or why not?
2. Do you enjoy watching violent television programs? Would you be upset if a "watchdog" group forced one of your favorite programs off the air? Explain.

CRAFT AND CONTENT

3. Evaluate the author's use of language in paragraphs 6, 7, 16, and 17. What does it reveal about people who wish to change television programming? Is this language likely to appeal to or anger his readers? Or does the answer depend on who is reading his column? Explain.
4. What phrases does Goodman repeat in his essay? Why do you think he repeats certain words?

CRITICAL THINKING

5. What is Goodman's opinion of parents who want to influence television programming? Do parents have a right to pressure Hollywood to change violent shows?
6. How might the other side respond to Goodman's claim that he has a right to watch violent programs if he wants to?

7. Goodman urges people to "vote with your remote." Is changing the channel the equivalent to "voting" on what programs should air on television? Is it a solution that could work? Or is it just a catchy phrase? Explain.
8. Goodman notes that "we have always been a violent country" (paragraph 14). Does this statement justify television violence? Why or why not?

WRITING ABOUT THE ISSUES

9. Goodman argues that if parents or other adults object to a television program, they should change the channel, or just turn off the television set. Is this a reasonable solution? Why or why not? Write about your thoughts on this issue in a short essay.
10. What is "art"? Are violent television programs, such as the ones Goodman cites (*Jackass, Oz, The Sopranos*), art? Does the claim that these programs are a form of artistic expression support Goodman's argument? Explain.
11. Write a short essay exploring the connection between censorship and television programming. Who is likely to control the airwaves? What programs would survive, and what would be cut? Explain.

Television's Global Marketing Strategy Creates a Damaging and Alienated Window on the World

George Gerbner

George Gerbner is professor of communications and dean emeritus of the Annenberg School of Communication in Philadelphia, where he directed a number of studies of mass communications and its effects on culture. For over 30 years, Gerbner and his team of researchers have studied the role of media violence in American society. He is also a founder of the Cultural Environment Movement, which is working to reassert democratic influence on the media. This article appeared in the Spring 1994 issue of *The Ecology of Justice*, published by the Context Institute.

CONNECTING TO THE TOPIC

George Gerbner headed the Cultural Indicators project, a research team probing the issue of media violence in America. One of the most disturbing estimates made by the project is that the average American child will have watched over 8,000 murders on television by the time he or she reaches 12 years of age. But is the argument over whether television violence causes real violence missing the point? In our desire to demonstrate a cause/effect relationship between violence on television and violent behavior, are we neglecting deeper issues? Gerbner argues that the alienating culture of television has replaced other forms of communication that once tied family and community together. It erodes culture by substituting social traditions in favor of general media messaging—and often this message is one of violence. Gerbner also advocates for impartial committees to democratically vote on television content, ensuring that alternative options are available to people who do not want violent programming.

WORDS IN CONTEXT

conglomerate: a corporation made up of a number of different companies that operate in different businesses
mythology: a body or collection of stories told by a particular people or culture that reveals their origin, history, deities, ancestors, and heroes and values
cultivate: to promote growth
paranoia: unfounded or unreasonable fear; delusional beliefs without logic or reason
pervasive: tending to spread throughout
empathize: to understand another's situation, feelings, and motives
hallmark: mark indicating quality or excellence
repression: holding back or controlling
de facto: exercising power or serving a function without being legally or officially established
foist: to impose (something or someone unwanted) upon another by trickery
levy: a tax or mandatory fee
subsidize: to financially assist
liberate: to free
abridge: to curtail; to shorten
allocate: to designate; to set apart for a special purpose
plurality: state of being multiple
monopoly: exclusive control by one group of the means of producing or selling a product or service
equitable: fair; balanced

1 For the first time in human history, children are hearing most of the stories, most of the time, not from their parents or school or churches or neighbors, but from a handful of global conglomerates that have something to sell. It is impossible to overestimate the radical effect that this has on the way our children grow up, the way we live, and the way we conduct our affairs.

2 People think of television as programs, but television is more than that; television is a mythology—highly organically connected, repeated every day so that the themes that run through all programming and news have the effect of cultivating conceptions of reality.

3 Violence on television is just one of the areas that causes a distorted concept of reality. Most of the violence we have on television is what I call happy violence. It's swift, it's thrilling, it's cool, it's effective, it's painless, and it always leads to a happy ending because you have to deliver the audience to the next commercial in a receptive mood.

4 Our studies have shown that growing up from infancy with this unprecedented diet of violence has three consequences, which, in combination, I call the "mean world syndrome." What this means is that if you are growing up in a home where there is more than say three hours of television per day, for all practical purposes you live in a meaner world—and act accordingly—than your next-door neighbor who lives in the same world but watches less television. The programming reinforces the worst fears and apprehensions and paranoia of people.

5 Another consequence of watching a lot of television is that one comes to believe that the violence portrayed on television is normal—that everybody does it, and that it's a good way of solving problems.

6 A more pervasive effect is that television desensitizes viewers to victimization and suffering; they lose the ability to understand the consequence of violence, to empathize, to resist, to protest.

7 The third consequence, and I think the most debilitating one, is the pervasive sense of insecurity and vulnerability. Our surveys tell us that the more television people watch, the more they are likely to be afraid to go out on the street in their own community, especially at night. They are afraid of strangers and meeting other people. A hallmark of civilization, which is kindness to strangers, has been lost.

8 That sense of insecurity and vulnerability is not randomly distributed. For every 10 violent characters on television there are about 11 victims; that's basically a tooth for a tooth. But for every 10 women who exert that kind of power—because violence is a kind of power—

there are 16 women victims, of young women there are 17; of women of color there are 22.

9 The mean world syndrome results in a reduced sensitivity to the consequences of violence along with an increased sense of vulnerability and dependence—and therefore a demand for repression from the government.

10 This has enormous political fallout. It's impossible to run an election campaign without advocating more jails, harsher punishment, more executions, all the things that have never worked to reduce crime but have always worked to get votes. It's driven largely, although not exclusively, by television-cultivated insecurity.

Images That Sell

11 Why are we awash in such a tidal wave of violent imagery despite the fact that 85 percent of the people in every poll say they are opposed to violent programming and it gets lower ratings? The reason is that violent programs travel well on the global market. Since there are only a few buyers of television programs, American producers can't break even on the domestic market, so they are forced onto the world market to make a profit. When you are forced onto the world market you are looking for a formula that will travel well, that needs no translation, and speaks action in any language.

12 So many of the stereotypes and violent images are the result of the imposition of a de facto censorship in the form of the marketing formulas that are imposed on the creative people who write, produce, direct, and act in them, and many of these people in Hollywood hate it. It is also foisted on children of the world; no country likes it, it doesn't serve any of our needs, but it is driven by the existing system of global marketing.

13 Cultural decision making is now out of democratic reach. It's highly centralized and run by an invisible Ministry of Culture of people whose names we don't know, who have never been elected, and who are supported by a form of taxation without representation.

14 That taxation is the price—the levy—that is included in the price of every advertised product and is turned over to the advertiser and then to the broadcaster, the magazine, and the newspaper publisher, and subsidizes—to the tune of $16 to 17 billion a year—popular

culture. That expenditure, which is also a tax deductible business expense, is public money channeled through private hands to serve private purposes.

15 That is why I call these conglomerates a private government that is as powerful as any public government and that exercises control that is out of democratic reach.

Reclaiming the First Amendment

16 We need to liberate cultural decision-making from the censorship that is imposed on the creative people in the media by these private governments, which the current interpretation of the First Amendment shields.

17 I believe the First Amendment should be extended to these private governments as well as to public government. No government—private or public—should abridge the freedom of speech. The First Amendment should be extended, according to its basic and original concept, to provide alternatives, to provide diversity, to provide freedom.

18 These issues have been discussed in European parliaments and even in South Asian countries for many years. Every democratic country has found a way of allocating resources to maintain a sense of plurality, a sense of choice, a sense of alternatives. For example, in France there is a tax on theater admissions and video tape, which funds loans for independent production, magazines, newspapers, and television programs and motion pictures. In some Scandinavian countries, there is a law that requires government to support opposition newspapers.

19 Every other democratic country has advisory committees working with broadcasters or with government ministries that run broadcasting. Sometimes these committees are elected. In a number of countries, there are laws that forbid the owners and those who run the finances to dictate editorial policy or program policy.

20 We're the only ones who have allowed the First Amendment to the Constitution to shield monopolies instead of provide freedom. The primary objective of the media to sell goods is legitimate in a limited sphere, but it should not drive the entire culture. We have to recognize and implement the right of a child to be born into a more diverse, more fair, more sane, more equitable cultural environment. ◆

CONSIDERING THE ISSUES

1. Before television, adults told children stories about their traditions, history, and culture as they sat around firesides, dinner tables, and on front porches. Where did you learn about the society you live in, the people in your culture, laws, traditions, and history? How important was television in informing your perspective on the world? What did it teach you? What messages are children likely to "hear" on television about their culture and society today?
2. If you were from another country and watched American television as a means to learn about American society, what do you think you would determine about American society based on prime time programming? Explain.

CRAFT AND CONTENT

3. Evaluate Gerbner's use of examples to support his essay's points. How effective are his examples? Do they seem credible and/or appropriate? Are they balanced and fair? Explain.
4. Gerbner coins several phrases to describe the type of violence we see on television and its effects. What is "happy violence"? What is the "mean world syndrome"? Do you think his creation of such phrases helps him make his point? Explain.

CRITICAL THINKING

5. What messages about violence does violent TV convey to children? According to Gerbner, what are the consequences of these messages? Explain.
6. What does Gerbner hope to achieve by writing this article? Identify areas of the essay that reveal his objective.
7. In his final section, Gerbner advocates for impartial committees to ensure that balanced programming options are available to everyone. Evaluate the quality and nature of television programming today. Is there something for everyone? Is it skewed toward particular audiences? Explain.

WRITING ABOUT THE ISSUES

8. Conduct a media study of your own. Track the number of violent acts in children's programming for a specific period of time, such

as during prime time or Saturday morning cartoons. Count and describe violent acts on a single network during the specified time period. Discuss the implications of your research in a short essay.

9. Review the definition of the word *mythology* given before the article. How does television construct our mythology? Write a short essay on how TV constructs our cultural mythology, referring specifically back to the definition provided. Give some examples from television programs to support your points.

Stop Blaming Kids and TV

Mike Males

Mike Males is the author of several books on media and youth culture, including *The Scapegoat Generation: American's War Against Adolescents* (1996), *Framing Youth: 10 Myths About the Next Generation* (1999), and *Kids and Guns* (2001). His articles have appeared in many journals and newspapers including the *New York Times, Los Angeles Times*, and *Washington Post.* He teaches at the University of California, Santa Cruz, and is a senior researcher at the Center on Juvenile and Criminal Justice in San Francisco. This article was written for the October 1997 issue of the *Progressive.*

CONNECTING TO THE TOPIC

Children learn many behaviors from their parents. This connection between children and parents is as old as the human race and is usually universally accepted. However, in the debate over kids and violence, the connection between parents and children is often overlooked in favor of placing the blame on television and the media. Could the home actually be more responsible for children's violent behavior than television? Do children learn violent behavior mostly by watching their parents? How responsible are parents (and elders) for youth violence today?

WORDS IN CONTEXT

exploitative: manipulative; influencing for one's own gain
mogul: a rich or powerful person
conservative: traditional; opposing change; associated with the political right

progressive: promoting or favoring progress toward new policies, ideas, or methods; associated with the political left
elicit: to draw out; to provoke
counterpart: that which closely resembles another thing of similar form or function
inherently: having as an essential characteristic or quality
candor: frankness; openness
perfidy: calculated violation of trust; treachery
impolitic: unwise
malleable: easily controlled or influenced

1 "Children have never been very good at listening to their elders," James Baldwin wrote in *Nobody Knows My Name.* "But they have never failed to imitate them." This basic truth has all but disappeared as the public increasingly treats teenagers as a robot-like population under sway of an exploitative media. White House officials lecture film, music, Internet, fashion, and pop-culture moguls and accuse them of programming kids to smoke, drink, shoot up, have sex, and kill.

2 So do conservatives, led by William Bennett and Dan Quayle. Professional organizations are also into media-bashing. In its famous report on youth risks, the Carnegie Corporation devoted a full chapter to media influences.

3 Progressives are no exception. *Mother Jones* claims it has "proof that TV makes kids violent." And the Institute for Alternative Media emphasizes, "the average American child will witness . . . 200,000 acts of [TV] violence" by the time that child graduates from high school.

4 None of these varied interests notes that during the eighteen years between a child's birth and graduation from high school, there will be fifteen million cases of real violence in American homes grave enough to require hospital emergency treatment. These assaults will cause ten million serious injuries and 40,000 deaths to children. In October 1996, the Department of Health and Human Services reported 565,000 serious injuries that abusive parents inflicted on children and youths in 1993. The number is up four-fold since 1986.

5 The Department of Health report disappeared from the news in one day. It elicited virtually no comment from the White House, Republicans, or law-enforcement officials. Nor from Carnegie scholars, whose 150-page study, "Great Transitions; Preparing Adolescents for a

New Century," devotes two sentences to household violence. The left press took no particular interest in the story, either.

6 All sides seem to agree that fictional violence, sex on the screen, Joe Camel, beer-drinking frogs, or naked bodies on the Internet pose a bigger threat to children than do actual beatings, rape, or parental addictions. This, in turn, upholds the doctrine that youth behavior is the problem, and curbing young people's rights the answer.

7 Claims that TV causes violence bear little relation to real behavior. Japanese and European kids behold media as graphically brutal as that which appears on American screens, but seventeen-year-olds in those countries commit murder at rates lower than those of American seventy-year-olds.

8 Likewise, youths in different parts of the United States are exposed to the same media but display drastically different violence levels. TV violence does not account for the fact that the murder rate among black teens in Washington, D.C., is twenty-five times higher than that of white teens living a few Metro stops away. It doesn't explain why, nationally, murder doubled among nonwhite and Latino youth over the last decade, but declined among white Anglo teens. Furthermore, contrary to the TV brainwashing theory, Anglo sixteen-year-olds have lower violent-crime rates than black sixty-year-olds, Latino forty-year-olds, and Anglo thirty-year-olds. Men, women, whites, Latinos, blacks, Asians, teens, young adults, middle-agers, and senior citizens in Fresno County—California's poorest urban area—display murder and violent-crime rates double those of their counterparts in Ventura County, the state's richest.

9 Confounding every theory, America's biggest explosion in felony violent crime is not street crime among minorities or teens of any color, but domestic violence among aging, mostly white baby boomers. Should we arm Junior with a V-chip to protect him from Mom and Dad?

10 In practical terms, media-violence theories are not about kids, but about race and class: If TV accounts for any meaningful fraction of murder levels among poorer, nonwhite youth, why doesn't it have the same effect on white kids? Are minorities inherently programmable?

11 I worked for a dozen years in youth programs in Montana and California. When problems arose, they usually crossed generations. I saw violent kids with dads or uncles in jail for assault. I saw middle-schoolers molested in childhood by mom's boyfriend. I saw budding teen alcoholics hoisting forty-ouncers alongside forty-year-old sots. I also

saw again and again how kids start to smoke. In countless trailers and small apartments dense with blue haze, children roamed the rugs as grownups puffed. Mom and seventh-grade daughter swapped Dorals while bemoaning the evils of men. A junior-high basketball center slept outside before a big game because a dozen elders—from her non-inhaling sixteen-year-old brother to her grandma—were all chain smokers. Two years later, she'd given up and joined the party.

12 As a result, teen smoking mimicked adult smoking by gender, race, locale, era, and household. I could discern no pop-culture puppetry. My survey of 400 Los Angeles middle schoolers for a 1994 *Journal of School Health* article found children of smoking parents three times more likely to smoke by age fifteen than children of nonsmokers. Parents were the most influential but not the only adults kids emulated. Nor did youngsters copy elders slavishly. Youths often picked slightly different habits (like chewing tobacco, or their own brands).

13 In 1989, the Centers for Disease Control lamented, "75 percent of all teenage smokers come from homes where parents smoke." You don't hear such candor from today's put-politics-first health agencies. Centers for Disease Control tobacco chieftain Michael Eriksen informed me that his agency doesn't make an issue of parental smoking. Nor do anti-smoking groups. Asked Kathy Mulvey, research director of INFACT: "Why make enemies of fifty million adult smokers" when advertising creates the real "appeal of tobacco to youth?"

14 Do ads hook kids on cigarettes? Studies of the effects of the Joe Camel logo show only that a larger fraction of teen smokers than veteran adult smokers choose the Camel brand. When asked, some researchers admit they cannot demonstrate that advertising causes kids to smoke who would not otherwise. And that's the real issue. In fact, surveys found smoking declining among teens (especially the youngest) during Joe's advent from 1985 to 1990.

15 The University of California's Stanton Glantz, whose exposure of 10,000 tobacco documents enraged the industry, found corporate perfidy far shrewder than camels and cowboys.

16 "As the tobacco industry knows well," Glantz reported, "kids want to be like adults." An industry marketing document advises: "To reach young smokers, present the cigarette as one of the initiations into adult life . . . . The basic symbols of growing up."

17 The biggest predictor of whether a teen will become a smoker, a drunk, or a druggie is whether or not the child grows up amid adult addicts. Three-fourths of murdered kids are killed by adults. Suicide and

murder rates among white teenagers resemble those of white adults, and suicide and murder rates among black teens track those of black adults. And as far as teen pregnancy goes, for minor mothers, four-fifths of the fathers are adults over eighteen, and half are adults over twenty.

18 The inescapable conclusion is this: If you want to change juvenile behavior, change adult behavior. But instead of focusing on adults, almost everyone points a finger at kids—and at the TV culture that supposedly addicts them.

19 Groups like Mothers Against Drunk Driving charge, for instance, that Budweiser's frogs entice teens to drink. Yet the 1995 National Household Survey found teen alcohol use declining. "Youths aren't buying the cute and flashy beer images," an in-depth *USA Today* survey found. Most teens found the ads amusing, but they did not consume Bud as a result.

20 By squabbling over frogs, political interests can sidestep the impolitic tragedy that adults over the age of twenty-one cause 90 percent of America's 16,000 alcohol-related traffic deaths every year. Clinton and drug-policy chief Barry McCaffrey ignore federal reports that show a skyrocketing toll of booze and drug-related casualties among adults in their thirties and forties—the age group that is parenting most American teens. But both officials get favorable press attention by blaming alcohol ads and heroin chic for corrupting our kids.

21 Progressive reformers who insist kids are so malleable that beer frogs and Joe Camel and Ace Ventura push them to evil are not so different from those on the Christian right who claim that *Our Bodies, Ourselves* promotes teen sex and that the group Rage Against the Machine persuades pubescents to roll down Rodeo Drive with a shotgun.

22 America's increasingly marginalized young deserve better than grownup escapism. Millions of children and teenagers face real destitution, drug abuse, and violence in their homes. Yet these profound menaces continue to lurk in the background, even as the frogs, V-chips, and Mighty Morphins take center stage. ◆

CONSIDERING THE ISSUES

1. How much violence or angry behavior did you witness in your family and community environment as a child? What impact, if any, did it have on you?
2. Males questions the claim by conservatives and progressives that television influences children's violent behavior. Consider

the things that influence children's behavior in addition to television. Make a list of these factors and rank them in order of what you feel has the greatest and least influence. Where does television fall in your list?

CRAFT AND CONTENT

3. In your own words, explain Males's quote from James Baldwin, "Children have never been very good at listening to their elders. But they have never failed to imitate them." How does this quotation support his argument?
4. Are you convinced by Males's argument that parents are the number-one source of violent behavior in children? What evidence or facts does he offer to convince you of his points? Do you agree with him? Why or why not?

CRITICAL THINKING

5. Despite the public outcry that America's teens are undergoing a violence crisis, Males cites several studies that claim the contrary. In your opinion, are America's youth indeed facing a crisis in youth violence? Are we overreacting? If so, what drives this perception that youth are out of control?
6. Males uses the example of teen smoking to support his argument on television and youth violence. Is this example parallel? What similarities exist between teen smoking behaviors and violent behavior in children? Explain.

WRITING ABOUT THE ISSUES

7. Males claims that juvenile violence is not due to television and media violence. Instead, he asserts that violence begins at home—that is where children learn to react to violence. Develop an essay where you illustrate the truth of Males's argument using an example you experienced or witnessed in your own childhood.
8. Males goes against the status quo by arguing that television is not to blame for violent behavior in children. Write a response to this article, addressing each of Males's primary points. You may support or question his viewpoint.

VISUAL CONNECTIONS

Through the Eyes of a Child

These drawings come from the book *Helping Young Children Understand Peace and War* (1985) by Diane Levin and Nancy Carlsson-Paige. (See the second article in this chapter for more information on Diane Levin.) Nancy Carlsson-Paige is a professor of education at Lesley University and the author of *Best Day of the Week,* a children's book about conflict resolution. She has coauthored (with Diane Levin) several books, including *Before Push Comes to Shove: Building Conflict Resolution Skills with Children* (1998). Together, they have consulted on a number of projects for public broadcasting, including the "Ready to Learn About Conflict" project.

CONNECTING TO THE TOPIC

Diane Levin observed in her book *Teaching Young Children in Violent Times* that "art and play allow children to work out what they've heard or seen about war and violence." Children will often draw what they don't want to talk about. Or they may inadvertently reveal what they are feeling in what they chose to draw and how they draw it. For example, while they may remember to draw a sun in the sky—a visual device common in children's drawings—they may depict the sun frowning. Sometimes it can be something or someone missing from the picture, such as a father or mother after a recent divorce or death. For many children, art can be a powerful tool for working out feelings about war and violence.

CONSIDERING THE ISSUES

1. Think back to the types of pictures you drew as a child. If you were not told what to draw, what types of pictures did you prefer to sketch? What colors did you like? Drawing tools? Subject matter? What do you think your pictures might have revealed about your state of mind?
2. Do you think art is a good way to help children work out their feelings? Explain.

CRITICAL THINKING

3. Take a look at these two pictures and analyze what is happening in each. Try to imagine what each child was thinking when they drew these pictures. What elements, if any, do you find surprising?
4. If you were a parent and your child brought home one of these pictures from school, how would you respond? Would you discuss the images with the child? What would you say?
5. Ask a child under the age of eight to draw a happy moment in his or her life, and a sad or scary one. After they have finished the pictures, try to analyze them, without first speaking to the child. Then, ask the child to describe in his or her own words what is happening in the drawing. How accurate were you in your interpretation of the drawings? Did anything the child said surprise you? Did you learn anything about child psychology through this exercise? Explain.

TOPICAL CONNECTIONS

GROUP PROJECTS

1. Prepare a questionnaire for your peer group that tests some of the claims made by the organizations and authors in this section. You could develop a survey on the connection between aggressive children and television violence. Or whether parents have a right to demand changes in television programming. Or whether the general public feels that children's television programs are too violent. Carefully consider and discuss the questions you will ask in order to get reliable information and feedback, and then evaluate the results.
2. Many television programs feature violent heroes. In fact, an entire genre based on violent heroes has developed to feed consumer demand for such programming. With your group, develop a list of programs that feature a specific violent hero or heroes. How many of these programs appeal to children? Discuss the

appeal of these programs and what effects, if any, they might have on young minds.

WEB PROJECT

3. There are several nonprofit organizations that focus on increasing public awareness of media violence. Visit the Media Awareness Web site at www.media-awareness.ca/english/issues/violence/violence_debates.cfm and review the debate on media violence. Write an essay explaining your view on the issue of media violence using examples from the information provided on the Media Awareness Web site and its linked articles.

FOR FURTHER INQUIRY

4. Several authors in this section mention that violent programs can influence children to act violently themselves, or to imitate what they see on TV. In several court cases, violent media (television, film, music) has been blamed as the reason why some young people have committed violent crimes. Research this issue in greater depth. What programs have been blamed for violent behavior? Is there any merit to the accusation that violent television programs and movies influence young people? Write a research paper exploring this topic.

9 Is Fast Food Responsible for a Crisis in Public Health?

In 2003, the reports looked dismal: an astonishing two-thirds of Americans are considered overweight. Half of this group is considered obese—and American physicians have started describing the situation as "epidemic." Perhaps even more distressing is the fact that despite the proliferation of health clubs and new exercise equipment, Americans are getting larger. An estimated 300,000 Americans die of obesity-related causes each year, and the direct medical costs of obesity are over $100 billion annually.

In addition to the proliferation of fast food restaurants and large portion sizes at regular eateries, America has become more sedentary—physical education programs have been cut from many schools, we spend more time in front of computers and television screens than we do engaging in activities outdoors, and time constraints often require that we grab a bite at the local fast food chain rather than go home and fix a healthy meal. The result of this combination of factors is visible—America may have a weight problem on its hands.

But who is responsible for this crisis in public health? Is it the fast food restaurants with their high caloric offerings and encouragement to increase the portion size for a few more cents? Several lawsuits filed in 2002 and 2003 indicated that some people thought so. This chapter examines the emerging controversy over the connection between the expanding American waistline and the perceived crisis in public health.

CRITICAL THINKING

1. What does this drawing depict? What message do you think it is trying to convey? Is there one message, or could this cartoon be interpreted in different ways by different people? Explain.
2. There is no caption accompanying this cartoon. What helps you understand it?
3. Would this cartoon have worked well thirty years ago? Explain.

Finding Fault for the Fat

Daniel Akst

Daniel Akst is the author of *Wonder Boy* (1990) and *St. Burl's Obituary* (1996), a novel about a fat man who becomes thin. His articles have appeared in many publications, including *Forbes*, *USA Today*, and the *Atlantic Monthly*. This essay first appeared in the December 7, 2003, issue of the *Boston Globe Magazine*.

CONNECTING TO THE TOPIC

Few people believe that fast food is healthy food. But should fast food companies share the responsibility for America's expanding waistline? And what about other possible sources for the obesity epidemic, such as a fundamentally flawed food pyramid, parents who fail to monitor children's eating habits, and schools that provide easy access to sugary and fattening items in vending machines? While there may be many factors at work, fast food companies are the ones on trial. Are lawsuits the answer? If so, whom do we blame?

WORDS IN CONTEXT

bristling: full
stupefying: amazing; astounding
tort: in law, damage, injury, or a wrongful act done willfully or negligently, involving strict liability, for which a civil suit can be brought
canard: something unfounded, false, or misleading
counterintuitive: contrary to what intuition or common sense would indicate
obligatory: required, as with a service or favor
per capita: per unit of population

1 My lunch with Richard Daynard is a lawsuit waiting to happen. We begin with a glass of wine and then let our waiter talk us into the classically rich New England clam chowder. We go for the fish and chips, which arrive practically sizzling from the fryer. Bristling with oily batter and potatoes, our lunches are accompanied by a bodyguard of artery-clogging tartar sauce, and the vegetable, if you'll pardon the expression, is coleslaw.

2 Dick Daynard, my dining companion, is a lean, gray-haired Northeastern University law professor who was chairman of the Tobacco Products Liability Project, which helped erect an intellectual framework for the legal assault on Big Tobacco. Over this stupefyingly caloric lunch, he's explaining his next big project: laying the groundwork for suing the pants off the food companies.

3 The professor notes that suing tobacco companies for making lethal products didn't work. "Juries want a story that involves moral fault," he explains. "If you focus on the product, the jury focuses on the failure of the plaintiff to quit using it." Thus, tort lawyers will pursue companies like McDonald's and PepsiCo not for making fattening food but for alleged deceptive practices. The companies will be accused of devious marketing, says Daynard, or perhaps commercial fraud. Most of all, they will be attacked for preying on the innocent—for targeting our precious children.

4 So here we are knowingly consuming enough calories to keep a village in sub-Saharan Africa going for a week. Doesn't personal choice enter the equation? Couldn't we simply have ordered a salad? Daynard himself says he doesn't often eat this way; he's usually careful, because he knows better. He lost 25 pounds a couple of years back, and when I ask him how, he says simply, "I ate a lot less." No jury trial was required.

5 What's to insulate Daynard's favorite fish restaurant from the consequences of its clam chowder? Or how about that all-you-can-eat Indian buffet? "These are tough questions," Daynard agrees. Even tougher is what these lawsuits might imply: that we're a nation of childish pigs who can't take responsibility for what we eat, how we live, and the fat bodies and ill health we have as a consequence. Who among us thinks Big Macs and french fries are health food? McDonald's doesn't say so. Why sue Big Food and not the media outlets that carry their ads? How about the fork makers? Can't we ever stop making excuses for ourselves? I mean, how American can you get? "It's a canard that Americans tend to blame others," Daynard insists calmly. "Americans tend to be extremely self-blaming and believe to a totally unrealistic degree that everything can be dealt with by willpower."

6 Just a few miles out Mass. Ave., Harvard economist Edward L. Glaeser begs to differ. Says Glaeser: "My whole worldview is about people taking responsibility for their actions." Glaeser, with colleagues David M. Cutler and Jesse M. Shapiro, has written a fascinating paper

that attributes much of the obesity problem to technologically inspired reductions in food preparation time, which they figure lowered our cost per calorie by a stunning 29 percent from 1965 to 1995. Time is money, remember, and the economists think lower food prices in this sense have raised consumption. It makes sense; it's easier to grab some KFC than to make fried chicken at home.

7 Like Daynard, Glaeser is thin, and he, too, works at it. The difference is that Glaeser thinks it's ridiculous to pin legal liability on Big Food. "I actually think McDonald's and the others have delivered social benefit," he says with counterintuitive relish. "I think they're actually good guys." Glaeser's rationale for suggesting that convenience foods are a social good is that, to judge from consumer behavior in the marketplace, people seem to prefer saving time to being thinner. And in economics, by and large, getting what you want is a good thing. Glaeser notes that until relatively recently, cheaper food (in terms of money as well as time) made us taller and healthier. Only in the past 25 years or so have diminishing returns set in.

8 Now that less is more when it comes to increased calorie intake, Glaeser expects the marketplace to correct the excesses he attributes to self-control problems. Glaeser can understand the need for regulation in the schools, or if food companies are misleading people. But he says: "I don't think anybody ate at McDonald's and thought it was good for them. I take a dim view of these lawsuits."

9 So who is right? Is it a question of willpower? Can the courts fix this problem for us? Or is obesity a disease, as some advocates have suggested? That might shift the burden of treatment costs onto health insurers, but would it also shift the burden of responsibility? In looking for someone to blame, it's important to remember that ours has always been a land of plenty; that's why people came here. But something changed around 1980, something other than our genes, and collectively, we started gaining weight.

10 Today a staggering two-thirds of Americans weigh too much, based on a standard measure relating weight to height called the body mass index (BMI). Put another way, only about a third of us weigh what the experts say we should; another third are overweight, and the rest are officially obese. Hardly anyone disputes that obesity is epidemic in this country.

11 Worse yet, we seem to be getting fatter.

12 When Rand Corp. health economist Roland Sturm analyzed data from telephone surveys conducted by the Centers for Disease

Control and Prevention, he found that the number of "morbidly obese" Americans—those whose body mass index is 40 or more—quadrupled between 1986 and 2000, to about 4 million. The number of super obese—those with BMIs topping 50—quintupled, to 500,000. The typical man in the latter group, at 5 feet 10 inches tall, weighed 373 pounds. Plain old obesity—a BMI of 30 or more—somehow only doubled during the period. Sturm's findings are especially troubling because people usually aren't completely honest about how much they weigh.

13 The consequences of our national weight gain ought to make anyone worried, even the skinny minority. Each year, according to the most widely accepted estimates, weight-related problems may cost the lives of 300,000 Americans and perhaps $100 billion. In studying obesity, Sturm has concluded that it is a bigger public health problem than drinking, smoking, or poverty.

14 Go shopping in some of the big-box stores and you can see the effects of America's ever-expanding waistline. Wal-Mart carries "extended sizes," meaning XXL and the like, and the men's department at Kohl's is full of pants with expandable waists. One pair of khakis I tried on, the Croft & Barrow Flexon model, offered an amazing 4 full inches of extra belly room by means of a cleverly designed tab hidden in the waistband Women's clothing has also changed. In 1985, the top-selling women's size was 8, but by 2002 it was a voluminous 14, according to Marshal Cohen, chief industry analyst for the NPD Group, a retailing consultancy in Port Washington, New York. This is to say nothing of size inflation; a size 8 in 1985 was smaller than an 8 today. Cohen says this "vanity sizing" is now widespread.

15 When the exertions of driving and shopping grow too much to bear, there is always something to eat at hand. Most malls feature the obligatory food court. The food court is a testament to a less-heralded factor in the expansion of the nation's waistline: the accompanying growth in tempting things to eat. One mall I visited has outlets selling Chinese, Indian, Japanese, and Italian foods, and the Cajun chicken place was offering free samples. The food court even has a children's play area. But a Haagen-Dazs ice cream outlet stands watch right next to it, as if children can't be expected to relax without the reassurance of high-calorie provisions always at hand. Not far away, exemplifying yet another factor in the fattening of America, there is a stand selling frothy, dessert-like coffees. The mocha chiller looked good, so I asked the fellow at the counter how many calories it has. "I have no idea," he said.

16 This is what drives the Dick Daynards of the world nuts. "Food companies can make very significant changes that will have a significant impact on obesity," says John F. Banzhaf III, an overweight law professor at George Washington University. Banzhaf says mom-and-pop delis have nothing to fret about; the harm they do would be outweighed by the cost of any remedy. It's the big fish that ought to be worried, and he and Daynard note that some food giants are already changing their behavior, which the professors insist is the real goal here. Fast-food outlets, for example, should at least prominently disclose nutritional information about their products. "If enough people had to face the fact that, my God, it has 900 calories," says Banzhaf, they might make other choices.

17 Consider fast food, on which Americans spend $110 billion a year—up from $6 billion 30 years ago. The number of fast-food restaurants per capita doubled in this country from 1972 to 1997. Fast food leads us to supersizing. "Portion sizes began to grow in the 1970s, rose sharply in the 1980s, and have continued in parallel with increasing body weights," says a 2002 study by New York University nutrition experts Marion Nestle and Lisa R. Young. Want something to drink with that? Annual soda consumption rose from 21 to 56 gallons per American from 1970 to 1997, observes science writer Ellen Ruppel Shell in her book *The Hungry Gene*. Shell further notes that "in the last decade, soda eclipsed coffee and tap water combined as the American beverage of choice."

18 But if liberals get to blame giant corporate food mongers, conservatives have their place at the banquet as well, starting with the "nanny state." It was government officials, after all, hand in hand with the medical establishment, who pushed all of us to eat more carbohydrates. They identified fat as the clear villain, and when a host of richly caloric products appeared on supermarket shelves boasting of little or no fat, consumers obligingly gorged themselves. "I have colleagues who told people it was only fat calories that made you fat," says Walter Willett, chairman of the nutrition department at the Harvard School of Public Health. "That was just completely wrong."

19 Perhaps the ultimate monument to wrongheaded expert advice is our own government's food pyramid, familiar to schoolchildren everywhere as an icon of nutritional piety. Willett considers this structure so badly out of whack that he published a pyramid of his own. In some ways, it turned the official pyramid upside down, mandating way more

fat, in the form of vegetable oils, while radically reducing white bread, white rice, potatoes, and pasta. He even found room for a little booze. It's enough to make a body wonder whether the lawyers ought to sue all those experts who made us miserable—and possibly even fat—all those years.

20 And what about mothers and fathers? Kelly D. Brownell, director of the Yale Center for Eating and Weight Disorders, reports in his book *Food Fight: The Inside Story of the Food Industry, America's Obesity Crisis, and What We Can Do About It* (coauthored by Katherine Battle Horgen) that more than half of the average child's daily calories now come from sodas, juices, and other high-calorie drinks, and that 10 percent of teenage boys suck down seven or more cans of soft drink a day. Forget the experts. Never mind Big Food. Maybe we ought to haul all those parents into court.

21 The food companies will have to change—and some already have, prodded in part by fears of liability and the social disrepute that afflicts cigarettes and, to a lesser extent, sport utility vehicles. But the government will also have to change, perhaps by requiring on-spot nutritional disclosure by restaurant chains, getting unhealthy foods out of the schools, and altering the zoning and other policies that help drive so many Americans into car-oriented suburbs.

22 Most of all, we have to change. As parents, we have to be tougher, getting our kids away from the TV and all the awful stuff they now eat. And we have to set an example by eating healthier ourselves and getting off our duffs to burn up more calories—something we might even do with our children. It's not complicated. Rena Wing can boil it down to one sentence: "If anybody eats less and exercises more," she says, "they will lose weight." ◆

CONSIDERING THE ISSUES

1. In paragraph 5, Daynard notes, "It's a canard that Americans tend to blame others. . . . Americans tend to be extremely self-blaming . . . ." Respond to this statement with your own opinion. Do you think Americans tend to blame themselves for their problems, or others? Explain.
2. Consider how often you purchase fast food. What do you buy? How often? Are your choices driven by necessity—that is, do you

pick foods that you can eat on the go? Do you try to find healthy items on the menu? Why or why not?

CRAFT AND CONTENT

3. Akst poses many questions throughout his essay. Compile a list of his questions in the order in which they appear in his essay. How many of them does he answer? Are some questions unanswerable? If so, which ones? Explain.
4. Akst notes the body shape, size, or weight of several of the people included in his essay. Why do you think he provides this information? Is it important to his essay? Why or why not?

CRITICAL THINKING

5. Akst provides several different sources contributing to America's obesity crisis. Identify each source he cites and then rank them according to your own viewpoint. Who is most responsible? Is any one source more at fault? Explain.
6. What are "vanity sizes"? How do they connect to America's growing obesity problem? Explain.
7. Daynard claims that the real motivation behind his and John Banzhaf's push to sue fast food is to get them to change their behavior. What do you think would happen if a fast food company were successfully sued for contributing to obesity? Explain.

WRITING ABOUT THE ISSUES

8. Edward L. Glaeser objects to Richard Daynard's assertion that fast food companies should assume the blame for America's obesity crisis. "My whole worldview is about people taking responsibility for their actions." Write a response to Glaeser's statement in which you agree or disagree, in whole or in part, with his statement. Focus your response on the relationship between the fast food industry and America's obesity problem.
9. Take a look at Walter Willett's revised food pyramid and compare it with the USDA food pyramid. Listen to a discussion of the revised pyramid on National Public Radio's "Science Friday" at www.sciencefriday.com/pages/2003/Jan/hour2_010303.html.

How are the two different? Do you think the government should use the Willett model? Why haven't they already done so? Write a short essay expressing your opinion, referring to points made in the interview on NPR.

Body Mass Index

National Institutes of Health

CONNECTING TO THE TOPIC

Body mass index (BMI) is a measure of body fat based on height and weight that applies to both adult men and women. According to the National Institutes of Health, BMI is a reliable indicator of total body fat, which has been found to increase your risk of disease and death. While the score is usually valid, BMI isn't perfect. It may overestimate body fat in athletes and others who have a muscular build, and underestimate body fat in older persons and others who have lost muscle mass.

▸ Individuals with a body mass index (BMI) of 25 to 29.9 are considered overweight, while individuals with a BMI of 30 or more are considered obese.

Source: National Institutes of Health

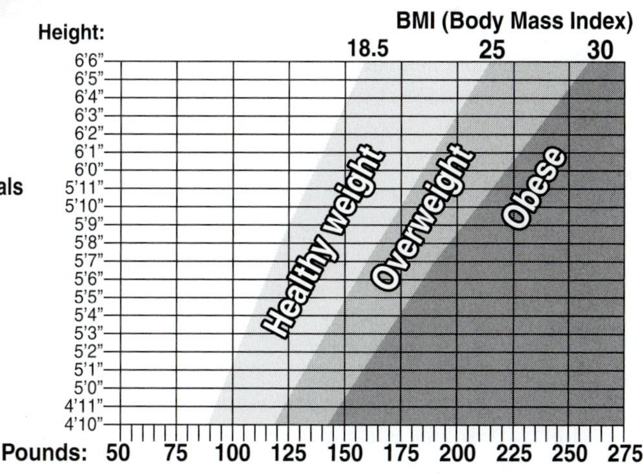

CRITICAL THINKING

1. Calculate your BMI with the body mass calculator provided by the National Institutes of Health at www.nhlbisupport.com/bmi/bmicalc.htm. (Please note that this calculator should be used as a guide only.) Where do you fall on the chart? Do you think the chart is correct or extreme? Explain.
2. Were you aware of the BMI? Did you know your BMI number before using the calculator? Do you think it is helpful as a guide for healthy living? Explain.

You Want Fries with That?

Richard Daynard

Richard Daynard is a professor in the School of Law at Northeastern University. He is well-known for his work to establish the legal responsibility of the tobacco industry for tobacco-induced death, disease, and disability, and currently serves as chair of the Tobacco Products Liability Project and editor-in-chief of the *Tobacco Products Litigation Reporter.* This essay was published in the May 2003 issue of *Northeastern University Magazine.*

CONNECTING TO THE TOPIC

Many people have heard about the lawsuits against big tobacco companies for deceptive practices. One comment made during the height of the cigarette litigation was that if tobacco could be sued, fast food and other "non-healthy" products would soon follow. In 2002, two teenage girls did just that—they sued McDonald's for making them fat. While their case was thrown out, it opened the door for similar, more targeted lawsuits. In the next piece, law professor Richard Daynard discusses why he feels the fast food industry is ripe for a lawsuit. Is the fast food industry responsible? Should they pay? Should they change?

WORDS IN CONTEXT

mantra: commonly repeated word or phrase
libertarian: one who advocates maximizing individual rights and minimizing the role of the state

purveyor: one that offers provisions, especially food
aesthetic: concerning the appreciation of beauty
inundate: to overwhelm, as in a flood
hedonism: pursuit of pleasure, especially the pleasures of the senses
epidemiological: concerning the branch of medicine that deals with the study of the causes, distribution, and control of disease in populations

1 When I was organizing lawsuits against the tobacco industry in the 1980s and 1990s, the tobacco companies' favorite spin became like a mantra: "First, they go after cigarettes. Next, it'll be red meat and dairy products!"

2 Recently, a writer for a libertarian magazine caustically reminded me my response had always been "No way." Yet here I am, a decade or two later, urging litigation against purveyors of meat and dairy (and sugar) products—fast-food and packaged-food companies, in particular.

3 What gives? Well, I had a conversion. It began in April 2002, after New York University nutritionist Marion Nestle wrote a book entitled *Food Politics*, and I was asked to comment on whether her thesis opened the door to obesity litigation.

4 Nestle argues that Americans are getting dangerously fat because we're consuming more food than we did twenty years ago, largely because food companies maximize their profits by maximizing the amount of food their customers eat.

5 The companies accomplish this through a variety of misleading marketing ploys, and by buying off or manipulating those who are supposed to protect us—politicians, dietitians' organizations, and school boards, for instance.

6 I found Nestle's argument plausible and disturbing. What really shocked me was the scope and seriousness of the obesity crisis. In 1978, 15 percent of Americans were obese (meaning, more than thirty pounds above a healthy weight). This was a modest uptick from 13 percent twenty years earlier.

7 But by 1999, the obesity percentage had more than doubled, to 31 percent. An additional 34 percent of the population was overweight (ten to thirty pounds above a healthy weight). In other words, 65 percent of Americans were too heavy. The statistics for children, though lower than those for adults, were escalating even more dramatically.

8 And the problem isn't just an aesthetic one: Overweight and obese people are developing diabetes, heart disease, cancer, and other medical conditions in huge numbers. Indeed, in 1999, annual premature deaths related to obesity were estimated at roughly 300,000, approaching the figure for tobacco-related deaths. Perhaps most striking is the epidemic of type 2 diabetes among children and adolescents; until recently, this disease was known as adult-onset diabetes.

9 But questionable behavior that contributes to a public-health crisis doesn't by itself add up to a viable lawsuit. The obvious differences between Big Macs and Marlboros made me question whether my experience with tobacco litigation was applicable to the food industry.

10 There's no such thing as "moderate" smoking, for example. Even a little is bad for you (though a lot is obviously worse). Eating, on the other hand, is a biological requirement; too little food for a sustained period is as bad as too much.

11 And there are other important distinctions. People who eat too much get immediate feedback, in the form of an expanding waistline; smokers can harbor lung cancer or heart disease for years without symptoms. Nicotine is strongly addictive, which explains why people continue to smoke even when they know the dangers. Finally, though cigarettes can injure or kill nonsmokers, there's no such thing as "passive eating."

12 Nonetheless, the more I learned about the food industry's operations—the massive marketing budgets; the deceptive health and low-fat claims; the rush to supersize everything; the inundation of soft-drink promotions and machines in schools; the extra sugars and fats added to seemingly healthy potato, chicken, and fish dishes at fast-food restaurants—the more I became convinced that changing the industry's behavior is the key to stopping the obesity epidemic.

13 True, the food industry isn't responsible for many factors that contribute to obesity: "bad" genes, inactivity, conflicting advice from nutrition experts, hedonism, lack of willpower.

14 But these factors don't account for our bigger belt sizes. The genetic makeup of a population doesn't change much over a few decades. Weakness of will and hedonistic desires are pretty much what they've always been. Average physical activity may have declined since the late 1970s, but it wasn't very impressive then. What's making us fat has to do with changes in the way we're eating. And the food industry is obviously responsible for a lot of these changes.

15 But where does litigation fit in? Back in 1988, I wrote an article for the *Journal of the National Cancer Institute* in which I described five possible public-health benefits of tobacco-industry litigation.

16 First, that holding tobacco companies financially responsible for even a fraction of the cost of tobacco-related medical care and lost productivity—more than $100 billion annually—would force them to raise prices, thereby discouraging consumption, particularly among children and adolescents. This has in fact happened: Dramatic price increases prompted by the industry's settlement of lawsuits brought by the states were followed by equally dramatic reductions in smoking among minors.

17 Second, that lawsuits would have an important educational effect, translating epidemiological statistics into easily understood cases of real people. This too has happened. Even the industry's "personal responsibility" defense—anyone stupid enough to smoke shouldn't complain about getting lung cancer—helps discourage smoking by underlining a causal link the tobacco companies otherwise used to deny.

18 Third, that the ability of plaintiffs' lawyers to obtain and publicize internal industry records documenting misbehavior would serve to delegitimize the industry, making legislative and regulatory remedies politically practicable. More than thirty million pages of such documents are now available. The shocking behavior they reveal has made "tobacco executive" a term of opprobrium and tobacco money a dangerous commodity for politicians.

19 Fourth, that health insurers would be able to seek industry reimbursement for money spent caring for tobacco victims. To date, tens of billions of reimbursement dollars have been paid to the states.

20 And fifth, that if the tobacco industry responded like other industries confronted with product-liability claims, it would change its behavior: make its products less deadly, for example, or its marketing less deceptive. This alone has not happened, the tobacco industry having apparently concluded that its only future lies on the "dark side."

21 Similar benefits can be anticipated from food litigation, whether it takes the form of product-liability suits on behalf of obese citizens or, more likely, consumer-protection suits on behalf of classes of customers ripped off by unfair or deceptive marketing practices.

22 For instance, there's no reason why the cheapest foods should be the least nutritious. Foods made with added sugars and fats are especially "obesigenic." If, as a result of litigation costs, the most obesigenic foods carry a higher price tag than simpler, more nutritious foods—the kind your parents or grandparents used to cook at home—that would make a big difference to the American waistline.

23 Food litigation has already produced an explosion of media coverage, which has spotlighted the obesity epidemic. Food-industry trade groups have responded—to the current suit against McDonald's, in particular—by insisting that everyone knows you shouldn't eat a steady diet of fast foods, despite the fact that most fast-food business comes from customers who do precisely that.

24 Unearthing documents that show how food companies manipulate and mislead consumers into buying their obesigenic products is likely to anger the public and complicate the benign image of food executives. And if health authorities can establish a causal connection between, for example, soft-drink concessions in schools, obesity, and the resulting health effects and costs, suits to recover these costs might be possible. Finally, if McDonald's has to pay for the harm caused by its Chicken McNuggets (which a court recently described as "Chicken McFrankenstein") or Filet-O-Fish, maybe it'll figure out how to formulate them without all the added fats and starches.

25 After all, food companies don't have to walk on the dark side. ◆

CONSIDERING THE ISSUES

1. Have you ever been on a diet? If so, what motivated you to go on one in the first place? Do you think the media influences how attractive we believe ourselves to be? If you have never considered your weight to be an issue, write about why it has not been a concern for you.
2. Consider the meaning behind Daynard's comment that the problem of obesity isn't simply an "aesthetic" one. Why does he use this word? What does it imply about obese and overweight individuals? Another way of looking at this question is to think about our common perceptions of beauty. What is a beautiful body? Is the obesity problem more connected to beauty, or health? What do you think?

CRAFT AND CONTENT

3. Daynard cites five benefits of tobacco-industry litigation. What is the relevance of this list to his argument supporting lawsuits against the fast food industry? Explain.
4. Daynard has been teaching law since the 1960s. In what ways could this essay serve as a lecture? Identify areas of his argument that seem as if you could be in a classroom listening to Daynard teaching. What questions would you ask him based on his lecture, and why?
5. In his conclusion, Daynard notes that a "court recently described" Chicken McNuggets as "Chicken McFrankenstein." What does this statement imply? Does it lead the reader to make a particular assumption about the opinion of the court? The judge who made this comment also threw out the lawsuit against McDonald's. If you did not know this, would you think that the judge was in favor of a lawsuit against McDonald's? Explain.

CRITICAL THINKING

6. Daynard proposes in paragraph 22 that the price of nutritious food be made cheaper so that people with lower incomes can afford it. What does food cost? Consider the differences in price for "junk food" verses "healthy food." Do you think Daynard makes a good point? Explain.
7. Following Daynard's example, create a similar list of five reasons why suing fast food companies is a good idea.

WRITING ABOUT THE ISSUES

8. Have the lawsuits filed in 2003 had any impact on fast food menu items? Take a look at some menu offerings on the Web sites at several large fast food chains such as McDonald's, Burger King, and Taco Bell. Do you think healthy additions to fast food menus will help alleviate the obesity epidemic? Why or why not?
9. Track your calorie intake over a two- or three-day period, keeping careful track of everything you eat. Don't change the way you normally eat so that the test can accurately measure your eating habits. Tabulate your total intake for each day and average

the number. Note your serving sizes (for example, a "serving" of macaroni and cheese is about 260 calories, but a whole box is about 780 calories). Did you consume more or less than you thought you would? What about serving size—is a serving an accurate way to measure how much you should eat of a particular item? Write a short essay about your experience and what it indicates about your eating habits.

We'll Have the Salad

Vic Cantone

Vic Cantone's cartoons were featured on the editorial pages of *The Brooklyn Papers* for many years. His work has also appeared in the *Daily News.* He is the recipient of a 2004 distinguished service award by the Deadline Club.

CRITICAL THINKING

1. What point is the cartoonist trying to make in this cartoon? What issue is he addressing? Who are the characters in the drawing, where are they, and what are they doing?
2. What can you judge about the situation based on the expressions on the faces of the characters behind the counter? Why do they look this way?
3. In what ways does this cartoon mimic what is going on with the fast food industry today? Explain.

Fast Food Isn't to Blame

R. A. Ames

R. A. Ames is a part-time student at a college in Massachusetts. He wrote this essay for a critical writing course in the fall semester of 2003.

CONNECTING TO THE TOPIC

In the next essay, writing student R. A. Ames asserts that the source of weight difficulties lies with people themselves, and not with the fast food industry. He acknowledges that his essay may seem harsh, but he believes that until people assume responsibility for their actions, the obesity problem will only get worse. How responsible are we for the things we eat? Is body size simply a matter of the will? Are fast food lawsuits just another way Americans can absolve themselves of personal culpability for their actions?

WORDS IN CONTEXT

metabolism: the process by which substances are broken down in the body
euphemism: the substitution of a mild, indirect, or vague term for a term considered harsh, blunt, or offensive

1 It seems like America has an obesity problem and it is getting worse. Frankly, I am a little sick of it. I have a part-time job as a clerk at a department store at the local mall, and I see many different types of

people. More and more of the store's patrons are shopping in the large size section. Later, I see them eating at the food court, putting thousands of calories into their mouths in a single sitting.

2 Now I don't mean to be insensitive here, as I am sure many overweight people are already thinking of a hundred angry retorts to my first paragraph. The fact is, I have been overweight myself and I know that it is no picnic (pardon the pun). I read those articles on "loving yourself" and tried to buy into the whole "fat is beautiful" propaganda. The truth is that it is a whole lot easier to get fat than to stay thin. And because of this, it is much more appealing to try and make yourself believe that cultural attitudes against obesity are the fault of advertisers, the fashion industry, society, you name it. And if you aren't blaming external forces, you cite internal ones—your metabolism or your genes. The only one you don't want to blame is yourself.

3 This essay is not about my "success story." The fact of the matter is, I was fat, I knew I needed to change, and I did. One day at a time. And over the course of two years, I got down to a healthy weight. But just as slimming down was an act of my will, so was getting fat. And this is the point that most overweight people seem to want to avoid. They are fat because they got themselves that way.

4 If you are fat, with the very rare exception of those suffering from specific diseases affecting metabolism (and such people are rather rare), the only finger to point is right at yourself. The food that you put in your mouth got in there because your hands lifted it there, plain and simple. No one tied you down and stuffed food into your mouth. You willingly ate yourself into the state that you are in. And the problem is that it is very, very easy to do. We live in a land of plenty—literally. The very luxury of choice makes it very hard—if we didn't have access to such temptation, we would probably be better off. But that doesn't mean that it is the restaurant's fault. Maybe you have no willpower to tell yourself "no," but it is still your responsibility. Overweight people need to own up to this unpleasant fact.

5 In my opinion, I have no right to tell anyone else what to do, as long as they aren't hurting me. I won't tell someone that they shouldn't smoke, even though the harmful affects of smoking are well-documented. Likewise, I won't tell someone not to eat himself or herself into a size XXL, as long as I don't need to sit next to them on a train on my way to school. (And this isn't because I think large people are unpleasant—it is just uncomfortable to be squished in between two overweight people with six stops left to go.)

6 I compare obesity to smoking because they are essentially very similar. The deadly health hazards of smoking—lung cancer, emphysema, bronchial infection, mouth cancer, etc., have been clearly established. The health hazards of obesity—diabetes, heart disease, and certain cancers, have also been well publicized. Both smoking and eating are something that you consciously do, perhaps addictively, but you still have to put a cigarette in your mouth the same way you put a candy bar. And now the two have one more thing in common—smokers and overeaters are blaming corporate industries for their acts of free will. To quote a famous news-journalist, "give me a break."

7 Now, instead of taking responsibility for their weight problem, fat people, like smokers, (and what about the obese people who also smoke . . . I would love to be their HMO), are blaming the fast food industry. They are even suing corporations such as McDonald's for financial restitution. (Hey, you didn't think that they would sue for a health club membership?)

8 Let's think this through. You are hungry, and you want to eat. What do you do? Do you drive to a supermarket and pick up some turkey breast from the deli and some whole wheat bread? No, you drive to Burger King and order a Double Whopper with Cheese with a King size fries (hey, it is just a few cents more). You eat the 1070 calorie Whopper sandwich and the 600 calorie fries, ingesting 100 grams of fat in the process. You wash it down with a 300 calorie large soda.

9 Lo and behold, you get fat. Amazing. How did this happen? Oh, that's right, the fast food companies. They made you fat with their tasty and tempting fattening foods and their sly way of offering super-sized versions of their already caloric offerings. You had better sue them.

10 Am I the only one who sees just how absurd this is? Why are overweight people even arguing about this? America is suffering—2/3 of its population is overweight. It is high time that the population wakes up and takes responsibility for its actions. There is a frightening trend going on in America—we are becoming a nation of whiners who refuse to accept responsibility for anything. We sue at the drop of a hat. We smoke ourselves into hospital beds, and yes, we are eating ourselves to death. The "land of the free" means that we are free to make our own decisions, but part of this freedom is the responsibility to own up to our choices. It doesn't mean free to do what we want and then blame someone else when we don't like the final results.

11 Unless we send a message as a society that this behavior is simply unacceptable, the problem is going to get worse. People respond to

social and financial pressure. Maybe one solution would be to demand higher health insurance premiums for obese people–their condition is something they can change, unlike a disease condition like cancer or Alzheimer's. And I say that we stop being so sensitive in how we discuss obesity. We don't want to offend anyone. We use euphemisms—overweight women wear "women's sizes" (how about calling them "overweight sizes"?) and obese men are called "portly." They are already deceiving themselves, we shouldn't help.

12 I know my view may be unpopular. I know it may sound mean. But I think that the very reason it may be unpopular is because it holds more than a kernel of truth. Obesity hits the very core of us—it has deeply emotional and psychological components. To admit that you are obese is hard. To admit that you got yourself in such a condition is even harder. I know that. But until we do—as individuals and as a nation—we are going to get worse. And that is a future I really don't want to think about, because our present is grim enough. ◆

CONSIDERING THE ISSUES

1. In your opinion, how personally responsible are we for our body size and shape? What factors can we control, and what factors are beyond our power? Do you hold yourself responsible for your physique? Explain.
2. What is the social view of obese people? Are they subjected to harsher social scrutiny? Are they treated differently? What about on television? How are overweight men and women portrayed on television? Explain.

CRAFT AND CONTENT

3. Why does Ames tell his audience that he has struggled with his own weight? Does this admission make his essay seem more valid? Do you think he feels that it does? Explain.
4. What is Ames's tone in this essay? What is your reaction to this tone? Explain.
5. In paragraph 5, Ames notes that he feels that he has "no right to tell anyone else what to do." Does he stick to this claim throughout the rest of his essay? Explain.

CRITICAL THINKING

6. At the end of his essay, Ames provides some possible solutions to America's obesity problem. Evaluate these solutions. Are they likely to work? Why or why not?
7. Evaluate Ames's comparison of smoking to eating. In what ways are the two similar, and in what ways are they different? How would Richard Daynard likely respond to this comparison? Explain.

WRITING ABOUT THE ISSUES

8. Write a response to Ames in which you either agree or disagree, in whole or in part, with his argument. Cite specific areas of his essay that you find of particular interest. Support your response with as much factual evidence as you can.
9. Write an essay in which you express your own opinion on the McDonald's obesity lawsuits. Do you think McDonald's should be held accountable, even in part, for America's obesity crisis? Do you think that the issue is one of personal or corporate responsibility? Explain.

Fat Foods: Back in Court

Laura Bradford

Laura Bradford is a writer for *TIME* magazine, in which this story was first published in its August 3, 2003, issue.

CONNECTING TO THE TOPIC

While the 2002–03 lawsuit against McDonald's never made it to trial, lawyers have been busy considering other ways to approach litigation against fast food companies and "junk food" vendors. New legal theories may revive the case against McDonald's and motivate other big food firms such as Pepsi to change their offerings. Will these lawsuits shift our sense of personal responsibility for our weight? Will they change what food is offered to us at fast food chains and in vending machines? And are such changes what we really want?

WORDS IN CONTEXT

derision: jeering laughter; ridicule
arsenal: stock of weapons
speculative: given to conjecture; questionable
allegation: statement without proof
tangible: possible to treat as valid
allege: claim, assert as true

1 When a group of obese teenagers sued McDonald's, claiming that it made them fat, the widely publicized case drew howls of derision. But the burger giant and its competitors aren't laughing anymore. When Federal Judge Robert Sweet threw out the teenagers' case last February, reasoning that customers knew the dangers of eating Big Macs and supersize fries, he went on—in less noted parts of his ruling—to set the stage for future lawsuits. He noted that "Chicken McNuggets, rather than being merely chicken fried in a pan, are a McFrankenstein creation of various elements not utilized by the home cook," including ground chicken skin, hydrogenated oils and dimethylpolysiloxane, an antifoaming agent, and he questioned whether customers understood the risks of eating McDonald's chicken over regular chicken.

2 Attorneys for the teens, grateful for the judge's guidance, filed a revised lawsuit alleging that McDonald's engaged in deceptive advertising, in part because it failed to adequately disclose additives and processing methods that make its food less healthful. The suit is back in front of Judge Sweet, in New York City, for another round. (McDonald's says its McNuggets contain the same ingredients found in grocery-store chicken and says the second suit is as baseless as the first.)

3 Whether the case ultimately succeeds, many more are sure to follow. And unlike the original lawsuit, the new ones may have staying power. Trial lawyers have been busy meeting with public-health experts, legislators and nutritionists, and have refined their arsenal against both fast-food and packaged-food firms. Some arguments are speculative, such as the allegation that certain companies manipulated addictive properties in their junk food, as some tobacco companies did with their products. Lawyers claim, for example, that some fast-food restaurants deliberately raise the temperature at which they cook their fries to increase the amount of fat absorbed. Terrie Dort, president of the National

Council of Chain Restaurants, calls such allegations "completely absurd and without scientific basis."

4 But two more tangible legal theories could pose a serious threat to the food firms. One is based on deceptive advertising, the other on aggressive marketing to children. Plaintiffs' lawyers are looking at school-board contracts that give big soda companies exclusive placement in school vending machines in return for cash payments. School boards from Seattle to New York City are reconsidering their partnerships with soda vendors. Thanks in part to the publicity generated by the initial lawsuit against McDonald's, "there has been a shift in perception," said Marion Nestle, chair of the Department of Nutrition and Food Studies at New York University, "from seeing obesity only as a personal or family responsibility to seeing it as a societal problem with societal solutions."

5 John Banzhaf, a longtime foe of tobacco and a professor of legal activism at George Washington University Law School, is among those leading the charge against firms he regards as junk-food peddlers. The idea of suing these companies came to him after a journalist called his attention to a 2001 Surgeon General's report noting that illness associated with obesity had cost the country $117 billion in the previous year alone. This figure was close to the average annual costs associated with smoking—$150 billion, according to the Surgeon General—and got Banzhaf wondering whether food companies were vulnerable to the same kind of lawsuits that have plagued Big Tobacco. "A fast-food company like McDonald's may not be responsible for the entire obesity epidemic," he says, "but let's say they're 5% responsible. Five percent of $117 billion is still an enormous amount of money." Walt Riker, a spokesman for McDonald's, responds, "That's absurd. People interested in the real issues are talking about the totality of an individual's lifestyle. McDonald's will do its part, but the lawsuits are publicity gimmicks."

6 Even so, food companies may be vulnerable to lawsuits that allege they have engaged in misleading advertising—whether by misstating calorie information or failing to disclose health risks when describing a food as nutritious. Plaintiffs' lawyers argue that consumers who rely on inaccurate information can't make informed decisions about what to eat.

7 Lawyers are already striking indirectly at food companies by examining their contracts with local school boards. In almost half of U.S. school districts, officials allow companies such as Coca-Cola and

PepsiCo to sell soda in school vending machines or on-campus stores. Some school districts have exclusive arrangements with a soda company, which gets an opportunity to build brand loyalty among young consumers. In return, cash-starved schools receive up-front payments and in many cases a percentage of sales. The National Soft Drink Association claims that less than 10% of school districts have these exclusive arrangements, but that could still be as many as 1,200 districts. Studies by the World Health Organization, among others, suggest a link between childhood soda consumption and obesity.

8 The Seattle School Board's five-year contract allows only Coca-Cola products to be sold in school vending machines, and nets about $400,000 a year for school activities. In July Banzhaf and a local attorney threatened to sue the district and each school board member if the contract was renewed. The board, after a delay of several weeks, voted 4 to 3 to renew the contract anyway, but included a cancellation option, mandated that juice and water be included among vending-machine offerings and gave individual schools the option of banning sodas altogether. Steve Brown, the board vice president, voted for renewal, saying, "We're in a serious budget situation."

9 Plaintiffs' lawyers argue that school boards are liable on this issue because they have a special duty to look after students while they are in school. "Taking money from food companies to encourage the use of harmful products is an egregious violation of that duty," says Banzhaf.

10 Some fear that the use of aggressive tactics will undermine quieter efforts to address health and nutrition issues. In several cities parents and teachers have succeeded in persuading school boards to remove junk food from hallways without resorting to lawsuits. A coalition of parents and teachers persuaded the Los Angeles Unified School District to ban soda sales in district schools beginning in 2004. In late August the school board will consider whether to set tougher nutrition standards for cafeteria menus and vending-machine snacks. In June the New York City Department of Education announced it would ban candy and soda from school vending machines and would reduce the fat content in cafeteria meals. Kelly Brownell, the director of the Yale Center for Eating and Weight Disorders and the author of a forthcoming book on the obesity crisis, *Food Fight,* worries that the public's perception of money-hungry lawyers trying to control food choice through the courts may cause a backlash against these and more measured public-health initiatives.

11 To others, the lawsuits seem a necessary evil. Jacqueline Domac, a nutrition teacher at California's Venice High School and an organizer of the Los Angeles coalition, says, "Just because we were able to get this done on a local level doesn't mean it will work everywhere. For some districts, it may take the threat of a lawsuit." Susan Roberts, a lawyer and consultant at the Agricultural Law Center at Drake University, agrees. "I've been involved in health policy for over 20 years," she says. "We haven't had a very large impact. Sometimes it takes litigation to get policies to change."

12 There's no shortage of people willing to consider litigation. Professor Daynard recently helped host a conference at Northeastern University School of Law to discuss "Legal Approaches to the Obesity Epidemic." More than 100 academicians, public-health experts and foundation representatives attended—along with several trial lawyers in training. Says Brian Murphy, a recent graduate of Rutgers Law School: "It's a very important and pressing issue, and its outcome will be with us for years to come. I'm hoping to be able to build a career out of this issue." ◆

CONSIDERING THE ISSUES

1. Do you have a favorite fast food? If so, what is its appeal? Why do you like it and how often do you indulge in it? Would you consider this item to be "addictive"? Why or why not?
2. Bradford reports on the concerns parents and teachers have expressed regarding vending machine offerings provided to students in school. Were there vending machines in your high school or middle school? If so, what types of food and beverages did they offer? Did the machines compete with more healthy choices in the school cafeteria?

CRAFT AND CONTENT

3. Evaluate the tone and style of this article. How important is the source of an article to how much we rely or depend on the truthfulness of the information provided in it? Explain.
4. How does the author incorporate factual information and quotes into her article? How does her use of outside sources and authorities support her article? Explain.

CRITICAL THINKING

5. What "tangible legal theories" pose a real threat to fast food companies? What makes these theories more serious than the 2002 lawsuit brought by two teenagers against McDonald's? Explain.
6. Banzhaf notes that if a fast food company like McDonald's was even five percent responsible for the obesity crisis (paragraph 5), "five percent of $117 billion is still an enormous amount of money." What does this statement imply about Banzhaf's motivations? Does he say where this five percent would actually go?

WRITING ABOUT THE ISSUES

7. Banzhaf observes that five percent of 117 billion dollars is a huge sum. Hypothetically, if the fast food industry were successfully sued for this amount (5.85 billion) for its role in America's obesity crisis, where should that money go? Write a short essay explaining how the money should be distributed, and why.
8. Should vending machines be allowed on school property? Are they making children fat? Write an essay in which you support or advocate for the removal of vending machines on school property. In your response, consider the financial incentives paid to schools. If machines were banned, how could schools recuperate this financial loss?

When America Relaxes, 'Food Police' Should Keep Quiet

Paul King

Paul King is senior editor of *Nation's Restaurant News,* in which this article was first published in the August 25, 2003, issue.

CONNECTING TO THE TOPIC

Americans love fast food. But if we try to blame the fast food industry for America's obesity problem, could we end up with "banned" foods? Could fast food companies deem some foods just too high a liability? What could happen to our freedom of choice? Could the "food police" ruin fast food?

1 The Walt Kelly cartoon character Pogo once uttered the now-famous line. "We have met the enemy, and they is us!"

2 In the quickly heating debate over obesity in America, nowhere was the inescapable truth of Pogo's statement more evident for me than during my recent vacation in Pittsburgh.

3 The scene was on The Boardwalk, the collection of eateries found at a water park called Sandcastle. It was a great place for people-watching, especially if you wanted to view out-of-shape adults in ill-advised swimwear.

4 It was also the first place I actually had encountered the fried Twinkie. I had heard and read about the fat-laden, cream-filled sponge cake, but I never had seen one. There it was, on the menu at one of the snack stands, alongside the funnel cakes and—believe it or not—fried Oreos.

5 I just had to taste the fried Twinkie—for research only, of course—and so while my children took one more slide down the Tornado water ride, I got on line to place my order, two Twinkies for $2.50.

6 For the uninitiated, making a fried Twinkie is simple. You take a chilled Twinkie—you have to chill it so the cream filling doesn't liquefy in the fryer—dip it in funnel cake batter and then quickly deep-fry it. The chilling-and-frying method gives you a hot-cold combination when you bite into it.

7 "Do you get many orders for these?" I asked the blonde teenager behind the counter while I waited for my made-to-order treat.

8 "Yeah, we get some," the girl answered. "But more people order the Oreos."

9 "Do you like them?" I asked.

10 "Nope," she said. "I think they're nasty. I just eat the funnel cakes."

11 As I waited, I noticed the heavy-set couple directly to my right, who were waiting for their order, the Funnel Cake Supreme. Sandcastle, which operates its own foodservice, makes that colossally caloric confection by taking its already artery-clogging fried dough and topping it with a thick ribbon of vanilla or chocolate soft-serve ice cream. Then, to gild the lily, your server pours a generous helping of syrupy strawberries on the ice cream.

12 For $4 the dessert is a real bargain in that it easily could feed four people. But the couple had ordered one apiece. I stared, slack-jawed, as they walked away to the seating area. I was so mesmerized by the sight that I didn't immediately hear my order being called.

13 As my family gathered around the table to taste our dessert, I mentally recalled all the stories I'd been reading over the past few months about lawsuits being filed against fast-food chains and about activists railing against soda and chips being sold to our nation's school-children.

14 In all truthfulness I think that the "food police" have a very valid point: Most Americans, given several nutritional paths, will choose the tastiest road. That way leads to madness, but many people gladly are willing to go crazy in that manner.

15 They also are right to be concerned about the message most food advertising sends to our young people and to try to counter that with nutrition education and some modicum of control over what foods our kids can buy while they are in the hands of our educators.

16 But do we really need John Banzhaf, the crusading attorney who blames the fast-food industry for the nation's obesity woes, and his ilk to save us from ourselves? Does our already litigious society need to clog the courts with nutrition lawsuits faster than our eating habits can harden our blood vessels? I don't think so.

17 I'll never eat a Funnel Cake Supreme. But when I'm treating my family to a day out, whether at an amusement park or a sports event, I expect to have the opportunity to have that choice. The enemy may be us, but I'll accept that. It's sweeter than the alternative. ◆

CONSIDERING THE ISSUES

1. In his essay, King watches with great interest an obese couple eating an excessively caloric dessert. Do you notice what other people eat around you? Do you make judgments about those people based on what they eat and how they look? Do you consider your own menu choices when you know others may see what you are eating? Explain.
2. Could lawsuits influence what kinds of foods we are offered at fast food chains in the future? How have lawsuits already affected menu offerings? Do you think Big Macs and Whoppers could face extinction? Why or why not?

CRAFT AND CONTENT

3. What is the purpose of the Walt Kelly quote at the beginning of King's narrative? How does this quote connect to his essay? Explain.

4. How does King describe Banzhaf and other lawyers in paragraph 16? What words does he choose? What does his word choice reveal about how King feels about fast food litigators?

CRITICAL THINKING

5. How does King feel about the large couple's choice of dessert? Does he feel that they should have ordered two Funnel Cake Supremes? Do you think he would have had the same opinion if the couple was more physically fit?
6. Who are the "food police"? What impact could they have on our fast food choices? Explain.

WRITING ABOUT THE ISSUES

7. Write a personal narrative mirroring King's experience. Go to a fast food outlet and order something on the menu. Note the people around you, and what they are eating. Write about your impressions of the experience.

We Eat; Therefore, They Are

Rosie Mestel

Rosie Mestel is a medical writer at the *Los Angeles Times.* In addition to the *LA Times,* her articles have appeared in many publications, including *New Scientist, Health* magazine, and *Discover.*

CONNECTING TO THE TOPIC

While many people assume that board-certified physicians help develop and approve the government's dietary recommendations, few are aware of the intense political lobbying that goes on behind the scenes influencing these recommendations. Food is big business in the United States. Companies that sell foods that are high in fat or sugar have a great deal riding on what dietary recommendations the government officially supports. As this article published in the August 10, 2004, edition of the *LA Times* explains, official recommendations may not be free of political influence.

WORDS IN CONTEXT

regally: as if holding court; with a kingly air
haggard: appearing worn or tired
castigate: to criticize severely
tepid: lacking enthusiasm; literally, lukewarm
ire: with anger
strenuous: requiring great effort or energy
blight: something that prevents or impairs growth; lacking in hope or ambition
rollicking: high-spirited and enthusiastic

1 Inside a packed ballroom at the local Holiday Inn, 13 government-appointed scientists sat regally around a table, debating servings of fish.

2 "What do we want to recommend for children? Fish twice a week?" asked chairwoman Janet King.

3 "Small fish," another panel member said.

4 "Children are advised to eat smaller portions of fish than adults?"

5 "Can we defer a vote on that?" pleaded another.

6 The august panel of nutrition researchers had been talking this way for 45 minutes. The ballroom was filled with silent listeners scribbling away on notepads. Some of the listeners were looking a little haggard. They had already witnessed exhaustive discussions on protein, sugar, fat, grains, breakfast, exercise and a record-breaking 2 1/2-hour standoff on vitamin D. "Mind-numbing isn't the half of it," said a woman in line for the restroom. "I want to strangle them."

7 After a year's work, the Dietary Guidelines Advisory Committee is in the final stages of overhauling the Dietary Guidelines for Americans, which will be formally adopted next year. Since 1980, the guidelines—consisting of seven to 10 short statements and an accompanying booklet—have been issued every five years by the departments of Agriculture and Health and Human Services.

8 School menus must comply with the guidelines; so must the Women, Infants and Children program, which provides food to low-income mothers. The food pyramid, currently receiving its own overhaul, is also based on the guidelines. America now waits hungrily for the latest update.

9 Do these scholars think we should still "choose a variety of fruits and vegetables daily" as the guidelines currently decree? Should we continue to "choose and prepare food with less salt," and "aim for a

Dietary Advice Through the Ages

1917: The Department of Agriculture releases a 14-page pamphlet, 'How to Select Foods,' encouraging Americans to eat from five food groups: milk and meat; cereals; vegetables and fruits; fats and fat foods; sugars and sugary foods.

1941: First recommended daily allowances released by the National Academy of Sciences.

1959: Nutrition researcher Ancel Keys and wife Margaret publish guidelines for avoiding heart disease, including 'do not get fat; if you are fat, reduce'; 'restrict saturated fats'; and 'be sensible about cigarettes, alcohol, excitement, business strain.'

1977: Dietary Goals for the United States – a report from the Senate Select Committee on Nutrition and Human Needs – recommends cutting back on salt, saturated fat, sugar and cholesterol. Food industry groups protest, as do some scientists and doctors.

1980: First edition of the Dietary Guidelines for Americans. People are told to avoid too much sugar, sodium, fat, saturated fat and cholesterol; to maintain an ideal weight; eat a variety of foods; and drink alcohol only in moderation.

1991: The Food Guide Pyramid is completed, sparking food industry protest. Agriculture Secretary Edward R. Madigan withdraws the pyramid, claiming it is confusing to children.

1992: The Food Guide Pyramid is released to the public.

Sources: 'Food Politics' by Marion Nestle, 2002; U.S. Department of Agriculture; Department of Health and Human Services. Researched by Times staff writer Rosie Mestel

healthy weight"? Would it remain wise to "choose beverages and foods to moderate your intake of sugars"?

10 To reach their conclusions, committee members—unpaid volunteers generally drawn from academia—have waded through thousands of pages of studies on fat, heart disease, television watching, obesity and the effect of fiber on stool weight. They have investigated the best way to wash broccoli and argued bitterly on the matter of sugar. They have been aided by testimony and letters from hundreds of groups and individuals, including the Sugar Association, the Grocery Manufacturers of America, the American Heart Association, People for the Ethical Treatment of Animals, the Bible-based Hallelujah Diet and scads of disciples of Dr. Joseph Mercola, author of "The No-Grain Diet."

11 The job is "enormous—probably one of the most difficult jobs I ever had," said Dr. Cutberto Garza, director of the division of nutritional sciences at Cornell University and chairman of the 2000 Dietary Guidelines Advisory Committee.

12 He didn't get paid, but he had some exciting times. Before the job was done, his committee sparked a lawsuit by an advocacy group claiming the panel had a pro-milk bias, was challenged by one senator

for being too positive about alcohol and castigated by 30 other senators for being too negative about sugar.

13 Writing the dietary guidelines is honor, toil, aggravation and tedium—in unequal measure. The results of the group's work are bland and seemingly obvious bits of advice that most Americans have never read.

14 "It is interesting to see how they put it all together," whispers one audience member. "It is a little bit boring, of course." [. . .]

15 Complaints surfaced from the moment the committee was appointed last year. The Center for Science in the Public Interest pointed fingers at seven of the 13 selected committee members for having financial relationships with industry groups, including the Sugar Association, the Campbell Soup Company and the American Cocoa Research Institute.

16 How, asked the consumer group, could Americans be sure the scientists were unbiased?

17 Richard Hanneman, president of the Salt Institute, was pretty ticked too. He has peppered the committee with letters complaining about the unfair and unscientific treatment given to salt in the 2000 guidelines, which told Americans to "choose and prepare foods with less salt."

18 "We could not accept that," said Hanneman, who hasn't missed a dietary guideline meeting since 1990. "We don't think there's evidence that the public should consume less salt."

19 The Sugar Association and the Grocery Manufacturers of America both wrote to say that the guidelines don't focus enough on physical activity—just on what people eat. The grocery manufacturers have suggested that the name of the guidelines be changed to the Dietary and Physical Activity Guidelines.

20 Such intensity about eating advice did not exist a century ago when the government began issuing guidelines, said Marion Nestle, a professor of nutrition, food studies and public health at New York University and author of the 2002 book, *Food Politics: How the Food Industry Influences Nutrition and Health.*

21 In the early days, the Department of Agriculture advised people to eat widely and plentifully, in keeping with its role promoting American agriculture. The advice has changed through the years—there were five food groups in 1917, 12 in 1933, eight in 1942 and either seven or 11 in 1943, depending on which pamphlet you consulted.

22 The tips were at times on the tepid side: The 1979 "Hassle-Free Guide to a Better Diet" told readers that many scientists felt diet contributed to chronic disease, but others did not, "so the choice is yours."

23 The trouble began when the government started advising people to start eating less of certain foods, Nestle said. One flap erupted in 1977 after a Senate committee report suggested Americans cut back on saturated fats, sugar, cholesterol and salt. The cattle, dairy, egg and sugar industries protested—and the report was revised, easing up on salt and cholesterol and dumping the phrase "reduce consumption of meat" for a friendlier "choose meats, poultry and fish which will reduce saturated fat intake."

24 The food pyramid also drew ire upon its completion in 1991 because its pointed shape indicated that some foods should be eaten less than others. Strenuous objections from the National Cattlemen's Association and National Milk Producers Federation—both of whose products were nearer the top of the pyramid—caused a one-year delay in the pyramid's release.

25 Creating the guidelines is still "political—from start to finish," said Nestle, who was on the 1995 Dietary Guidelines Committee. "It's science politics. It's politics politics. It's corporate politics." She recalled tensely standing her ground to ensure that a phrase she hated—"there is no such thing as a good or bad food; all foods are part of a healthy diet"—was not included in the 1995 guidelines.

26 Nestle bemoaned the fact that even as Americans fatten up, no one is ever told to eat less of any specifically identified food—not even a candy bar or soft drinks. And she snorted at the guideline about sugar, which as far as she's concerned has been infected by a creeping blight of wishy-washiness.

27 In 1980, people were flatly told to "avoid too much sugar." By 2000, the committee was going to tell Americans to "choose beverages and foods to limit your intake of sugar"—but the word "limit" was tossed out at the last minute by the government (after industry protests) and replaced with the weaker word "moderate." This time, people are holding their breath to see if there will be a sugar guideline at all. [. . .]

28 [The May] meeting of the committee was supposed to be the last, but a rollicking debate about vitamin D threw everything off schedule. No one was certain when the meeting would end. "I'm figuring midnight," said a USDA employee, placidly stitching away on a patchwork quilt to pass the time. Fresh science, it seemed, had emerged since 2000, revealing that many people are deficient in the vitamin. But some committee members were nervous about recommending a big jump in intake.

29 Brisk progress was made on some subjects: Eight draft guidelines were crafted advising Americans to "keep food safe to eat," "monitor your body weight to achieve health," "choose and prepare foods with less salt" and "be physically active every day."

30 For the first time, the committee planned to recommend Americans slash their intake of trans fats, those hardened, partially hydrogenated vegetable oils found in stick margarines and many baked goods.

31 But sugar was a sticky mess. As the committee took up the issue again, an excited rustle went through the audience like so many candy bars being unwrapped. Dr. Carlos Camargo, assistant professor of medicine and epidemiology at Harvard University, cited three recent studies reporting that kids drinking the greatest number of sugary soft drinks ended up plumper later on.

32 Nutrition researchers Teresa Nicklas, professor of pediatrics at Baylor College of Medicine, and Joanne Lupton, professor of nutrition at Texas A&M University, lobbed back other types of studies that didn't find that link.

33 Camargo, noting his position as president of the American College of Epidemiology, said that the other types of studies were inferior in design.

34 Well, Lupton said, if we're going to ignore them for sugar, we have to ignore those kinds of studies for other issues too.

35 "We're here to make a difference," Camargo said.

36 "I don't think we are here to make a difference," Lupton said. "I think we are here to evaluate the science."

37 The mood began to lighten when sugar was put off again and matters drifted on, past cholesterol and fish to a discussion of alcohol, in which nothing, as usual, was left unquestioned. The panel debated a recommendation that alcohol be avoided by children and those operating heavy machinery. One committee member asked for the pertinent data.

38 They forged ahead, moving on to fiber's impact on heart disease and bowel motion. Lupton explained that there had been more than 100 studies on the effect of fiber on stool weight and its consequent speedier passage through the bowel. "So there is a very strong . . . are you laughing at me for talking about this?" she said.

39 Some committee members were giggling.

40 "It is interesting where we, as a society, have placed our research efforts . . . 100 trials on stool," Camargo said. Lupton tried to explain

that constipation is one of the most common disorders in Western countries, affecting up to 10% of children and maybe 20% of people aged 65 and older. A blond woman five rows back was laughing so hard she was crying.

41 Some people in the audience took advantage of the uproar and sneaked out for an evening snack. ◆

CONNECTING TO THE TOPIC

1. Does the U.S. government, with its "official" food pyramid, have a responsibility for the overall public health? Why or why not?
2. Do you follow the Dietary Guidelines for Americans? For example, do you look at the nutritional information on the sides of food products? Does the information on the panel influence what you eat? Explain.

CRAFT AND CONTENT

3. In paragraph 27, Mestel describes how the very words used to caution Americans on sugar intake became a subject of great debate. The recommendation changed from "avoid" to "limit" to "moderate." What do these words mean to the average consumer? Would you be influenced to eat less sugar if you were told to "limit" your intake as opposed to "moderate" it? Explain.
4. In paragraph 36, in response to Dr. Carlos Camargo's charge that the committee was there "to make a difference," professor Joanne Lupton replied, "I don't think we are here to make a difference." "I think we are here to evaluate the science." What does she mean? Do you agree with Camargo's position or Lupton's position, and why?

CRITICAL THINKING

5. Before reading this article, were you aware of how the Dietary Guidelines for Americans was determined? What assumptions regarding government recommendations did you have? After reading this article, are you more or less confident in the government's strategy for developing the new guidelines? Explain.

6. Marion Nestle expresses frustration that while Americans are obviously dealing with health problems related to expanding waistlines, "no one is ever told to eat less of any specifically identified food—not even a candy bar or soft drinks." Should certain foods carry warnings? Is it up to the individual to know which foods are healthy and which ones are not? Is it the government's responsibility to guide the public? Explain.

WRITING ABOUT THE ISSUES

7. Write an essay exploring your own eating habits as they are influenced—or not influenced—by the guidelines set forth by the government or on the sides of prepared-food packages. Include in your response the nutritional information cited online by fast food companies such as McDonald's. Is this information helpful? Why or why not?
8. Mestel provides a glimpse behind the inner workings of a government panel responsible for developing the Dietary Guidelines for Americans. Based on what you have read, explain how you feel about this panel and its effectiveness. If you wish, make recommendations of your own on how the Dietary Guidelines for Americans should be drafted.

VISUAL CONNECTIONS

Now What Do We Eat?

CONNECTING TO THE TOPIC

Over the last two decades, thousands of schoolchildren were taught the "food pyramid" approved by the United States Department of Agriculture. Many Americans believed that they understood what healthy eating habits comprised, even if they didn't actually have such habits themselves. But the food pyramid has come under fire as Americans begin to

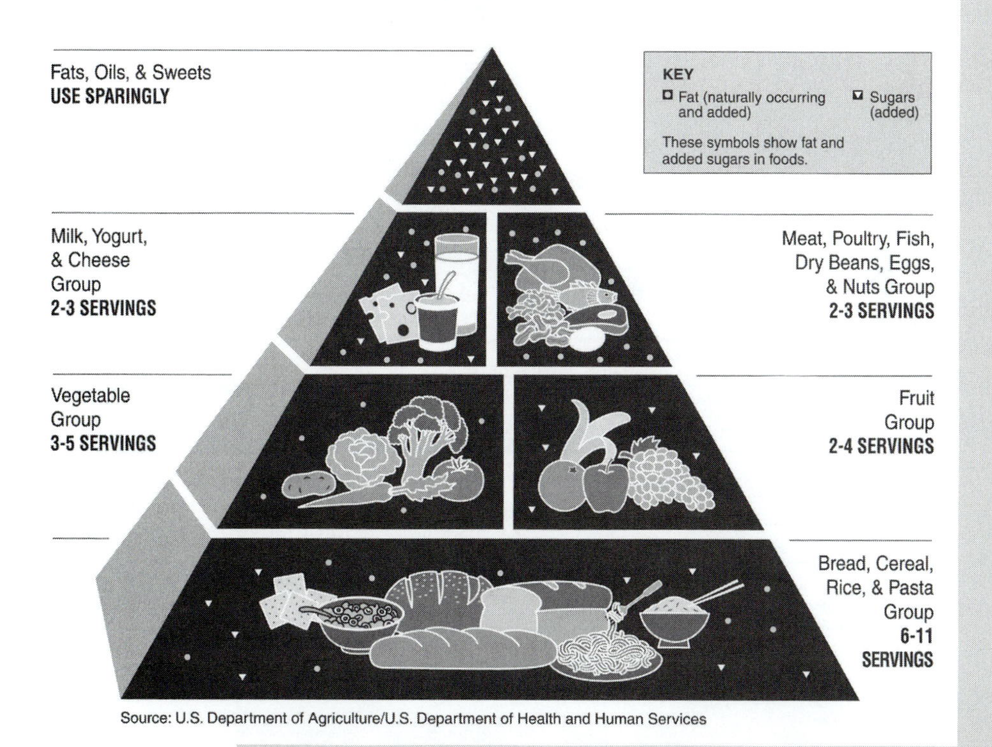

Source: U.S. Department of Agriculture/U.S. Department of Health and Human Services

recognize a growing obesity crisis nationwide. Is it time to revise the food pyramid? Walter Willett of the Harvard School of Public Health thinks it is. He has created a new food pyramid and has published a book, *Eat, Drink, and Be Healthy,* encouraging all Americans to change their eating habits in order to enjoy more healthy lives. A graphic of the traditional food pyramid, familiar to most people from their days in health class, appears on page 315, and Willett's revised pyramid can be seen below.

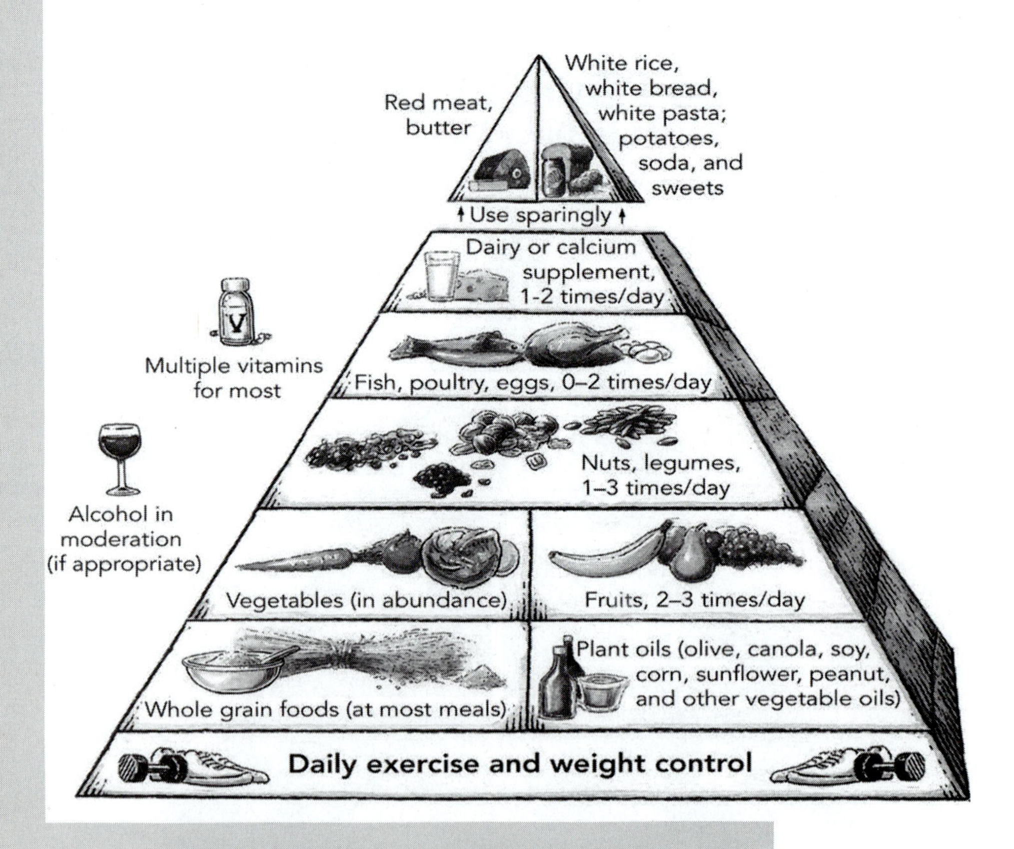

CONSIDERING THE ISSUES

1. Do you try to follow the recommendations of the USDA food pyramid? How much food, based on servings, do you think you would eat if you followed the traditional pyramid? Explain.
2. What information do you need to know in order to understand what is happening in this picture? Explain.

CRITICAL THINKING

3. Review the recommendations of each pyramid carefully. Consider how your dietary habits compare to each graph. What pyramid seems more healthy, and why? How does your diet compare to the recommendations in each graph? Explain.
4. The pyramid on the facing page was designed by a professor of health, and has not yet been approved by the USDA. Based on what you read in Mestel's article, do you think it is likely that Willett's pyramid will be approved for the general public? Why or why not?

TOPICAL CONNECTIONS

GROUP PROJECTS

1. Discuss in your group the following question: If you could be either very beautiful or very wealthy, what would you choose? Explain the motivation behind your choice. Based on your group's multiple responses, can you make any conclusions about the influence of body size, beauty, and social acceptance in today's society?
2. Together with your group, develop a lawsuit against a popular fast food chain. Identify the reason behind the suit, on whose behalf you are suing, and the expected restitution. Refer to specific points made in the essays in this chapter.

WEB PROJECTS

3. One of the issues explored in this chapter is whether the fast food industry should assume some financial responsibility for health issues connected to obesity in this country. In Colorado, laws protect certain industries and workers, such as dude ranches and ski-lift operators, from "frivolous lawsuits." In January 2004, the Colorado legislature submitted a bill to protect fast food industries against obesity lawsuits. Research this issue in greater depth on the Internet (try newspapers such as www.denverpost.com). Should states pass such bills? Are they a good idea? Why or why not?
4. In April of 2005, the U.S. Department of Agriculture revised the traditional food pyramid. View the new pyramid at www.pyramid.gov and compare it to the two other pyramids featured on pages 315 and 316. Which pyramid do you prefer, and why? Do we need a visual to explain how we should eat? If you were in charge of the USDA, how would you approach the issue of explaining dietary recommendations to children and adults? To support your project, research additional information on nutrition online at www.nal.usda.gov/fnic and www.nutrition.org.

FOR FURTHER INQUIRY

5. The obesity crisis is not just an adult problem—childhood obesity rates have tripled over the last 20 years. Disease conditions such as type 2 diabetes, more commonly called "adult onset" diabetes, and heart disease are striking children at an alarming rate. Research the issue of childhood obesity. Why are children getting heavier? What can be done to stop this disturbing trend? And what could happen if we don't? Visit the Kid Source Web site addressing childhood obesity at www.kidsource.com/ kidsource/content2/obesity.html for more information. The National Institutes of Health also provides a good Web site on this issue at www.nih.gov/news/WordonHealth/jun2002/childhoodobesity.htm.

10 Why Do We Work?

While the question as to why we work may seem obvious on the surface—to support ourselves and our loved ones—there are many reasons why we work. Some reasons, such as ambition, a drive to succeed and excel, and the desire to make the world a better place are considered noble reasons to work. They can help determine the career paths we take and how we will ultimately measure our success. But there are some reasons we might be less willing to admit, such as the ability to buy more expensive luxuries, drive better cars, support a particular lifestyle, or even to get away from our chaotic home lives.

Most college students enter their two- or four-year training programs in order to develop skills that will allow them to better compete in the working world. But what are our expectations of the working world? What do we hope to get out of a job besides a regular paycheck? What satisfaction do you expect from a job? What defines a career? What is your idea of "making it"—of achieving success? An early retirement? Fame? Respect? This chapter explores some of the issues connected to why we work.

CRITICAL THINKING

1. What is happening in this cartoon? Can you tell who the people are in the cartoon? What are they discussing? Explain.
2. Do you think this cartoon presents a stereotype of the American work ethic? What issue does it intend to hold up for public scrutiny? Explain.

Why We Work

Andrew Curry

Andrew Curry is a general editor of *Smithsonian* magazine. His articles have appeared in many publications, including the *Washington Post*, the *Christian Science Monitor*, the *Miami Herald*, and the *Guardian*. This article appeared in the February 24, 2003, issue of *U.S. News and World Report* when Curry was an associate editor for that publication.

CONNECTING TO THE TOPIC

Although most of us work because we have to, we also assume that this work will ultimately improve our lives. But is the pursuit of the American dream becoming just that, a dream? It seems as if Americans are working harder than ever before, with less leisure time. Today, American society is dominated by work. But there was a time when people could have followed a different path, when we could have opted as a nation to actually work *less*. When did the American workforce make the choice to have more stuff over less time? And was it the right choice?

WORDS IN CONTEXT

eccentric: behaving differently from the norm, as an oddball
starkly: bluntly
precarious: lacking in stability
affluent: wealthy
smelter: an iron works
ample: in large number or quantity
apex: highest point
propaganda: methodical and persistent distribution of a message advocating a particular cause or idea
persistence: the refusal to give up
autonomy: the ability to make one's own decisions; independence

1 Some do it for love. Others do it for money. But most of us do it because we have no other choice.

2 In 1930, W. K. Kellogg made what he thought was a sensible decision, grounded in the best economic, social, and management theories of the time. Workers at his cereal plant in Battle Creek, Michigan, were told to go home two hours early. Every day. For good.

3 The Depression-era move was hailed in *Factory and Industrial Management* magazine as the "biggest piece of industrial news since [Henry] Ford announced his five-dollar-a-day policy." President Herbert Hoover summoned the eccentric cereal magnate to the White House and said the plan was "very worthwhile." The belief: Industry and machines would lead to a workers' paradise where all would have less work, more free time, and yet still produce enough to meet their needs.

4 So what happened? Today, work dominates Americans' lives as never before, as workers pile on hours at a rate not seen since the Industrial Revolution. Technology has offered increasing productivity and a higher standard of living while bank tellers and typists are replaced by machines. The mismatch between available work and those available to do it continues, as jobs go begging while people beg for jobs. Though Kellogg's six-hour day lasted until 1985, Battle Creek's grand industrial experiment has been nearly forgotten. Instead of working less, our hours have stayed steady or risen—and today many more women work so that families can afford the trappings of suburbia. In effect, workers chose the path of consumption over leisure.

5 But as today's job market shows so starkly, that road is full of potholes. With unemployment at a nine-year high and many workers worried about losing their jobs—or forced to accept cutbacks in pay and benefits—work is hardly the paradise economists once envisioned.

6 Instead, the job market is as precarious today as it was in the early 1980s, when business began a wave of restructurings and layoffs to maintain its competitiveness. Many workers are left feeling insecure, unfulfilled, and under-appreciated. It's no wonder surveys of today's workers show a steady decline in job satisfaction. "People are very emotional about work, and they're very negative about it," says David Rhodes, a principal at human resource consultants Towers Perrin. "The biggest issue is clearly workload. People are feeling crushed."

7 The backlash comes after years of people boasting about how hard they work and tying their identities to how indispensable they are. Ringing cell phones, whirring faxes, and ever-present E-mail have blurred the lines between work and home. The job penetrates every aspect of life. Americans don't exercise, they work out. We manage

our time and work on our relationships. "In reaching the affluent society, we're working longer and harder than anyone could have imagined," says Rutgers University historian John Gillis. "The work ethic and identifying ourselves with work and through work is not only alive and well but more present now than at any time in history."

8 It's all beginning to take a toll. Fully one third of American workers—who work longer hours than their counterparts in any industrialized country—felt overwhelmed by the amount of work they had to do, according to a 2001 Families and Work Institute survey. "Both men and women wish they were working about 11 hours [a week] less," says Ellen Galinsky, the institute's president. "A lot of people believe if they do work less they'll be seen as less committed, and in a shaky economy no one wants that."

9 The modern environment would seem alien to pre-industrial laborers. For centuries, the household—from farms to "cottage" craftsmen—was the unit of production. The whole family was part of the enterprise, be it farming, blacksmithing, or baking. "In pre-industrial society, work and family were practically the same thing," says Gillis.

10 The Industrial Revolution changed all that. Mills and massive iron smelters required ample labor and constant attendance. "The factory took men, women and children out of the workshops and homes and put them under one roof and timed their movements to machines," writes Sebastian de Grazia in *Of Time, Work and Leisure*. For the first time, work and family were split. Instead of selling what they produced, workers sold their time. With more people leaving farms to move to cities and factories, labor became a commodity, placed on the market like any other.

11 Innovation gave rise to an industrial process based on machinery and mass production. This new age called for a new worker. "The only safeguard of order and discipline in the modern world is a standardized worker with interchangeable parts," mused one turn-of-the-century writer.

12 Business couldn't have that, so instead it came up with the science of management. The theories of Frederick Taylor, a Philadelphia factory foreman with deep Puritan roots, led to work being broken down into component parts, with each step timed to coldly quantify jobs that skilled craftsmen had worked a lifetime to learn. Workers resented Taylor and his stopwatch, complaining that his focus on process stripped their jobs of creativity and pride, making them irritable.

Long before anyone knew what "stress" was, Taylor brought it to the workplace—and without sympathy. "I have you for your strength and mechanical ability, and we have other men paid for thinking," he told workers.

13 The division of work into components that could be measured and easily taught reached its apex in Ford's River Rouge plant in Dearborn, Michigan, where the assembly line came of age. "It was this combination of a simplification of tasks . . . with moving assembly that created a manufacturing revolution while at the same time laying waste human potential on a massive scale," author Richard Donkin writes in *Blood, Sweat and Tears.*

14 To maximize the production lines, businesses needed long hours from their workers. But it was no easy sell. "Convincing people to work 9 to 5 took a tremendous amount of propaganda and discipline," says the University of Richmond's Joanne Ciulla, author of *The Working Life: The Promise and Betrayal of Modern Work.* Entrepreneurs, religious leaders, and writers like Horatio Alger created whole bodies of literature to glorify the work ethic.

15 The first labor unions were organized in response to the threat of technology, as skilled workers sought to protect their jobs from mechanization. Later, semi- and unskilled workers began to organize as well, agitating successfully for reduced hours, higher wages, and better work conditions. Unions enjoyed great influence in the early 20th century, and at their height in the 1950s, 35 percent of U.S. workers belonged to one.

16 Union persistence and the mechanization of factories gradually made shorter hours more realistic. Between 1830 and 1930, work hours were cut nearly in half, with economist John Maynard Keynes famously predicting in 1930 that by 2030 a 15-hour workweek would be standard. The Great Depression pressed the issue, with job sharing proposed as a serious solution to widespread unemployment. Despite business and religious opposition over worries of an idle populace, the Senate passed a bill that would have mandated a 30-hour week in 1933; it was narrowly defeated in the House.

17 Franklin Delano Roosevelt struck back with a new gospel that lives to this very day: consumption. "The aim . . . is to restore our rich domestic market by raising its vast consuming capacity," he said. "Our first purpose is to create employment as fast as we can." And so began the modern work world. "Instead of accepting work's continuing

decline and imminent fall from its dominant social position, businessmen, economists, advertisers, and politicians preached that there would never be 'enough,'" says University of Iowa Professor Benjamin Hunnicutt, author of *Work Without End: Abandoning Shorter Hours for the Right to Work*. "The entrepreneur and industry could invent new things for advertising to sell and for people to want and work for indefinitely."

18 The New Deal dumped government money into job creation, in turn encouraging consumption. World War II fueled the fire, and American workers soon found themselves in a "golden age"—40-hour workweeks, plenty of jobs, and plenty to buy. Leisure was the road not taken, a path quickly forgotten in the postwar boom of the 1950s and 1960s.

19 Decades of abundance, however, did not bring satisfaction. "A significant number of Americans are dissatisfied with the quality of their working lives," said the 1973 report "Work in America" from the Department of Health, Education and Welfare. "Dull, repetitive, seemingly meaningless tasks, offering little challenge or autonomy, are causing discontent among workers at all occupational levels." Underlying the dissatisfaction was a very gradual change in what the "Protestant work ethic" meant. Always a source of pride, the idea that hard work was a calling from God dated to the Reformation and the teachings of Martin Luther. While work had once been a means to serve God, two centuries of choices and industrialization had turned work into an end in itself, stripped of the spiritual meaning that sustained the Puritans who came ready to tame the wilderness.

20 By the end of the '70s, companies were reaching out to spiritually drained workers by offering more engagement while withdrawing the promise of a job for life, as the American economy faced a stiff challenge from cheaper workers abroad. "Employees were given more control over their work and schedules, and "human relations" consultants and motivational speakers did a booming business. By the 1990s, technology made working from home possible for a growing number of people. Seen as a boon at first, telecommuting and the rapidly proliferating "electronic leash" of cellphones made work inescapable, as employees found themselves on call 24/7. Today, almost half of American workers use computers, cellphones, E-mail, and faxes for work during what is supposed to be non-work time, according to the Families and Work Institute. Home is no longer a refuge but a cozier extension of the office.

21 The shift coincided with a shortage of highly skilled and educated workers, some of whom were induced with such benefits as stock options in exchange for their putting the company first all the time. But some see a different explanation for the rise in the amount of time devoted to work. "Hours have crept up partly as a consequence of the declining power of the trade-union movement," says Cornell University labor historian Clete Daniel. "Many employers find it more economical to require mandatory overtime than hire new workers and pay their benefits." Indeed, the trend has coincided with the steady decline in the percentage of workers represented by unions, as the labor movement failed to keep pace with the increasing rise of white-collar jobs in the economy. Today fewer than 15 percent of American workers belong to unions.

22 In a study of Silicon Valley culture over the past decade, San Jose State University anthropologist Jan English-Lueck found that skills learned on the job were often brought home. Researchers talked to families with mission statements, mothers used conflict-resolution buzzwords with their squabbling kids, and engineers used flowcharts to organize Thanksgiving dinner. Said one participant: "I don't live life; I manage it."

23 In some ways, we have come full circle. "Now we're seeing the return of work to the home in terms of telecommuting," says Gillis. "We may be seeing the return of households where work is the central element again."

24 But there's still the question of fulfillment. In a recent study, human resources consultants Towers Perrin tried to measure workers' emotions about their jobs. More than half of the emotion was negative, with the biggest single factor being workload but also a sense that work doesn't satisfy their deeper needs. "We expect more and more out of our jobs," says Hunnicutt. "We expect to find wonderful people and experiences all around us. What we find is Dilbert." ◆

CONSIDERING THE ISSUES

1. Curry begins his essay with the statement "Some do it for love. Others do it for money. But most of us do it because we have no other choice." Respond to this statement. What motivates you to work? Do you do it for the love of the job? For the money? Because you must? A little of each? Explain.

2. In this essay, Curry traces the historical origins of the American workforce and observes that there was a time before World War II when Americans made a choice to have more material things instead of having more leisure time. Which would you rather have? More money or more time? Explain.
3. Curry observes that e-mail, voice mail, cell phones, faxes, and computers have created "electronic leashes" that blur the boundaries between home and work. How much do you rely on this equipment? Would your quality of life be less if you did not have access to a cell phone? To e-mail? Do such devices keep us "on" 24/7? Why or why not?

CRAFT AND CONTENT

1. Curry quotes several authors and professors who have researched transformations in the American workforce and work ethic. How do these authors, and the quotes he cites, relate to his overall point that American workers have "chosen a path of consumption over leisure"? Explain.
2. In paragraph 14, professor Joanne Ciulla observes that it "took a tremendous amount of propaganda" to convince people to work 9 to 5. What is propaganda? What do we associate with the word *propaganda*? What does it imply? Does it seem to fit this context? Why or why not?
3. What is the author's opinion of the state of the American worker? Identify specific statements in this essay that reveal his viewpoint.

CRITICAL THINKING

4. Who was Frederick Taylor? How do his theories, and the science of management, relate to the state of the modern worker?
5. Participants in a study on Silicon Valley culture noted how they brought work-culture home in the form of "family mission statements," conflict resolution "buzzwords," and even flowcharts to organize Thanksgiving gatherings. Is work intruding on family life?

WRITING ABOUT THE ISSUES

6. What is your definition of "the American Dream"? How important is money in your version of the dream? What priorities do you give to leisure time? Write an essay in which you compare the points

Curry makes in his essay on the nature of the modern American workforce and your own lifestyle choices, now and in the future.

7. At the end of his article, Curry quotes consultants Towers Perrin, who found Americans in general to be deeply dissatisfied with work. Americans expect more and get less out of their jobs. Write an essay about your expectations of job satisfaction now and in the future. Have you ever held a job that you truly loved? Do you expect to find one that provides you with a sense of achievement and satisfaction? How has your experience in the workforce thus far measured up to your expectations? Explain.

Work Is Life

Oliver Libaw

Oliver Libaw is a reporter and writer for ABC News.

CONNECTING TO THE TOPIC

Is work life? For many twenty- and thirty-somethings, work is where they socialize, form friendships, define personal identities, and form support networks. While most sociologists agree that Americans are working more than ever, they disagree as to why. Do we work because we have to, or are we driven by deeper emotional and psychological reasons? Could we be working so hard because we actually *want* to?

WORDS IN CONTEXT

autonomy: the ability to make one's own decisions; independence

encroach: to push back or take over established boundaries with a gradual, almost imperceptible persistence

1 In a sense, Phil Chavez is always at work—and that's the way he likes it.

2 "This is 24/7. I get calls at all hours of the night," says Chavez, a 29-year-old sports agent in Madison, Wisconsin.

3 In representing professional athletes and coaches, he plays the role of friend, counselor, motivator and confidant, and that means being accessible to his clients. The stress level is through the roof, he says.

Major Occupational Groups and Mean Annual Wages

Management:
employed: 6,653,480; wage: $82,790

Business and Financial Operations:
employed: 4,924,210; wage: $55,550

Computer and Mathematical:
employed: 2,827,010; wage: $63,240

Architecture and Engineering:
employed: 2,376,650; wage: $59,230

Life, Physical, and Social Science:
employed: 1,113,130; wage: $53,210

Community and Social Services:
employed: 1,615,610; wage: $35,420

Legal:
employed: 951,510; wage: $78,910

Education, Training, and Library:
employed: 7,831,630; wage: $40,660

Arts, Design, Entertainment, Sports, and Media:
employed: 1,538,150; wage: $42,620

Healthcare Practitioners and Technical:
employed: 6,173,760; wage: $55,380

Healthcare Support:
employed: 3,208,770; wage: $22,750

Protective Service:
employed: 2,999,630; wage: $34,090

Food Preparation and Serving:
employed: 10,216,620; wage: $17,290

Building and Grounds Cleaning and Maintenance:
employed: 4,260,380; wage: $21,060

Personal Care and Service:
employed: 2,988,590; wage: $21,380

Sales and Related:
employed: 13,534,180; wage: $31,250

Office and Administrative Support:
employed: 22,678,010; wage: $28,260

Farming, Fishing, and Forestry:
employed: 461,630; wage: $20,200

Construction and Extraction:
employed: 6,085,510; wage: $36,650

Installation, Maintenance, and Repair:
employed: 5,226,080; wage: $36,210

Production:
employed: 10,488,450; wage: $28,710

Transportation and Material Moving:
employed: 9,414,920; wage: $27,600

Occupational Employment and Wages, U.S. Department of Labor: May 2003

4 But, Chavez insists, "I wouldn't want it any other way."

5 Chavez is typical of a growing trend in the workforce, affecting both white and blue-collar employees, says Terry Alan Beehr, a Central Michigan University psychology professor who studies business organization and occupational stress.

6 "A lot of professional jobs are rewarding," he says, as employers emphasize the qualities that drive people to feel invested in their job. Workers naturally drive themselves harder if their position provides them with autonomy, variety, feedback, and shows tangible results, says Beehr.

7 "I do this for personal satisfaction. I really enjoy it," says Adam Lewinson, a 34-year-old project director at Lifetime Television in Los Angeles. "I have a set of personal goals for my life, and my job is part of that." Lewinson's attitude reflects the growing importance of work in our lives.

8 A century ago, work was more commonly seen as a means to an end, says Benjamin Hunnicutt, a sociologist at the University of Iowa. Other aspects of life, like community, family and religion, were considered more important than one's job.

9 "Today, work defines our identity. It gives us direction and purpose," he argues. Work today not only shapes our self-conception, it also provides us with an increasingly important social group. More and more, people build their social network around their colleagues instead of their neighbors or family. "Who do you invite over for dinner—your neighbors or people you work with?" asks Angela Hattery, a Wake Forest University sociologist.

10 "It's an age thing," says Harvard Business School professor Rosabeth Moss Kanter. "When you're younger and don't have family responsibilities, [work] is also your social life." Some companies have seized on the social aspects of work, and actually encourage interoffice dating, she notes.

11 Kanter and others insist these attitude shifts are the primary reason people are working harder than ever. For the vast majority of white-collar workers putting in long, stressful hours, salary is only a secondary consideration, she argues. Instead people work hard because they get satisfaction from doing their jobs well, and from being a part of a group achievement.

12 Kate Mellema, an administrator at a software company in Washington State, reflects these qualities. "I love coming to work each day; I feel a sense of purpose about our accomplishments," she says.

13 Her views are echoed by Sarah MacMillan, a recent college graduate working for a Boston medical supply company. "I work hard not only because I like it, but because I get treated seriously," she says.

14 For some, however, letting work become the center of life leads eventually to frustration over missed opportunities. "Why are we working so much? It's because we believe that our job will pay off somehow," says Hunnicutt.

15 "We let the workplace invade us," says Bill Gillmore, a computer programmer and engineer in Richardson, Texas. Gillmore says the excitement of working in a new and evolving field spurred him to work long hours throughout his career. Now, however, the heavy demands of his job have taken a toll, he admits. People chasing their career goals "don't notice the workplace encroaching into every aspect of their personal lives."

16 Now, he says, he's "burned out, fed up, and waiting to get laid off." ◆

CONSIDERING THE ISSUES

1. Do you have a full- or a part-time job? If so, how much time do you spend working? Do you work more than you would like to? Less? If you do not currently hold a job, speak to someone who holds the job you expect to have someday and ask them how many hours a week they spend, on average, working. Does their answer surprise you? Why or why not?
2. Think about the things that define you as a person. Describe how these things help to create your personal identity. Does work or career factor into your self-definition? Why or why not?

CRAFT AND CONTENT

3. What is the tone of this article? In what ways does the source of the article reflect our expectations of the tone and style of the piece? Explain.
4. In paragraph 5, Libaw notes that Chavez is a typical example of a growing trend in the workforce, "affecting both *white* and *blue collar* employees." What do these terms mean? Do the examples of workers profiled in the article reflect both these work types?

CRITICAL THINKING

5. In paragraph 9, professor Benjamin Hunnicutt states that in many ways, "today, work defines our identity." Do you agree with this statement? In what ways do you think your current or your future career will define your identity? Is this a bad thing? Why or why not?
6. Rosabeth Moss Kanter, a professor at Harvard Business School, argues in paragraph 11, "For the vast majority of white-collar workers putting in long, stressful hours, salary is only a secondary consideration." Do you agree with her statement? Explain.

WRITING ABOUT THE ISSUES

7. In a short essay, compare Libaw's article that most Americans like to work because it makes them happy, to Curry's article, which leans more toward the idea that Americans work because "they have to." Which argument do you agree with more, and why?

8. Imagine that one of your close friends told you that he or she was tired of a job, like Bill Gillmore at the end of this article. The friend is "burned out, fed up, and waiting to get laid off." Respond to this friend in a letter referring to points made in this article and your own personal work experience. What would you tell your friend to do?

Measuring Success

Renee Loth

Renee Loth is the editor of the editorial page of the *Boston Globe,* in which this essay first appeared.

CONNECTING TO THE TOPIC

The Declaration of Independence describes our inalienable right to "life, liberty, and the pursuit of happiness." But what, exactly, is "the pursuit of happiness"? As the document has been interpreted, it often means the right to financial independence and success. Many college students enter the workforce with just such a sense of idealism. Time and experience often test this optimism, forcing many to redefine "the pursuit of happiness" along more realistic and mature lines. What is success? Does our definition change with time? What could college students learn about success from their more experienced friends and family?

WORDS IN CONTEXT

callow: young; lacking in experience and maturity
approbation: expressions of approval or appreciation
mutable: changeable
superfluous: more than is necessary or than what is required
optimist: one who sees the positive side of things, who expects a favorable outcome
fickle: highly changeable or unstable
chagrined: embarrassed

1 Back when I was a callow college student, I devised a neat grid system for what I hoped would be my life's achievements. I could count my life a good one, I thought, if I could attain both success and happiness. So I set about analyzing the component parts of each: Happiness I subdivided into sections labeled health and love; success, I determined, was composed of wealth and fame.

2 Once I actually entered the world of work, however, I learned that success is not so easy to define. For one thing, when I made my simple calculation, I never took into account the joy of creation; the approbation of one's peers; the energy of collaboration; or the sheer satisfaction of a job well done. These are real qualities of success that live outside of wealth or fame.

3 Also, I found that definitions of success are mutable, shifting along with our changing values. If we stick with our chosen fields long enough, we sometimes have an opportunity to meet our heroes, people we thought wildly successful when we were young. A musician friend told me that he spent most of his youth wanting to play like the greats, until he started getting to know some of them. To his surprise, many turned out to be embittered, dulled by drink or boredom, unable to hold together a marriage, or wantonly jealous of others. That's when he realized he wanted to play like himself.

4 Success is defined differently by different people. For some, it is symbolized by the number of buttons on the office phone. For others, it is having only one button—and a secretary to field the calls. Some think the more nights and weekends they spend at the office, the more successful they must be. For others, success is directly proportional to time off.

5 And what about those qualities I did include in my handy grid system? Wealth—beyond what is needed to provide for oneself and one's family, with a little left over for airfare to someplace subtropical in January—turned out to be superfluous. And the little experience I had with fame turned out to be downright scary.

6 Several years ago, I had occasion to appear on a dull but respected national evening television news show. My performance lasted exactly six minutes, and my name flashed only twice. But when I got home from the live broadcast, my answering machine had maxed-out on messages.

7 I heard from a woman I had last seen in Brownie Scouts. I heard from former boyfriends, conspiracy theorists, and celebrity agents. I even got an obscene phone call—what kind of pervert watches PBS?—from someone who might have been an old friend pulling my leg. At least, I hope so.

8 For weeks afterward, I received tons of what an optimist might call fan mail. One fellow insisted that if I froze a particular frame of a political campaign ad I had been discussing, I could see the face of Bill Clinton in the American flag. Somebody sent me a chapter of a novel in progress with a main character disturbingly like me. Several people sent me chain letters.

9 I was relieved when the fickle finger of fame moved on to someone else.

10 When I was young and romanticizing about success, I liked a particular Joni Mitchell lyric: "My struggle for higher achievement and my search for love don't seem to cease." Ah, but the trouble with struggling and searching is that it keeps us in a permanent state of wanting—always reaching for more. The drive to succeed keeps us focused on the future, to the detriment of life in the moment. And the moment is all we ever really have.

11 When I look back at my simplistic little value system, I am a bit chagrined at how absolute I thought life was. But I am also happy to report that the achievements that have come my way are the ones that count. After 20 years of supercharged ambition, I have stumbled upon this bit of wisdom. Who needs wealth and fame? Two out of four ain't bad. ◆

CONSIDERING THE ISSUES

1. Loth begins her essay by explaining how, as a college student, she developed a grid system that she felt would define her life's achievements. Following Loth's example, create your own list or grid in which you define what you think your life's achievements might be. How do you define *happiness*? How do you define *success*?
2. What is your definition of wealth? To what extent is it connected to your definition of success? How important is it to your definition of success? Explain.

CRAFT AND CONTENT

3. In paragraph 1, Loth recalls the days when she was "a callow college student." How does this word choice help establish both the tone and the theme of this essay? Explain.
4. In paragraph 10, Loth says in reference to the Joni Mitchell lyric she quotes, "The trouble with struggling and searching is

that it keeps us in a permanent state of wanting." What does she mean by this statement? How does it relate to the point of this essay overall?

CRITICAL THINKING

5. How does Loth redefine her early notion of success? Why do you think this happened?
6. Loth also changes her definition of fame and abandons it as a goal of success. Why does she do this? Why do you think she wanted fame? Do you? Why or why not? Explain.

WRITING ABOUT THE ISSUES

7. Write your own essay definition of happiness and/or success. Be sure to employ the same strategies Loth does: think of your own experience, the things that make you feel happy and successful, and talk to friends and family for their insights.
8. Since you too might be described as "a callow college student" at this point in your life, create a series of questions that you will then ask older and more experienced friends, family, and acquaintances about happiness and success. Ask all sorts of people your questions, regardless of your own opinions of their happiness or success. Review your notes and write an essay in which you argue what success and happiness really mean based upon your interviews.

The Right Way to Answer the Question: "Mommy, Why Do You Have to Work?"

Sue Shellenbarger

Sue Shellenbarger is an award-winning columnist who writes weekly on issues connected to work and family for the *Wall Street Journal.* She has talked to thousands of people about the "work/life balance" in today's society. She is the author of *Work & Family: Essays from the "Work and Family" Column of the Wall Street Journal.* This essay appeared in her weekly column on October 29, 2004.

CONNECTING TO THE TOPIC

Most parents dread the question from a pleading youngster, "Why do you *have* to go to work?" Many respond with excuses—they must pay bills, put food on the table, and keep their children clothed. They feel guilty for leaving their child, and even more guilty for preferring to go to work rather than staying home. But what if parents answered children truthfully—that they liked work, or enjoyed helping people, or they liked the challenges they encountered while on the job? Some psychologists say showing enthusiasm for your job is better for children, who may otherwise begin to think of work as "a four-letter word."

WORDS IN CONTEXT

amid: in the middle of
comparable: similar in nature; alike
intrinsic: essential to the nature of a thing

1 Ilya Welfeld faced a dilemma common among working parents: Leaving for work every day, how could she explain to her crying toddler why she was going away?

2 "'Honey, we need to buy groceries,' didn't really make a lot of sense" to a 2-year-old, says Ms. Welfeld, then a corporate vice president in communications.

3 Parents play a dominant role in shaping children's lifelong attitudes about work. Yet amid the emotions raised by leaving kids to do our jobs, many moms and dads fumble the ball, mumbling explanations that are a bad fit developmentally or just plain wrong. In fact, parents' influence on kids' work ethic plays out not only in words, but in emotions, behavior, and attitudes, in different ways at different stages of a child's life—and often not in the way we think.

4 Parents generally are failing to convey positive feelings about work to their kids. In a national survey of 605 parents, 69% of mothers say they like their work a lot. But in a comparable sample of 1,023 third- through 12th-graders, only 42% of the kids say their mothers like their jobs a lot, according to the study, reported in "Ask the Children" by Ellen Galinsky of the Families and Work Institute, New York. The same gap existed with fathers; 60% of dads say they like their jobs a lot, but only 41% of children see that positive attitude in their fathers.

5 Some parents fear acting as if they like their jobs will hurt their kids' feelings. Thus, they try to reassure them by acting as if they don't have a choice, saying, as I used to tell my toddler, "Honey, I'm sorry, I have to go to work." Other parents simply feel sad at separating from their children, and focus too much on those feelings.

6 In fact, those emotions speak more loudly to babies and toddlers than any words a parent might utter. "You can explain to a 2- or 3-year-old until you're blue in the face that you need to pay the mortgage," says Jane Healy, a Vail, Colo., educational psychologist and author. "What they're going to pick up is your emotional attitude toward work and what they see it doing to you." A child may feel, "If there's something making my mother miserable, there must be something to be frightened of." Before long, "work" becomes a four-letter word.

7 A better route: Focus on the positive, such as, "I'm really glad I have interesting work to do. And you have interesting work to do, too, when the babysitter comes and you help her put away the groceries," Dr. Healy suggests. Promise to do something together when you return; small children aren't very aware of the passage of time, and looking forward to, say, hearing stories from your workday will help them stay upbeat through the day.

8 Ms. Welfeld saw the power of parental attitude when she quit corporate life last year to start a business in her Bergenfield, N.J., home. In the past, the stress of her corporate job seeped into home life, straining leave-takings from her two children, now three and one. But now, "my attitude toward work is so positive" that she has seen a change in her son: He has relaxed and is more optimistic, and he loves preschool.

9 The next stage, ages five through the elementary-school years, is perhaps most important of all in building a work ethic. Dr. Healy calls this the "age of industry," when children love to accomplish things. This is the time to foster the good feelings that can arise from accomplishment. Celebrate jobs completed, with words or perhaps an outing.

10 Some parents mistakenly assume at this stage they need to take charge of their kids' work habits and direct them in an authoritative way. But studies show parents who support self-reliance—who encourage kids to make their own choices, rather than applying pressure or controls—are more likely to raise hard-working kids.

11 In talking about work with kids of this age, draw positive parallels between your job and their play and school. When Michael Weinberger's 5-year-old daughter asks, "Why do you have to go to work today?" he

replies, "I get to go to work today. It's the same way with you. You get to go to school." He emphasizes that he loves his work as a portfolio manager at a New York hedge fund.

12 Tell your kids about your own intrinsic motivation, Dr. Healy says. For example: "I feel good about what I did today because I helped some people," or "The products I sold today are going to make people comfortable."

13 By middle-school age, kids are ready to understand the values, moral reasoning and financial needs that underlie work choices—why we work and how our job relates to household needs, to other people and to the world at large.

14 At this point, you will begin to see in your kids the results of your teachings. Aaron Dobrinsky, CEO of RoomLinX, Hackensack, N.J., has long told his kids: "You will only excel at what you love. If you hate getting up to go to work every day, you're not going to excel at it." They seem to be listening; his 16-year-old daughter loves working with special-needs children and plans to make it a career; she has started job-shadowing special-ed professionals.

CONSIDERING THE ISSUES

1. Shellenbarger observes that many children think that their parents do not like their jobs very much. Think about how you would answer a child's question, "Why do you have to work?" Would you answer honestly? Would you be concerned that you could hurt your child's feelings by being enthusiastic about going to work? If you are a parent, how have you addressed this question in the past?
2. Recall your own parents' attitudes about work. Did one or both of your parents work outside of the home? Did you think your parents liked their jobs? Have their attitudes influenced your own view of work? Explain.

CRAFT AND CONTENT

3. Shellenbarger refers to several parents and psychologists to support the points she makes in her column. Do some comments seem more credible than others? Explain.
4. Shellenbarger offers advice to parents on how to answer the question "Why do you have to go to work today?" Evaluate her

advice. How do you think a child would respond to the solutions she offers? Explain.

CRITICAL THINKING

5. In paragraph 6, psychologist Jane Healy warns that expressing a distaste for work in order to spare children's feelings could actually frighten children and give a negative impression of work. What do you think? Are children growing up fearful of work and its responsibilities? Are there any trends in popular culture that reflect this view? Explain.
6. Shellenbarger cites Ms. Welfeld (paragraph 8) as an example of "the power of parental attitude." Is Welfeld's situation compelling support for Shellenbarger's essay? How might a critic react to this particular example? Explain.

WRITING ABOUT THE ISSUES

7. Shellenbarger cites a national survey of 605 parents and 1,023 children on their feelings about work. Conduct your own survey. Poll at least 20 parents and 20 to 30 children. Include fathers in your survey. Did children think that one parent was more likely to like his or her job than the other? Discuss your results in a short essay explaining how your data match or counter the survey conducted by Ellen Galinsky.
8. In your opinion, are mothers more likely to hear the question expressed in this essay's title than fathers? Why or why not? Are there any social assumptions that come into play? Explain.

There's No Place Like Work

Arlie Russell Hochschild

Arlie Russell Hochschild, a professor of sociology at the University of California at Berkeley, is the author of *The Second Shift*. This essay has been excerpted from her book *The Time Bind: When Work Becomes Home and Home Becomes Work*.

CONNECTING TO THE TOPIC

Where are you happiest, at work or at home? If you inherited a fortune, would you quit your job? If you had your choice, would you spend more or less time with your family? What do you want your family life to look like in five years? Why do people work in the first place? These are some basic questions that you will soon face once in the job force. These are also questions that Arlie Russell Hochschild put to scores of people in researching the book from which this essay came. According to Hochschild, family life in America is suffering seriously from the demanding work schedules of parents and spouses. In fact, many people find work preferable to home life in the way it nurtures and stimulates.

WORDS IN CONTEXT

counterintuitive: the opposite of what common sense would suggest
paradox: a seemingly contradictory statement that may nonetheless be true
incentive: something that serves to motivate, either by punishment or by reward
premise: a statement or belief upon which an argument is based
evade: to avoid
talisman: an object believed to confer on its bearer magical powers or supernatural protection
devoid: completely lacking
paternity leave: time off of work granted to fathers of newborn children

1 It's 7:40 A.M. when Cassie Bell, 4, arrives at the Spotted Deer Child-Care Center, her hair half-combed, a blanket in one hand, a fudge bar in the other. "I'm late," her mother, Gwen, a sturdy young woman whose short-cropped hair frames a pleasant face, explains to the child-care workers in charge. "Cassie wanted the fudge bar so bad, I gave it to her," she adds apologetically.

2 "Pleeese, can't you take me with you?" Cassie pleads.

3 "You know I can't take you to work," Gwen replies in a tone that suggests that she has been expecting this request. Cassie's shoulders droop. But she has struck a hard bargain—the morning fudge bar—aware of her mother's anxiety about the long day that lies ahead at the center. As Gwen explains later, she continually feels that she owes Cassie more time than she gives her—she has a "time debt." . . .

4 Gwen used to work a straight eight-hour day. But over the last three years, her workday has gradually stretched to eight and a half or nine hours, not counting the E-mail messages and faxes she answers from home. She complains about her hours to her co-workers and listens to their complaints—but she loves her job. Gwen picks up Cassie at 5:45 and gives her a long hug.

5 At home, Gwen's husband, John, a computer programmer, plays with their daughter while Gwen prepares dinner. To protect the dinner "hour"—8:00–8:30—Gwen checks that the phone machine is on, hears the phone ring during dinner but resists the urge to answer. After Cassie's bath, Gwen and Cassie have "quality time," or "Q.T.," as John affectionately calls it. Half an hour later, at 9:30, Gwen tucks Cassie into bed.

6 There are, in a sense, two Bell households: the rushed family they actually are and the relaxed family they imagine they might be if only they had time. Gwen and John complain that they are in a time bind. What they say they want seems so modest—time to throw a ball, to read to Cassie, to witness the small dramas of her development, not to speak of having a little fun and romance themselves. Yet even these modest wishes seem strangely out of reach. Before going to bed, Gwen has to E-mail messages to her colleagues in preparation for the next day's meeting; John goes to bed early, exhausted—he's out the door by 7 every morning.

7 Nationwide, many working parents are in the same boat. More mothers of small children than ever now work outside the home. . . . Meanwhile, fathers of small children are not cutting back hours of work to help out at home. If anything, they have increased their hours at work. . . . All in all, more women are on the economic train, and for many—men and women alike—that train is going faster. . . .

8 I contacted Bright Horizons, a company that runs 136 company-based child-care centers associated with corporations, hospitals and Federal agencies in 25 states. Bright Horizons allowed me to add questions to a questionnaire they sent out to 3,000 parents whose children attended the centers. The respondents, mainly middle-class parents in their early 30's, largely confirmed the picture I'd found at Amerco. A third of fathers and a fifth of mothers described themselves as "workaholic," and 1 out of 3 said their partners were.

9 To be sure, some parents have tried to shorten their hours. Twenty-one percent of the nation's women voluntarily work part time, as do

7 percent of men. A number of others make under-the-table arrangements that don't show up on surveys. But while working parents say they need more time at home, the main story of their lives does not center on a struggle to get it. Why? Given the hours parents are working these days, why aren't they taking advantage of an opportunity to reduce their time at work?

10 The most widely held explanation is that working parents cannot afford to work shorter hours. Certainly this is true for many. But if money is the whole explanation, why would it be that at places like Amerco, the best-paid employees—upper-level managers and professionals—were the least interested in part-time work or job sharing, while clerical workers who earned less were more interested?

11 Similarly, if money were the answer, we would expect poorer new mothers to return to work more quickly after giving birth than rich mothers. But among working women nationwide, well-to-do new mothers are not much more likely to stay home after 13 weeks with a new baby than low-income new mothers. . . . A second explanation goes that workers don't dare ask for time off because they are afraid it would make them vulnerable to layoffs. . . . But when I asked Amerco employees whether they worked long hours for fear of getting on a layoff list, virtually everyone said no. . . .

12 Were workers uninformed about the company's family-friendly policies? No. Were rigid middle managers standing in the way of workers using these policies? Sometimes. But when I compared Amerco employees who worked for flexible managers with those who worked for rigid managers, I found that the flexible managers reported only a few more applicants than the rigid ones. The evidence, however counterintuitive, pointed to a paradox: workers at the company I studied weren't protesting the time bind. They were accommodating to it.

13 Why? I did not anticipate the conclusion I found myself coming to: namely, that work has become a form of "home" and home has become "work." The worlds of home and work have not begun to blur, as the conventional wisdom goes, but to reverse places. We are used to thinking that home is where most people feel the most appreciated, the most truly "themselves," the most secure, the most relaxed. We are used to thinking that work is where most people feel like "just a number" or "a cog in a machine." It is where they have to be "on," have to "act," where they are least secure and most harried.

14 But new management techniques so pervasive in corporate life have helped transform the workplace into a more appreciative, personal sort of social world. Meanwhile, at home the divorce rate has risen, and the emotional demands have become more baffling and complex. In addition to teething, tantrums and the normal developments of growing children, the needs of elderly parents are creating more tasks for the modern family—as are the blending, unblending, reblending of new stepparents, stepchildren, exes and former in-laws. . . .

15 Current research suggests that however hectic their lives, women who do paid work feel less depressed, think better of themselves and are more satisfied than women who stay at home. One study reported that women who work outside the home feel more valued at home than housewives do. . . . Many workers feel more confident they could "get the job done" at work than at home. One study found that only 59 percent of workers feel their "performance" in the family is "good or unusually good," while 86 percent rank their performance on the job this way. . . .

16 Using modern participative management techniques, many companies now train workers to make their own work decisions, and then set before their newly "empowered" employees moral as well as financial incentives. At Amerco, the Total Quality worker is invited to feel recognized for job accomplishments. Amerco regularly strengthens the family-like ties of co-workers by holding "recognition ceremonies" honoring particular workers or self-managed production teams. Amerco employees speak of "belonging to the Amerco family," and proudly wear their "Total Quality" pins or "High Performance Team" T-shirts, symbols of their loyalty to the company and of its loyalty to them. . . .

17 If Total Quality calls for "re-skilling" the worker in an "enriched" job environment, technological developments have long been deskilling parents at home. Over the centuries, store-bought goods have replaced homespun cloth, homemade soap and home baked foods. Day care for children, retirement homes for the elderly, even psychotherapy are, in a way, commercial substitutes for jobs that a mother once did at home. Even family-generated entertainment has, to some extent, been replaced by television, video games and the VCR. . . .

18 The one "skill" still required of family members is the hardest one of all—the emotional work of forging, deepening or repairing family relationships. It takes time to develop this skill, and even then things

can go awry. Family ties are complicated. People get hurt. Yet as broken homes become more common—and as the sense of belonging to a geographical community grows less and less secure in an age of mobility—the corporate world has created a sense of "neighborhood," of "feminine culture," of family at work. Life at work can be insecure; the company can fire workers. But workers aren't so secure at home, either. Many employees have been working for Amerco for 20 years but are on their second or third marriages or relationships. The shifting balance between these two "divorce rates" may be the most powerful reason why tired parents flee a world of unresolved quarrels and unwashed laundry for the orderliness, harmony and managed cheer of work. People are getting their "pink slips" at home.

19 Amerco workers have not only turned their offices into "home" and their homes into workplaces; many have also begun to [manage] time at home, where families are succumbing to a cult of efficiency previously associated mainly with the office and factory. Meanwhile, work time, with its ever-longer hours, has become more hospitable to sociability—periods of talking with friends on E-mail, patching up quarrels, gossiping. . . .

20 [Many families] respond to their time bind at home by trying to value and protect "quality time." A concept unknown to their parents and grandparents, "quality time" has become a powerful symbol of the struggle against the growing pressures at home. It reflects the extent to which modern parents feel the flow of time to be running against them. The premise behind "quality time" is that the time we devote to relationships can somehow be separated from ordinary time. Relationships go on during quantity time, of course, but then we are only passively, not actively, wholeheartedly, specializing in our emotional ties. We aren't "on." Quality time at home becomes like an office appointment. You don't want to be caught "goofing off around the water cooler" when you are "at work."

21 Quality time holds out the hope that scheduling intense periods of togetherness can compensate for an overall loss of time in such a way that a relationship will suffer no loss of quality. But this is just another way of transferring the cult of efficiency from office to home. . . .

22 Children often protest the pace, the deadlines, and the grand irrationality of "efficient" family life. Children dawdle. They refuse to leave places when it's time to leave. They insist on leaving places when it's not time to leave. Surely, this is part of the usual stop-and-go of

childhood itself, but perhaps, too, it is the plea of children for more family time, and more control over what time there is. This only adds to the feeling that life at home has become hard work. . . .

23 [Another] way working parents try to evade the time bind is to develop what I call "potential selves." The potential selves that I discovered in my Amerco interviews were fantasy creations of time-poor parents who dreamed of living as time millionaires.

24 One man, a gifted 55-year-old engineer in research and development at Amerco, told how he had dreamed of taking his daughters on a camping trip in the Sierra Mountains: "I bought all the gear three years ago when they were 5 and 7, the tent, the sleeping bags, the air mattresses, the backpacks, the ponchos. I got a map of the area. I even got the freeze-dried food. Since then the kids and I have talked about it a lot, and gone over what we're going to do. They've been on me to do it for a long time. I feel bad about it. I keep putting it off, but we'll do it, I just don't know when."

25 Banished to garages and attics of many Amerco workers were expensive electric saws, cameras, skis and musical instruments, all bought with wages it took time to earn. These items were to their owners what Cassie's fudge bar was to her—a substitute for time, a talisman, a reminder of the potential self.

26 Obviously, not everyone, not even a majority of Americans, is making a home out of work and a workplace out of home. But in the working world, it is a growing reality, and one we need to face. Increasing numbers of women are discovering a great male secret—that work can be an escape from the pressures of home, pressures that the changing nature of work itself are only intensifying. Neither men nor women are going to take up "family friendly" policies, whether corporate or governmental, as long as the current realities of work and home remain as they are. For a substantial number of time-bound parents, the stripped-down home and the neighborhood devoid of community are simply losing out to the pull of the workplace. . . .

27 So where do we go from here? There is surely no going back to the mythical 1950's family that confined women to the home. Most women don't wish to return to a full-time role at home—and couldn't afford it even if they did. But equally troubling is a workaholic culture that strands both men and women outside the home.

28 For a while now, scholars on work-family issues have pointed to Sweden, Norway and Denmark as better models of work-family balance.

Today, for example, almost all Swedish fathers take two paid weeks off from work at the birth of their children, and about half of fathers and most mothers take additional "parental leave" during the child's first or second year. Research shows that men who take family leave when their children are very young are more likely to be involved with their children as they grow older. When I mentioned this Swedish record of paternity leave to a focus group of American male managers, one of them replied, "Right, we've already heard about Sweden." To this executive, paternity leave was a good idea not for the U.S. today, but for some "potential society" in another place and time.

29 Meanwhile, children are paying the price. In her book "When the Bough Breaks: The Cost of Neglecting Our Children," the economist Sylvia Hewlett claims that compared with the previous generation, young people today are more likely to "under-perform at school; commit suicide; need psychiatric help; suffer a severe eating disorder; bear a child out of wedlock; take drugs, be the victim of a violent crime." But we needn't dwell on sledgehammer problems like heroin or suicide to realize that children like those at Spotted Deer need more of our time. If other advanced nations with two-job families can give children the time they need, why can't we? ◆

CONSIDERING THE ISSUES

1. Consider the rhetorical question Hochschild poses at the end of this essay. "If other advanced nations with two-job families can give children the time they need, why can't we?" What sort of family did you grow up in? Did both of your parents work? Were you raised by only one parent or guardian? Do you feel that your caregivers were able to spend enough time with you? Alternatively, if you are a parent yourself, do you feel that you are able to balance work and family? Explain.
2. In paragraph 13, Hochschild says that "work has become a form of 'home' and home has become 'work.'" What ideas do we typically associate with home? With work? Explain.

CRAFT AND CONTENT

3. Hochschild begins her essay by telling the story of a day in the life of Cassie Bell and her parents. Why does she tell this story? What kinds of issues does each establish?

4. What are the management philosophies Hochschild refers to in this article? How does she relate these philosophies to home management issues?

CRITICAL THINKING

5. What does Hochschild say about the changing role of women in American society? In what ways is their role not actually changing? How are these concerns important to the argument overall?
6. What is the "potential self"? How does this potential self function in the situations Hochschild describes? How does it contribute to the problem?
7. Hochschild notes, "Increasing numbers of women are discovering a great male secret." What is the great male secret? Why does she identify it this way? Do you agree with her viewpoint on this allure of the workplace? Explain.

WRITING ABOUT THE ISSUES

8. Hochschild focuses primarily on the role of women and their particular concerns with regard to work and family time. Do you agree that this is primarily a female issue? What are the roles of men in families? In business? Who, ultimately, is responsible? Explain your perspective in a short essay drawing from some of the points Hochschild raises in her essay.
9. Hochschild polled many people in preparation for her essay, but her discussion focuses primarily on adult issues. Interview some children who live in such "time-starved" families and prepare a response to Hochschild that represents *their* perspective. Try to formulate your questions based on your understanding of the issues and concerns most relevant to young people.

VISUAL CONNECTIONS

Juggling Family and Work

CONNECTING TO THE TOPIC

In the previous article, Arlie Russell Hochschild identified some of the many issues families face when dealing with home life and work life. Parents claim to be overwhelmed with "time crunches," yet are working longer hours than ever before. As our lives become more efficient, from instant oatmeal and breakfast bars, to microwave gourmet meals and Internet shopping, we seem to have less time to do all the things we say we want to do. Which begs the question of the chapter, "Why do we work?"

CONSIDERING THE ISSUES

1. What are our expectations of working mothers? Are they different than those for working fathers? Explain.
2. In the previous article, Arlie Russell Hochschild explained that women who work outside the home are less likely to be depressed and are overall more satisfied with their lives. If you had a choice (money is not an issue) to stay at home with your child or work outside the home, what choice would you make? Do you think this choice should be influenced by your gender? Why or why not?

CRITICAL THINKING

3. What is happening in this photo? What can we presume about the mother? The father? The baby? Their lifestyle? Explain.
4. Does this photo challenge any social clichés? Explain.
5. Would our interpretation of this photo be different if it featured a man waving good-bye to the child, with the woman standing on the porch? What if the man were not dressed in a business suit? Explain.

TOPICAL CONNECTIONS

GROUP PROJECT

1. Hochschild interviewed many individuals who worked in corporations and industry about the reasons they worked. As a group, develop a list of questions and interview at least five to eight people each about why they work outside the home. Make sure your questions are likely to elicit truthful responses. Collect and discuss the data and compare it to the conclusions Hochschild reaches in her essay. Prepare a short report on your findings.

WEB PROJECTS

2. In his essay, Andrew Curry mentions author Horatio Alger and his works that "glorified the work ethic." Who was Horatio Alger? Look up more information on this nineteenth-century author and the genre that became synonymous with his name at www.city-journal.org/html/10_4_urbanities-the_moral.html. For Alger's heroes, what was the defining principle of work? Explain.
3. Visit the Work to Live Web site (www.worktolive.info) and read more about the state of the American workweek. Visit the "World Desk" and view information on the number of vacation days many nations afford workers. Write an essay in which you explore the concept of vacation time and its importance—or nonimportance—to the average American worker.

FOR FURTHER INQUIRY

4. Watch a movie that explores different aspects of the American dream—*Death of a Salesman*, *The Great Gatsby*, *Wall Street*, *Field of Dreams*, etc. What arguments does the movie put forth about why we work and the connection between work and happiness?
5. Few teenagers have escaped the question "What are you going to do with your life?" from a curious, perhaps even concerned, relative. What they are really asking is what sort of *work* you intend to do as an adult. Many people never find the answer. Author Po Bronson has written a book asking this very question, interviewing hundreds of successful and struggling people for their perspective on life, work, and happiness. Visit his Web site and read some of the testimonials at www.pobronson.com under the link "What Should I Do with My Life?" After reading a few excerpts and other material on his Web page, write your own essay exploring this question.

Credits

Image Credits

Page 13: Steve Greenberg/*Seattle Post Intelligencer*, November 11, 1996; page 41: Use of the Registered Honda trademarks is courtesy of American Honda Motor Co., Inc. Photography by Mark Laita; page 42: Courtesy of VF Corporation; page 44: Courtesy of beyond petroleum; page 46: Courtesy of the Michael J. Fox Foundation for Parkinson's Research. Photograph by Mark Seliger; page 48: "© Apple Computer, Inc. Used with permission. All rights reserved. Apple ® and the Apple logo are registered trademarks of Apple Computer, Inc." Photographer, Matthew Welch, Matthew Welch Photography. Represented by @radical.media, inc.; page 50: Courtesy of www.adbusters.org; page 55: Mike Keefe/*The Denver Post*, November 16, 2002/Cagle Cartoons; page 73: Courtesy of the United States Postal Service (USPS); page 83: Ira Wyman/CORBIS Sygma; page 87: Larry Wright/*The Detroit News*, May 29, 2003/Cagle Cartoons; page 99: Melissa Gerr; page 116: © Jim Borgman/Zits partnership. King Features Syndicate; page 121: Edward Koren/*The New Yorker*, February 5, 2001; page 147: Courtesy, Scott Messinger/Chris Stokes/ Bucknell University Conservatives Club; page 151: Jeff Parker/*Florida Today*, February 23, 2004/Cagle Cartoons; page 169: Dan Wasserman/ *The Boston Globe*, November 3, 2004/Tribune Media Services; page 175: *Quad City Times*, February 14, 2004; page 179: Mike Keefe/*The Denver Post*, 2001; page 208: Courtesy of the American Civil Liberties Union, October 2001; page 213: Mike Keefe/*The Denver Post*, 2001; page 242: Gandee Vasan/Stone/Getty Images; page 247: Mike Keefe/*The Denver Post*, 2002; page 274: both: from "Teaching Young Children in Violent Times" by Diane Levin and Nancy Carlsson-Paige/The National Association for the Education of Young Children. Drawing courtesy of the NAEYC; page 279: Lauzan/Cagle Cartoons, March 1, 2004; page 294: Vic Cantone/*O'Dwyer's PR Services Report*, March 2003; page 315: Courtesy of the USDA and the US Department of Health and Human Services; page 316: from *Eat, Drink, and Be Healthy: The Harvard Medical School Guide to Healthy Eating* by Dr. Walter C. Willett. Published by Simon &

Schuster 2001; page 321: Jeff Parker/*Florida Today*, October 4, 2002/Cagle Cartoons; page 349: Photodisc/Getty Images.

Text Credits

Daniel Akst, "Finding Fault for the Fat." *Boston Globe Magazine*, December 7, 2003. Reprinted by permission.

Jonathan Alter, "Who's Taking the Kids?" *Newsweek*, July 29, 2002. Reprinted by permission.

American Civil Liberties Union, "National ID Cards: 5 Reasons Why They Should Be Rejected." www.aclu.org. Reprinted with permission.

American Psychological Association. "Violence on Television—What Do Children Learn? What Can Parents Do?" www.apa.org/pi/pii/vio&tv.html. Copyright © 2003 by the American Psychological Association. Reprinted with permission.

Ross Alden Ames, "Fast Food Isn't to Blame." Reprinted with permission of the author.

Peter Belmonte, "Brand Cool." *Adbusters*, September–October 2003. Reprinted by permission of the author.

Jane Black, "When Cameras Are Too Candid." *Business Week*, September 26, 2002.

Myrna Blyth, "The Female Fear Factor." From *Spin Sisters: How the Women of the Media Sell Unhappiness—and Liberalism—to the Women of America* by Myrna Blyth. Copyright © 2004 by the author and reprinted by permission of St. Martin's Press, LLC.

Laura Bradford, "Fat Foods: Back in Court." *TIME*, August 3, 2003. Copyright © 2003 TIME, Inc. Reprinted by permission.

Austin W. Bramwell, "Censor This?" *The Record*, November 2002. Reprinted by permission.

Margaret Carlson, "The Case for a National ID Card." *TIME*, January 14, 2002. Copyright © 2002 TIME, Inc. Reprinted by permission.

Damien Cave, "On Sale at Old Navy: Cool Clothes for Identical Zombies!" *Salon*, November 22, 2000. Reprinted by permission.

Denise Chaykun, "Free Speech Sucks!...But Censorship Sucks Even More." *Counterweight*, March 27, 2003. Reprinted by permission.

Jonathan A. Colvin, "Me, My Clone, and I." *The Humanist*, May 2000. Reprinted by permission.

Council for Responsible Genetics, "The Genetic Bill of Rights." www.gene-watch.org. Reprinted with permission.

Andrew Curry, "Why We Work." *U.S. News and World Report*, February 24, 2003. Copyright © 2003 U.S. News & World Report, LP. Reprinted with permission.

Richard Daynard, "You Want Fries with That?" *Northeastern University Magazine*, May 2003. Reprinted by permission.

Richard Delgado, "Hate Cannot Be Tolerated." *Insight on the News*, June 24, 1996.

Emory University, "Policy Statement on Discriminatory Harassment." From the Emory University homepage, www.emory.edu/EEO/dhindex.htm.

Laurie Essig, "Same-Sex Marriage." This article first appeared on Salon.com, at www.salon.com, July 10, 2000. An online version remains in the Salon archives. Reprinted with permission.

Laura Fokkena, "Are You a Terrorist, or Do You Play One on TV?" *Pop-Politics*, issue 7. Reprinted by permission of the author.

George Gerbner, "Television's Global Marketing Strategy Creates a Damaging and Alienated Window on the World." *The Ecology of Justice,* Context Institute, (IC#38), Spring 1994.

Nancy Gibbs, "Baby, It's You and You and You." *TIME*, February 12, 2001. Copyright © 2001 TIME, Inc. Reprinted by permission.

Tim Goodman, "Hate Violence? Turn It Off." *San Francisco Chronicle*. April 29, 2001. Reprinted by permission.

Arlie Russell Hochschild, "There's No Place Like Work." Excerpt from "The Waving Window" from *The Time Bind: When Work Becomes Home and Home Becomes Work* by Arlie Russell Hochschild. Reprinted by permission of Henry Holt and Company, LLC.

Wendy Kaminer, "I Spy." *The American Prospect*. Reprinted with permission from *The American Prospect*, volume 11, number 18: August 14, 2000. *The American Prospect,* 11 Beacon Street, Suite 1120, Boston, MA 02108. All right reserved.

Randall Kennedy, "Blind Spot." *The Atlantic*. Reprinted by permission.

Paul King, "When America Relaxes, 'Food Police' Should Keep Quiet." *Nation's Restaurant News*, August 25, 2003. Reprinted by permission.

Michael Kinsley, "Abolish Marriage." *Slate*, July 2003. Article reprinted by permission of Newspaper Enterprise Association, Inc.

Diane E. Levin, "Beyond Banning War and Superhero Play: Meeting Children's Needs in Violent Times." *Young Children*, May 2003. Reprinted with permission from the National Association for the Education of Young Children.

Oliver Libaw, "Work Is Life" at www.ABCNews.com. Reprinted courtesy of ABCNews.com.

Renee Loth, "Measuring Success." *Boston Sunday Globe Magazine*. March 14, 1996, p. 12. Reprinted with permission.

William Lutz, "With These Words I Can Sell You Anything." *Doublespeak*, HarperCollins, 1989. Reprinted by permission of the author.

Heather Mac Donald, "What Looks Like Profiling Might Just Be Good Policing." *Los Angeles Times*, January 19, 2003. Reprinted by permission.

Mike Males, "Stop Blaming Kids and TV." *The Progressive*, October, 1997. Reprinted by permission from *The Progressive*, 409 E. Main St., Madison, WI 53703 www.progressive.org.

Bill McKibben, excerpts from *Enough: Staying Human in an Engineered Age* by Bill McKibben. Copyright © 2003 by Bill McKibben. Reprinted by permission of Henry Holt and Company LLC.

Rosie Mestel, "We Eat; Therefore, They Are." *Los Angeles Times*, August 10, 2004. Reprinted by permission.

Peter Phillips, "Heads Above the Hype." *Briarpatch Magazine*, October 2001. Reprinted by permission.

David Plotz, "Privacy Is Overrated." As David Plotz revised it, August 26, 2004. Reprinted by permission of the author.

Sasha Polakow-Suransky, "Racial Profiling Goes Beyond Black and White." *Africana*, November 2001. Reprinted by permission.

Dorothy Rabinowitz, "Difficult Conversations." *Wall Street Journal*, November 19, 2002. Reprinted with permission.

Douglas Rushkoff, "A Brand by Any Other Name." *The London Times*, May 6, 2000. Copyright © 2000 by Douglas Rushkoff. Reprinted by permission of William Morris Agency, Inc. on behalf of the author.

Sam Schulman, "Gay Marriage—And Marriage." Reprinted from *Commentary*, November 2003, by permission. All rights reserved.

Sue Shellenbarger, "The Right Way to Answer the Question: 'Mommy, Why Do You Have to Work?'" *Wall Street Journal*, October 29, 2004.

Harvey A. Silverglate, "Muzzling Free Speech." Reprinted with permission from the October 7, 2002 edition of *The National Law Journal*. Copyright © 2002 ALM Properties, Inc. All rights reserved. Further duplication without permission is prohibited.

Jane Ellen Stevens, "The Violence Reporting Project: A New Approach to Covering Crime." Originally titled "Integrating the Public Health Perspective into Reporting Violence." *Nieman Reports*, December 22, 1998. Reprinted by permission.

Gregory Stock, "The Last Human." From *Redesigning Humans: Our Inevitable Genetic Future*, by Gregory Stock. Copyright © 2002 by Gregory Stock. Excerpted by permission of Houghton Mifflin Company. All rights reserved.

John Stossel, "Extreme Reality: How Media Coverage Exaggerates Risks and Dangers." www.ABCNews.com. Reprinted with permission.

Andrew Sullivan, "The 'M'-Word: Why It Matters to Me." *TIME*, February 16, 2004. Copyright © 2004 TIME, Inc. Reprinted by permission.

Train, "Calling All Angels," from the album *My Private Nation* (2003), written by Charlie Colin, Patrick T. Monahan, Jimmy W. Stafford, and Scott Underwood. EMI Music Publishing.

Alton Fitzgerald White, "Ragtime, My Time." *The Nation*, October 11, 1999. Reprinted by permission.

Index of Authors and Titles